Acknowledgments

I wish to thank the organizations, churches and families that shared their experience with the project. We are particularly grateful to active members of our advisory committee: Reverend Olen Arrington Jr., Olatoye Baiyewu, Guida Brown, Tony Garcia, Pat Kiefer, Dan Melyon, Adeline Robinson and Julian Thomas, for their guidance and support throughout the project. Funding for the project came from the Aspen Institute Non-profit Sector Research Fund and the Palmer Foundation. Ethnographic research was conducted by a team which included Theresa Embury, Maria Lydia Spinelli, Carol Jones, Calvin Lucas, Tania Rodriquez, Karen Szalapski, Elda Torres, Traci Rabelhoffer, Marin Rocha Jr, Latisha Riser and Meghan Mumford.

The Employer's Study was designed in partnership with the Kenosha Women's Commission and Leadership Kenosha. Data collection for the project was conducted by Kenosha Women's Commission, Leadership Kenosha and three University of Wisconsin-Parkside research methods classes (Spring 1999, Weekend College Fall 1999 and Spring 2000) and some students in Anne Statham's class. Students active in survey collection included Yvonne Mancussi, Amy Queen, Amanda Salo, Cari Campagna, Jaclyne Buzzell, Vicente Correa, Richard Davis, Michael Graczyk, Lisa Helgesen, Cynthia Moore, Nicholas Potter, Kathryn Schaefer, Jeanie Schober and Jason Vanacker.

Institutional and office support for the project came from the Center for Community Partnerships at University of Wisconsin-Parkside, the Sociology Department at Indiana University of Pennsylvania, the Mid-Atlantic Addiction Training Institute (MAATI) at Indiana University of Pennsylvania, and Ram Cnaan and staff at the Center for Research on Religion and Urban Civil Society at the University of Pennsylvania. Regina Miller, Crystal Deemer, Robert McConnell, Lane Blaquiere, Jason Brady, Michael Graczyk, Alfredo Mercado and Brenda Underwood provided clerical, research and editorial assistance on the project.

Photographs and the cover design were produced by Tom Fritz Studio. The Kenosha map was created by Helen Metz. Publications design was created by the publications office at Indiana University of Pennsylvania.

Table of Contents

Kenosha Social Capital Study Education Report Executive Summary

ii

Kenosha and the Surrounding Area

The *Kenosha Social Capital Study* examined the role of non-profit organizations and churches in the African American and Hispanic/Latino communities in Kenosha, Wisconsin. 1990 U.S. Census figures listed a population of approximately 80,000 people. Ninety percent were white, five percent African American and another six percent were Hispanic/Latino. Hispanic/Latinos in Kenosha and their descendants come mostly from either Mexico or portions of Texas annexed by the United States in the last century. This population also includes a group of central American migrants.

The *Kenosha Social Capital Study* was an action research project developed and carried out with the guidance of Kenosha community representatives. The research was conducted by a team of faculty, research associates and students from University of Wisconsin-Parkside. Most of the research included observations of activities in organizations, churches and community events. We also interviewed key leaders throughout Kenosha and typical Hispanic/Latino and African American families. Finally, the project included a survey

of Kenosha employers regarding their hiring practices.

Project Goals Overall, the project focused on 1) how African Americans and Hispanic/Latinos support their families, 2) the role of community organizations and churches in this process, and 3) the

dynamic between communities and their organizations. Through social capital we can also understand the reasons behind people from these two groups utilizing or not utilizing the support services available through non-profits and government. Research focused on the following questions:

- What are the community dynamics and needs within the Hispanic/Latino and African American communities?

- What roles do community-based organizations and churches play in supporting community residents?

- What is the relationship between these two communities and the Kenosha County Job Center (the government agency providing most social welfare services)?

- In general, what role do community-based organizations play in facilitating or hindering communication between organizations providing government-funded welfare reform services and the populations served by these programs?

- What role does race and immigration status play in this process?

A Note on Group Labels

People in Kenosha use several different names to talk about peoples of African descent and people from Spanish-speaking countries. In this report, I use African Americans to mean people whose ancestors migrated from Africa. Most people from Spanish speaking backgrounds in the community call themselves Hispanics. In order to accommodate current preference for the term Latino, I use Hispanic/Latino throughout this document.

Project Description and Methods

The *Kenosha Social Capital Study* was an ethnographic project designed to answer these questions by creating a description of the development of social capital through non-profit organizations and churches in this community during the study period. Anthropological ethnography provides a holistic picture of community processes through multiple methods.

Research methods combined the following data collection techniques:

1. **Ethnography of organizations and inter-organizational dynamics in these two communities.** This research component involved regular observations in participating social service organizations and churches for an eight month period. Students, faculty and research associates observed day to day activities in the agencies, board meetings, coalition meetings and public events sponsored by these organizations.

2. **Open-ended interviews with 25 key organization, church and community leaders.**

3. **Family study of 26 typical families (15 Hispanic/Latino and 11 African American).** This component consisted of open ended interviews with typical families from a variety of backgrounds about their work and education history, involvement with organizations and churches, and experiences with diversity.

4. **Analysis of secondary source material such as newspaper articles, agency and church documents, affirmative action reports and other government reports**

5. **A survey of 121 Kenosha employers focused on the nature of their labor force, hiring practices, and use of the Kenosha County Job Center**

Understanding Social and Cultural Capital

Most people are familiar with the idea of *capital*: money that people use to start businesses, invest in property, pay for education and training or save for the future. Capital put to work in any of these ways creates more money that people can use for a variety of purposes. Without capital, people have limited options.

Economists and social scientists also use capital to refer to several other kinds of assets that individuals, organizations and communities may have to sustain and improve their way of life. All of these types of capital are intertwined. *Economic capital* refers to money required for an activity. *Human capital* means education and skills needed to fulfill a goal. *Cultural capital* means knowing how to act, dress, talk and otherwise present oneself in order to fit in.

Social capital provides the means to get access to the other kinds of capital. It refers to social networks that help people obtain their goals. However, social capital involves more than simply knowing who to contact to get money, obtain skills or learn appropriate cultural habits.

Social scientists see social capital as the social relationships and patterns of trust that enable people to gain access to resources like government services or jobs. For organizations, social capital includes social relationships through both organizations and individuals that help organizations find funding, volunteers, employees, information, program participants and other things that an institution needs to survive.

Social capital consists of two ingredients: 1) relationships based in enforceable trust with people or organizations who have access to resources needed to meet basic necessities and fulfill goals, and 2) knowledge of cultural cues which indicate that an individual is a member of a group and should be given access to those relationships. The first half of the definition includes three parts: connections, trust and networks with appropriate information. The second half of the definition refers to access to cultural capital essential to use social networks. Social and cultural capitals are separate concepts, but they work together to help people and organizations to fulfill their goals.

While all people have social capital, not everyone's networks can help them achieve their goals. For example, Janice was a young African American woman from a strong family that worked together to meet everyone's needs. However, her family could not help her gain access to the resources required to move into professional employment. Other adults also did nothing to provide the guidance needed to obtain human capital through education.

Eventually, Janice did find people through non-profit organization activities, church and school clubs who offered the advice and support she needed to succeed in college. These same mentors suggested courses, helped her choose colleges and later offered emotional support to

iii

iv

continue through college. She chose a career helping others partly based on this kind of trusting support.

Janice's story shows that knowing the courses to take is as important as having someone to provide an introduction for an education program or a job. Familiarity with the steps needed to get an education, find a job or obtain funding for an organization is the second part of the definition of social capital. Behaving in ways considered appropriate by the people who are part of social capital networks is as important as having the right contacts. This knowledge about education, employment or organizational development systems and the appropriate ways to behave and speak in order to succeed is called *cultural capital*. People need to know how to use the right cultural capital for a given goal like getting an education in order to have access to the trusting relationships of a social capital network.

Appropriate ways to behave are specific to local communities. The right way to behave, dress or act can be different for African Americans and Hispanic/Latinos than for whites in the same community.

Social and cultural capital are linked to human and economic capital. As Janice's story shows, lacking social and cultural capital meant that she did not take the high school courses she needed for college. Some people do not have access to economic capital to meet their goals. Sometimes, coming from environments without access to human or economic capital means that people do not know how to move outside of familiar patterns. In other cases, social capital can provide important links to family supporting jobs. Social capital also supplies support for child care, social support and other family needs.

Social and cultural capital are developed in dense networks often found in family, neighborhoods or churches. There are two kinds of social capital: closed and bridging.

Both are equally important for individuals and organizations.

Closed social capital involves strong ties within sub-communities, like a neighborhood or ethnic group. Closed social capital networks develop strong supports for the people in those communities. Everyone belongs to at least one closed social capital network. It may be family, people who graduated from a certain school or simply local community networks. People in these closed networks are familiar with each other, practice the same culture and trust each other.

Bridging social capital means that people have developed strong, trusting ties across sub-community groups. Bridging social capital tries to create trusting relationships between closed social capital networks. Building bridges is an intentional and slow process. We saw many examples of bridging social capital in Kenosha. We also learned that bridging social capital depends on closed social capital networks.

Kenosha History

Kenosha is best described as an auto manufacturing town which has rebounded from the loss of its major employer in the 1980s. Rural parts of the county still are agricultural. Anticipating a planned plant closing, Kenosha business and government leaders stepped in early to ensure that Kenosha did not experience high unemployment, crime and poverty levels. Chrysler offered retraining and relocation packages for unemployed auto workers, government worked with local banks to avoid home loan defaults, and business and government together recruited small manufacturers and service employers to Kenosha. Around the same time, the outskirts of the city began to develop as a bedroom community for northern Illinois. This led to an increase in construction employment as well as an influx of more professional residents. By the mid 1990s, unemployment hovered at approximately 3.5 percent. However, many of the good paying, unionized

jobs had been replaced by smaller employers offering lower wages and benefits. The company town atmosphere had also been replaced by a larger number of commuting families.

The workforce for industry largely came from migration. As in other U.S. cities, the late nineteenth century immigrants from Italy and Eastern Europe who came to Kenosha for factory jobs experienced prejudice in housing, employment and all other aspects of life. As a result, they developed tight communities focused on church, fraternal and benevolent societies to provide social support As unions developed, social life also began to focus on the union hall. By the 1990s, the initial ethnic enclaves had broken down, but social capital and community still focused on the small group of known people developed through church, union, family, neighborhood and school ties. Given economic prosperity through union employment, Kenosha was slow to develop non-profit and government supports for low income people.

The history of the African American and Hispanic/Latino communities mirrors the experience of the earlier immigrants. However, like similar communities, people of color experienced even more extreme prejudice than the white immigrants and still face discrimination in education, employment and other daily life experiences today. These two groups have been labeled "invisible people" due to their small numbers and the tendency to maintain passive, closed communities. This characterization was just beginning to change during the study period.

Both African Americans and Hispanic/Latinos still experience discrimination in hiring and promotion. However, like most social capital resources in Kenosha, people with ties through already established networks can find good paying working class jobs. Many African Americans and Hispanic/Latinos have had a very difficult time finding work in professional and some service sector employment related to the new Kenosha economy because they lack social ties to people connected to such jobs.

The history of Kenosha and its communities of color show this small city to be a place where people migrate to find work, first in factories and now in a combination of factories and service businesses. It is a place where people are expected to support themselves, but where strong communities based on closed social capital networks provide resources to find work, housing, to socialize, worship and find other supports when needed. Churches remain a source of support and community in the 1990s. The non-profit sector is relatively new and reflects community history and values.

Kenosha Culture

Anthropologists define *culture* as the whole way of life of a people, including patterns of work, ideas and behavior. People who study organizations or poverty often use *culture* to mean values or habits particular to one organization or a group of people. This section describes unique aspects of Kenosha culture as in the second definition. Specific behaviors and beliefs are shaped by economic structures and other systems in a community.

Every culture has both positive and negative traits. In many cases, cultural habits that are helpful to many people within a community can cause trouble for people who do not understand community rules. This is particularly true for communities made up of multiple closed social capital networks like Kenosha. Each cultural trait discussed below was mentioned by many people as impacting on the lives of people living in Kenosha, especially African Americans and Hispanic/Latinos.

People working with other communities may find much in common with Kenosha culture. Preference for known insiders is typical in most localities, particularly smaller cities or towns. Highlighting parochial knowledge over education is familiar in many working-class communities. Patterns of individualism and expectations that others are available as needed come from wider Midwestern cultural traits. These traits come together to form unique patterns for Kenosha. Understanding how local culture is similar and different to that in other communities becomes essential in developing programs in any locality.

Kenosha is a study in contrasts. Widely described as a blue-collar, conservative town, it also developed internationally known models for social welfare. Understood as twenty years behind most areas in the U.S. in developing affirmative action and anti-racism initiatives, this community also offered good paying factory jobs to many African Americans and Hispanic/Latinos. There are few segregated neighborhoods and most people of color report positive relationships with whites.

Kenosha culture comes out of its history as a migration point for people from many different backgrounds seeking factory work. Much of

Kenosha's unique way of life stems from close, supportive networks of people working together to meet their needs through churches, neighborhoods and factory employment.

Kenosha culture is a tension among several seemingly contradictory elements. People negotiate these contradictions in everyday life, learning them as they are socialized into the culture. Newcomers learn Kenosha culture through trial and error, sometimes getting help from established insiders.

This study found the following elements in Kenosha culture that influenced social and cultural capital development for people in this community:

Rules and Allowances for Insiders: The first contradiction involves a balance between a wide variety of rules known only by insiders and the ways that the community makes allowances for known people who break those rules. This pattern shows how the community sets boundaries and tells people about how things work in Kenosha. As with many parts of Kenosha culture, these traits come from wider regional patterns.

- **Localized Knowledge**: People learn set patterns through personal knowledge. Many presume that anything outside of their personal experience is either wrong or does not exist. Information is not readily shared with outsiders and established Kenosha residents assume that others already know the expected patterns.

- **Conformity:** Community rules worked well for those familiar with them and who could live within them, but caused large problems for those who did not follow them. Many people reported that Kenosha is resistant to change, and following community cultural patterns is one aspect of fearing change. Since cultural patterns are transmitted through informal socialization rather than readily available written information or widespread education, newcomers are judged on whether or not they fit existing patterns. People who look and act differently are expected to learn to conform.

- **Support for Insiders:** The positive side of Kenosha culture is that people within the known social capital circle are provided with every kind of support. Rules are bent when the person breaking the rules belongs to the same group.

Insider Status Comes from Social Contact, Not Simply Racial Background: While this study documented many cases of negative behaviors toward people of color, the research consistently also found that individual ties developed through school or work were far more important than race or other group identity. We found two patterns:

1) Closed racial/national communities. Often, people had instrumental social supports exclusively within one race/national community because most of their social contacts were developed within race-based community networks and institutions.

2) Cross-race networks. These people developed closed social capital networks based on living and working in mixed neighborhoods, workplaces and schools.

Individual Attention and Boundaries through Rules: Another tension in Kenosha culture involves the conflict between providing attention to the individual versus the need for time boundaries in the completion of expected tasks. The many rules in an office establish boundaries. These rules are negotiated around the expectations of individual support. Kenosha culture involves two contradictory strategies to deal with this trend:

- **Individual Attention:** Part of supporting insiders involves being available to help them whenever they are in need. Previous obligations fall by the wayside as the staff person seeks to please the next request. This results in people failing to respond in a timely manner to less present requests as they always focus on the most immediate problem.

- **Boundaries through Rules and Egalitarian Ethos:** The many rules serve as a buffer from these expectations of always-available support. Always available support is only available to those who follow approved community patterns.

In order to counteract the trend toward helping known, personally present insiders before others, organizations often resort to lotteries or other first-come-first-served strategies to get around accusations of favoritism. In order to get around these solutions to allocating resources through closed social capital networks, people developed insider knowledge in order to make sure that they got resources first. For example, tickets for popular events may be sold out before they are advertised to the general public because insiders bought them before formal notification was published.

Presentation Patterns: Another aspect of Kenosha culture involves approved ways of interacting with others. People are calm and polite. On the surface they appear friendly. To people within their networks, friendliness is genuine—insiders receive every consideration. Outsiders, on the other hand may be politely ignored.

Communication patterns combine with communication styles. In addition to only talking with known individuals, insiders and outsiders are distinguished by their ability to maintain a calm, surface-friendly demeanor. People who exhibit emotions, talk more loudly than expected, move more quickly than locals or use hand gestures are considered potentially violent or crazy.

Education and the Egalitarian Ethos: As a community in transition, Kenosha residents had to address the need for more education against a history of factory work. Shop-floor culture privileged the camaraderie of line workers against educated or skilled outsiders. This played out in Kenosha as a suspicion of people with advanced education or who sought status through credentials.

Kenosha's egalitarian and anti-intellectual ethos played out differently among the educated middle class. Here, education and credentials were played down in favor of a low key, casual approach to others with similar ideas. We saw open reception to people offering good ideas to support the community. While being established in Kenosha mattered, the educated middle class was more open to newcomers who made a commitment to the area. Much of the creative social service activities came from the educated middle class melding ideas to fit the local community.

Reactions of Kenosha African American and Hispanic/Latino Communities to Kenosha Culture: People of color responded to Kenosha culture in three ways: 1) developing passive, invisible closed social capital networks within the Kenosha community, 2) blending into existing community patterns by adopting Kenosha culture and establishing cross-group networks, and 3) maintaining alternative cultural styles and fighting for group rights in Kenosha. The first two strategies were most welcomed by established Kenosha culture and were most prevalent until recently. Leaders were beginning to practice the third strategy shortly before this research project. Kenosha responded through resistance and slow change.

Economics and Social Capital: Employers

Types of Employers: The portrait of employment in Kenosha reveals a community that largely consists of a diverse, secondary sector employment base. Secondary sector firms are small companies. Currently, firms fall into two general categories. Half are *family supporting, education required* firms, offering family supporting wages and benefits primarily to well-educated male workers. The other half are *lower wages, wider range of opportunity* firms, providing lower wages, more part-time work and less benefits to people with varying educational backgrounds. This second group of firms offers more opportunities for people with limited education and semi-skilled or unskilled work experience. More women and minorities are employed in these firms.

In order to examine available employment more carefully, businesses were grouped by similar characteristics. Analysis revealed several very different kinds of employment opportunities for people seeking work in Kenosha. We found the following five clusters of business:

1. **Small retail and service sector businesses, sixty-two percent skilled labor force, moderate to high wages.** Forming twenty-one percent of the sample, companies in this group included small doctor's offices and high-end retail employers like a shop that makes and sells computers. Only twenty percent of the employees in these firms were part-time workers. Sixty-four percent of these companies had less than ten employees. On average, forty percent of their employees were female. All paid wages of over nine dollars an hour to their employees. Eighty-six percent of these businesses offered health insurance benefits to their employees.

2. **Small service and manufacturing firms offering high wages and requiring skilled employees.** Forming twenty-six percent of the sample, firms in this group included professional service organizations like law and doctors' offices and small manufacturing firms hiring skilled craftsmen. Seventy-seven percent of their labor force was skilled. Eighty-nine percent of the workers earned more than eleven dollars an hour. Ninety-seven percent of these companies offered

health insurance and only fifty-three percent expected employees to contribute to the costs of their health insurance. On average, sixty-one percent of the people employed in these firms were men.

3. **Service sector and manufacturing firms paying moderate wages, fifty-three percent skilled labor force, one-third labor force part-time.** Forming thirty-five percent of the sample, firms in this category included beauty parlors and small manufacturers. Most jobs paid between seven and eleven dollars an hour. These employers offered an even mix of skilled and unskilled jobs. Seventy percent of these employers offered health insurance to their workers.

4. **Middle size to large retail and non-profit firms paying low to moderate wages, over fifty percent part-time workers.** Forming ten percent of employers in the sample, examples were large chain stores, nursing homes, and large youth serving agencies. These employers offered the most unskilled and semi-skilled jobs. On average, forty-seven percent of their workforce was paid less than seven dollars an hour and the rest of the workers earned less than eleven dollars an

hour. Only twenty-eight percent of the workers in these companies were skilled. On average, seventy-one percent of the workers in these organizations were women. Seventy percent of these organizations offered health insurance.

viii

5. **Small to middle size retail and service companies paying low wages and offering part-time hours.** Forming eight percent of the sample, employers in this group were very similar to group four, but were smaller operations. Examples include small restaurants, house cleaning services and small stores. Half of their employees were part-time. Eighty-five percent of their workers earned less than seven dollars an hour. On average, sixty percent of the labor force was female. Only half of the employers in this group offered health insurance. Even when employees could get insurance through their work, they were expected to pay for the insurance themselves.

Hiring and Retention: Most people hope for jobs in companies like those in the first two groups. However, not everyone can find work in these firms. Just as there are two divergent types of employers in Kenosha, employees are tracked into either low-wage or high-wage employment. This tracking partly comes from the human capital and cultural capital characteristics of employees themselves. Ways that jobs are advertised and employer hiring practices which bring social capital into play also influence who finds jobs in different kinds of firms.

Advertising and Hiring Practices: On average, employers reported that one-third of their referrals came from friends and family, thirty-one percent came from newspaper advertising, sixteen percent from walk-ins, eight percent from training programs, two percent from unemployment, and nine percent from other means. The nine percent "other" category included hiring through temporary agencies. Temporary agency employment is a

particular concern to some anti-poverty agencies because temporary employees rarely receive benefits and often do not graduate to full time, permanent jobs. On the other hand, employers like temporary agencies because they screen their employees for them and allow them a flexible workforce.

The types of advertising used to garner applicants varied depending on the size of the company. Small companies were more likely to get referrals from friends and family while larger firms were more likely to advertise in the newspaper or use the unemployment office.

Hiring in Kenosha is usually done by one individual in each comany. The owner or chief executive was responsible for hiring decisions thirty-nine percent of the time. A manager or department head made hiring decisions forty-three percent of the time. Four percent of the hiring decisions were made by human resources. Owners and executives primarily did the hiring in small companies while managers and department heads were responsible in chains and large firms. Only nine percent of the companies used team hiring to decide on workers. Team hiring primarily occurred in small, professional service establishments where people need to work together.

Individualized decision-making meant that employees may have little say in who worked with them. On the other hand, employers might rely on employee referrals in deciding among applicants. Combined with the fact that managers and owners often had a lot of say regarding benefits, this meant that the employer had a lot of power in employment relationships. In the small firms where most employees come from similar cultural capital backgrounds and share social capital connections, the power dynamics between employee and employer may not become cause for concern.

However, in companies hiring people different from themselves,

individualized hiring and employment decisions meant that the employer set the tone for employment decisions. For example, we noticed several employers who would not consider an applicant from a different racial and ethnic group. A few other businesses actively recruited a diverse workforce.

Retention: The tone of the workplace also influenced the ability of employers to keep employees. In a tight labor market like Kenosha, churning—or quick turnover of employees—is a real concern for both employers and people hoping to place low-income workers into stable employment. The value of a supportive workplace is particularly important in a community with closed social capital networks relying on individualized knowledge and cultural practices.

The *Kenosha Employers Survey* sought to understand this process by asking about mentoring available for new employees on the job. Sixty-eight percent of the employers reported that they think mentoring is important and assign a mentor to newcomers. However, mentoring largely turned out to mean orientation by a supervisor or more established employee.

Limited mentoring means that employees need to learn quickly the rules of the workplace. Adjusting to a new workplace may be easy if they fit into the unspoken culture because they come with appropriate cultural capital or they already have friends in the workplace due to social capital networks that encouraged them to apply. Those lacking either appropriate social or cultural capital may have a harder time.

The Role of the Kenosha County Job Center: The *Kenosha Employers Survey* and the observation data suggest that few employers need to use a government service to find employees. The *Kenosha Employers Survey* found that only thirty-four percent of the organizations in the study used the job center. These employers fell into three types: sixty-nine percent of the manufacturers;

seventy-one percent of government agencies; and sixty-four percent of non-profits in the study used the job center. Interviews and observations revealed that these organizations used the job center due to social capital. Government and non-profit organizations have strong ties to the job center due to contracting and information-sharing networks. Manufacturers are tied to the job center because KABA, their professional organization, works closely with the job center to recruit employers to Kenosha and facilitate employment in the area.

Implications for Policy and Programs:

This picture of employment in Kenosha suggests the following concerns for people intent on finding stable employment for families:

- *Employment and support practices need to be targeted toward small, secondary sector firms.* The prevalence of small companies in Kenosha suggests that many of the strategies to support working families developed for large companies, such as good employer-based health insurance, on-site day care and employer-sponsored transportation, will not work in this community. Instead, local government and agencies need to design childcare, health insurance benefits and transportation strategies that are employer pooled or community based. Ideas like small business health insurance pools, neighborhood based childcare, and car donation and repair services may work better in this type of community.

- *Employment development strategies need to address the needs of two divergent types of employers in Kenosha.* Both types of employers are needed in the Kenosha economy. Since the tight labor market has already increased wages and benefits, simply calling for improving basic wage levels will not improve conditions for Kenosha

families. Given the small size of these firms, many cannot remain in business if solutions simply focus on employer driven strategies. Given the strong sense of individuality common in Kenosha culture, mandates are not likely to be well received. Therefore, more individualized strategies to improve wages, working conditions and employment prospects are important in Kenosha.

- *Targeted training combined with links between employer and potential employees will work best for some Kenosha firms.* This research suggests that half of the employers offer good benefits and wages to a skilled workforce. Developing targeted training initiatives to help Kenosha residents develop the skills needed for these jobs will improve working and training conditions for half of the employers and employees in Kenosha. However, given the limited number of jobs of this nature in Kenosha, trying to move everyone into these jobs will not succeed in fulfilling the needs of either employees or employers in this community. While some companies may be drawn to Kenosha if it had a more educated workforce, it is equally possible to saturate the job market. Producing too many employees in one category may lower wages and benefits. Education and training for higher skilled jobs is important, but must be combined with initiatives for low-skilled workers.

- *Community support strategies need to be developed for people in low-wage sectors of the economy.* The other half of the jobs in Kenosha are with service, retail, non-profit and government firms that offer low wages, limited benefits and part-time hours due to available funding and common business practices in these sectors. Given that many of these firms cannot or will not be able to improve wages and working conditions, strategies for these firms

should improve supplements for childcare, wages, benefits and transportation through government and non-profits.

- *Supports for entrepreneurs could provide additional family-supporting jobs in Kenosha.* Given the trend toward self-employment already evident in Kenosha, providing supports for these kinds of initiatives through small loans, technical support, pooled insurance plans and community-based marketing assistance could provide employment opportunities for some people struggling to find family-supporting work. These kinds of supports would also benefit existing small employers.

- *Social and cultural capital play a role in employment decisions in Kenosha.* Most employers in Kenosha use a combination of friends, family and word-of-mouth referrals to find applicants. Hiring decisions, benefits and supports on the job depend on the good will of the individual in charge of the organization. This means that employees need to develop ties to these organizations and develop the cultural capital appropriate to sustain employment.

Economics and Social Capital: Family survival strategies

Overall, the *Kenosha Social Capital Study* found three types of families in Kenosha:

- **Rising Educated Middle Class:** These families included wage earners with some college education who worked in professional or managerial occupations. In some cases, where there were two adult workers in the family, one may have worked primarily in stable factory or clerical employment.

- **Stable Working Class:** These families consisted of people with long-term good paying jobs in either factory or clerical

ix

employment. These individuals may have had some specific vocational training like a union apprenticeship or clerical training, but did not have a college education. In families with two adult wage earners, men frequently worked in factories while women worked either in factory work, clerical work or social service work.

- **Low-skilled Workers:** Low-skilled workers spent most of their work life in jobs that required limited skills and education. They alternated between spells on welfare and working in low-wage jobs. Examples included people who worked in low-wage secondary sector factories or service sector occupations like gardening, nursing assistant or cleaning houses. Many had completed high school and some had vocational training. People in this group were most likely to use welfare when times became difficult because they lacked the savings or on-the-job wages and benefits to survive without government support.

Social capital universally served as the entry point for jobs, education and other social supports in Kenosha. Almost everyone found work through family, friends and occasionally church or formal social service contacts. Educational decisions were made in the same way. Often, work and education decisions were influenced by cultural capital too. Social and cultural capital also influence strategies to deal with childcare, health care, transportation and other social supports.

Families in the three categories of *Rising Educated Middle Class*, *Stable Working Class* and *Low-skilled Workers* each have access to different kinds of social and cultural capital. We also found different levels of trust within closed social capital networks and among bridging networks for people in each of these three categories.

Most educated, middle-class African American and Hispanic/Latino families have found links to college and middle-class employment through supportive teachers, co-workers, supervisors or church members. These supports provided both the cultural and social capital to move into professional employment. People in this category also were able to use their credentials to find jobs even without strong social networks. The study found that people in this group were more comfortable using citywide resources like the Kenosha County Job Center computer network or professional organizations where they may not have a personal contact to find resources.

This comfort with published sources came from familiarity and trust of "mainstream" white resources. They also felt competent to judge among resources found through formal systems like listings of doctors or childcare facilities. Educated, middle-class people more easily bridged into other social capital networks among people with similar education and work experience backgrounds. For example, educated African Americans and Hispanic/Latinos were more likely to participate in organizations outside of their ethnic and racial communities.

Most stable working-class families rely primarily on friends and family to find work. Closed social capital networks also come from their churches. Most of their resources for childcare, transportation and other needs come from the same closed social capital networks. Many of the children of stable working-class families tend to develop similar career paths using the same kinds of networks. Given changes in the economy, the next generation also either moves down into the low-skilled worker category or moves into the educated middle class if they receive appropriate supports.

As with families in the first two categories, low-skilled workers also had strong closed social capital networks that helped them find work. The same networks helped with childcare, transportation, housing and a variety of basic needs. Low-skilled workers often turned to other family members, friends or neighbors for support. The same was true when cars broke down, people were evicted or they ran out of food. The difference between low-skilled workers and the families with more stable incomes is that these people do not have networks that can get them into more stable work. Low-skilled workers are also more likely to simply walk in and fill out applications for jobs than people in the stable working class because they lack direct connections to many jobs. Since people in the low-skilled worker category often lack the requisite work history to get jobs beyond their previous low-skilled employment, filling out applications for better jobs often leads nowhere.

Formal social service agencies are part of the social capital resources of low-skilled workers. Church social services are known in the same way. Through word-of-mouth knowledge within closed friend and family social networks, people learn which agencies to contact and, often, which services may be most helpful. Knowledge about how to use these services is also part of the cultural capital of these communities. Unlike the stable working-class, who are often ashamed to use government supports, the culture of communities that needs social services by necessity involves understanding how formal services can provide help when family, church and community networks cannot offer enough aid. While many low-skilled workers dislike using formal services because they are sometimes treated badly by agency staff, they do not feel shame when turning to an outside agency for help.

Implications for Programs and Policy

- *Formal supports are best advertised through informal networks.* People found resources through their closed social capital networks of friends, family, neighborhood and church. They learned about formal services like jobs, educational opportunities and other resources through the same channels. The best way to spread information given this tendency is to develop bridging contacts in closed social capital networks.

- *Supports are based on trust and cultural capital, not just information.* We found that people evaluated both organizations and individuals based on the good report of people or organizations that they trusted already. Much of that trust came from shared cultural capital. For organizations offering services or trying to develop workers, contact needs to go beyond simply sharing information. Agencies need to develop strong relationships with the people they work with and be prepared to modify cultural expectations to reach across communities.

- *Moving between communities involves developing both cultural and social capital.* The families who were most successful and resilient in this study could move between several closed social capital networks. These skills come from trusted, long term, positive involvement with people in different communities. Bridging social capital means more than connections or short-term interactions among people from different closed social capital networks.

The Kenosha Welfare System

The Kenosha welfare system experienced rapid change during the study period. Wisconsin's new welfare reform program, W-2, requires low-income families receiving government assistance to participate in work-related activities in an effort to rapidly move them into the labor force. Kenosha succeeded in achieving W-2 goals of reducing the welfare caseload. In September, 2000, 176 families were receiving cash assistance and another

126 were enrolled in case management or related services. This change was due to a combination of Kenosha's booming economy and W-2's emphasis on moving welfare recipients rapidly into the workforce.

While few families are involved in W-2, many more receive supports from government in the form of food stamps, medical assistance and subsidized childcare. W-2 emphasizes supporting working poor families through these kinds of supplements. Given that many of the jobs in Kenosha's new economy are service sector or small factory employment offering low wages and limited benefits, these kinds of supports are particularly important. In September, 2000, 4,901 families received food stamps, Medicaid or a combination of the two. The majority of these families, 3,080, only used government supports for medical assistance. A small proportion of Kenosha families, 818, were enrolled in subsidized childcare.

Kenosha differed from most of the United States in its approach to providing assistance to families in need through government. In keeping with Kenosha's egalitarian ethos of helping everyone in its community to become self-supporting, the Kenosha County Job Center did not distinguish between public assistance recipients and other community residents when offering job search and other related services. The Kenosha County Job Center was available to everyone looking for work in this community. The Kenosha County Job Center also developed close links to organizations offering housing, energy assistance, childcare, parenting, education and other services needed to support a working family. Through contracts and well-developed coalitions, the Kenosha County Job Center epitomized the one-stop-shop system that has become the ideal for social supports in the United States in recent years.

Despite goals of serving all Kenosha

residents, funding for the Kenosha County Job Center largely came from state welfare funds. From 1997 to 1999, roughly seventy percent of the Kenosha County Job Center budget came from W-2 and related contracts. Given the sharp reduction of people on public assistance after W-2 started, new state contracts implemented halfway through the *Kenosha Social Capital Study* reduced funding by approximately thirty-seven percent. As a result, Kenosha is now trying to offer the same universal program with less money, resulting in some staff and program cuts.

Implications for Policy and Programs:

Like many government systems, the Kenosha County Job Center has much promise but sometimes fails in executing its program fully. Problems come from: 1) a combination of limited funding that in turn limits services; 2) Kenosha cultural views about government aid that influence staff behavior; and 3) limited information about Job Center services stemming from localized knowledge within closed social capital networks. Low-income eligibility cut-offs associated with many government programs also limit the ability of the job center to provide assistance to a wide range of families that would benefit from assistance. Kenosha County Job Center's challenge involves creatively expanding its networks so that community residents increasingly use needed services while contending with budget cuts, as the state presumes that the working poor are completely self-supporting because they do not use government aid systems. The following changes to government policy and programs would help the Kenosha County Job Center and facilities like it throughout the United States better serve community residents:

- *Determine funding for government services based on community income figures rather than government program use.* The Kenosha partnership between government and non-profits that provides holistic service to some low-income residents is currently at risk because the government center has had to cut services due to funding which is formula-based on numbers of people using W-2. If the goal of welfare reform is to support low-income families through work, case management supports, childcare assistance, medical care and other services available through government become increasingly important in order to maintain these families in a secondary sector economy. Basing government funding to communities on data on families with incomes below the median wage or the number of workers employed in firms offering low wages and limited benefits would allow government to better meet this goal.

- *Raise income limits for support services like medical assistance, childcare assistance and training.* As with many other studies of working people in the United States, the *Kenosha Social Capital Study* finds that the lack of universal benefits common in most countries for health care, education and assistance raising children makes life difficult for all families. Given political realities which suggest that universal benefits will not be developed soon in this country, I recommend raising income eligibility levels so that more families who do not have access to these resources through work can get the help they need to thrive. Allowing more families to qualify for assistance may, in turn, increase support for government services throughout the community.

- *Ensure that staff providing information to the public seeking services have full training and have developed empathy for people using government aid.* One of the weaknesses of the Kenosha County Job Center system involves poor

services provided by front-line workers. Paying extra attention to the training and behavior of these workers would increase use of the Kenosha County Job Center and improve perceptions of the agency in the community.

- *Enlarge networks of organizations involved in coalition activities with the Kenosha County Job Center in order to improve service and expand community knowledge of government services.* The project found many examples of good service provided through a team of non-profit and government providers. However, agencies likely to be most in-touch with the closed social capital communities needing services are sometimes left out of these networks. Creating bridges to agencies within communities of color and their churches may improve supports for families in need and enhance knowledge of government services throughout Kenosha.

- *Use social capital links through agencies, employers, churches, schools, unions and other venues that are used by a wide array of Kenosha residents to share information about programs and the Kenosha County Job Center.* While anti-poverty agencies had information about government programs that were shared with program participants, many other organizations either did not have information or did not readily share it with all Kenosha residents. The Kenosha County Job Center needs to better advertise all of its services through presentations to people at places where they regularly congregate. In order to best facilitate use of services throughout the community, education sessions for gatekeepers within the organization such as teachers, floor supervisors, counselors, pastors and agency staff might best serve this goal. Given Kenosha's emphasis on providing employment supports to

all Kenosha residents, information fliers and presentations should stress the egalitarian goals of government services to help everyone eligible for assistance.

Social Service Agencies and Social Capital

The *Kenosha Social Capital Study* concentrated on Kenosha's non-profit organizations that provided a service to families in need or who were understood as located within the African American and Hispanic/Latino communities. The research focused on three organizations chartered to serve everyone in Kenosha with a particular need and five non-profit organizations identified with the African American and Hispanic/Latino community.

We found two types of organizations that provided services to the African American and Hispanic/Latino communities in Kenosha. On the one hand, citywide anti-poverty organizations provided services to a population that disproportionally consisted of people of color. These organizations were considered "strong" and "well run" by the city power structure.

On the other hand, organizations based in communities of color actually served people throughout the community because they each had contracts for citywide services. These organizations struggled more for funding than the mainstream organizations. These organizations had their core mission activities aimed at their communities, but also provided these services to people outside of their communities. While citywide opinion of each of these organizations varied, all had a reputation for "weak" governance and most had experienced financial scandals in the past. People in the Kenosha power structure were less sure of the quality of these organizations.

Part of this difference of opinion regarding these minority-based organizations came from the fact that

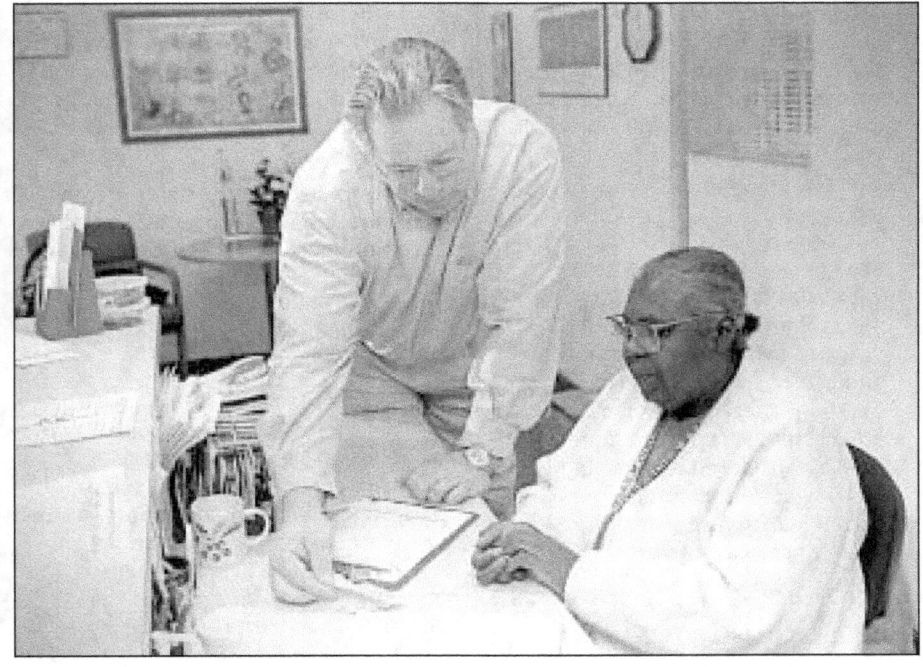

obligations, these individuals were more likely to put their energies into fundraising and governance for the organizations they perceived as providing more consistent service. They remained on community of color organization boards because they felt an obligation to community self-support despite misgivings about the direction of the organizations. As a result, they did little to help the weak organizations improve. The continued limited performance of these weak organizations became a self-fulfilling prophecy as under funded organizations struggled to meet their mission.

Citywide power brokers supported organizations in communities of color through contracts to provide services to everyone in Kenosha. These contracts had two opposite effects. On the one hand, contracts brought needed funds into these organizations. On the other hand, agencies already pulled in several directions found more of their resources focused on activities outside of their core mission. Community-wide support sometimes limited their ability to serve their closed social capital networks.

In an effort to offer bridging social capital, citywide power brokers created tensions in these minority community-focused institutions that were not easily resolved. Citywide solutions to crisis in these organizations reflected efforts to broaden social capital through connections to mainstream networks. Other organizations associated with communities of color continue to struggle to maintain their mission activity and build bridges to the larger Kenosha community.

they did not have uniformly good social capital relationships with the city power structure. Concerns also came from media perceptions. Finally, community perceptions of "good" leadership and citywide criteria for governance were not always the same. These factors together influenced citywide perceptions of these organizations. Perceptions, in turn, influenced the ability to get funding and staff for these organizations, creating a self-fulfilling prophecy that made it difficult for these organizations to successfully fulfill their missions.

Analysis of non-profit agencies providing services to the needy or to communities of color revealed a mixed picture. On the one hand, agencies received strong support from their community and worked together well. On the other hand, Kenosha organizations suffered from chronic under funding typical of small non-profit organizations. This was exacerbated by Kenosha's understanding of non-profits as charity for the deserving poor. The resources available to each institution depended on the resources of the social networks it was tied to. While citywide power brokers were concerned about caring

for African Americans and Hispanic/Latinos, they judged organizations by their ability to obtain resources from the wider community and create strong social capital ties throughout Kenosha.

At the same time, this perception of weak organizations came from lack of visibility for these organizations and their constituent communities in citywide social capital networks. Decision makers often were leery to believe these agencies' reports because they have no direct knowledge of their activities.

Often, non-profit organization analysts attribute poor organization performance to weak boards. This is not the case in Kenosha. In fact, we found overlapping board memberships including some of the same competent power brokers in the city in most Kenosha social service organizations we studied. All of these boards were racially integrated. In several cases, we found strong boards working actively for their communities that lacked the social capital resources to easily realize their missions. In other cases, boards consisted of people with access to citywide social resources who were on several boards. Torn between multiple

Implications for Policy and Programs

Nonprofit funding levels in Kenosha are too low to ensure adequate staffing, salaries and other tools to meet agency missions. Nonprofits become one employment source for workers, particularly in the African American and Hispanic/Latino communities. All agencies suffered from limited staffing due to insufficient funds. In order to adequately serve its community, funding and salary levels for small Kenosha non-profits need to rise to levels common in similar organizations elsewhere. Given generous community support already, additional resources may need to come from outside Kenosha.

Citywide contracts need to be better integrated into mission-based service provisions in order to better fulfill agency missions and build bridging social capital. Citywide services sometimes stretch the missions of the organization as well as their limited staff resources. Boards and staff at these organizations need to develop stronger mechanisms to link these programs to the core programs for the agency.

- *Organizations based in communities of color need to develop mechanisms to bring mainstream stakeholders into the agency to become more familiar with activities.* African American and Hispanic/Latino organizations sometimes lose out on citywide funds because key decision makers do not have direct knowledge of their activities. Mechanisms like placing these individuals on boards, inviting them to view activities, and regular conversations can better develop these links.

- *Agency heads need to develop strong personal social capital connections throughout Kenosha.* Bridging individuals were able to obtain resources for their agencies because they participated in citywide activities and made a practice of cultivating trusting relationships with politicians, businessmen and others throughout Kenosha. Newer key agency staff need to develop similar relationships in order for their agencies to thrive.

- *Front-line contacts like receptionists need to be paid staff with strong knowledge of agency programs and good communication skills.* Often agencies lose out on both funding and use of service because the person managing communications is a constantly changing volunteer. While considered expendable by many agencies, front-line communication staff are often key agency representatives.

Social Service Agency Use and Social Capital

Staff Practices: While many people reported getting good service from the Kenosha non-profits, we found that under-staffing did impact on service provision in agencies. Kenosha social service agency staff behavior reflected the patterns of support within closed social capital networks common in Kenosha culture. People observed that they had to wait a long time to get services or could not reach the staff person they needed to find. For example, one person tried to obtain a specialized service, only to have the appointment time reset over and over because staff would be pulled away for other emergencies.

Kenosha social service organizations also follow Kenosha culture patterns of working with people as they appear, not according to appointments. Some staff provide better service to people who are known to them. As a result, people needing help would identify a helpful staff person and rely on them to provide access to a variety of services.

However, we equally found organizations that would go out of their way to help someone that they had never met before. Staff would use their contacts to gain service throughout the city. In this way, Kenosha social service agency staff became the social capital conduit between people who lacked jobs, goods and services, and those who could fulfill that particular need.

Analysis of agencies revealed strong collaboration among agencies primarily based on individual social capital ties among staff. Caseworkers knew which agencies had contracts for which services and who might have a better connection for furniture or another basic need.

Usually, this involved a combination of direct referrals to other agencies and, if program participants had trouble navigating the communication practices at the other agency, caseworkers stepping in to ensure that their program participant received the requested service. This two-step process became necessary when the front line staff at the second organization did not relay messages to the requested caseworker due to limited time and training. Sometimes a new applicant to an agency had trouble accessing services because they did not fit into the social and cultural capital community of front-line agency staff. The front-line gatekeeper ignored newcomers or treated them badly because they were different.

Ways that People in Need Access Services: People accessed services at a particular agency in Kenosha for two reasons: 1) that agency was the only one providing the service; or 2) they had heard through closed social capital networks that an agency worker provided good service. As with employment and other aspects of Kenosha life, information was spread largely through word of mouth referrals. Social capital provided most of the information that people needed in order to find services. Within communities needing particular services, there was little need to advertise because people provided the information to others in their social capital network.

People coming to an agency to obtain a specific service often simply came to achieve their goal and left. We rarely witnessed people coming into an agency for these specific services asking about other programs offered by that agency. This observation implies that, while government contracts to provide citywide services brought money and people into these small community-based agencies, these activities did little to expand the number of people who used other programs or enhance bridging social capital among closed communities.

This pattern shows that closed community patterns extended to nonprofit organization use. People in need would first turn to their churches and then to organizations with a reputation for supporting people in their social capital networks. Organizations needed to establish trusting relationships in the same way as individuals. For people of color, this often meant going to a trusted staff person at one of the organizations based in communities of color.

Results of Service: Comparisons Across Types of Agencies: We found two patterns among social service agencies in Kenosha. In some cases, agency workers provided help that met direct needs for program participants but maintained a boundary that maintained inequality and existing closed social capital networks. Mainstream agency staff were more likely to practice this pattern. For example, one direct service worker offered an array of services to clients, but presented advice in a rigid and patronizing manner. While offering help, the worker maintained a boundary through her manner that suggested that the clients were objects to serve, not neighbors in need. No social capital connections or trust were offered or built through this transaction. The program participants patiently accepted the service, but did not try to bridge the gap between provider and participant.

The tendency for organizations to provide help, but not always a step up, varied based on several factors:

• **The relationship between staff and program participants.** In most cases, we found that people of color in need seldom developed strong egalitarian relationships with mainstream white agency staff because those staff held subtle beliefs that program participants were culturally different from themselves. On the other hand, agency staff from any background that see program participants as potential equals and promote their development can make a real difference in the lives of the people they serve.

• **The cultural habits and closed social capital networks bringing program participants to the agency.**

• **The social and cultural capital networks developed within programs among agency participants.** For example, program participants in one anti-poverty program developed a close network that continued after participants finished the program. These participants worked together to find childcare and housing, and fulfill other basic and social needs. While these networks provided important support for these individuals, they also limited the ability of network members to seek additional outside supports. Since all of these people were low-skilled workers returning to low-skilled jobs, they did not develop either networks or skills to move beyond their current social and economic status.

Organizations based in communities of color and mainstream organizations often have different social and cultural capital related gifts to offer people in their programs. While mainstream agency staff often did little to create bridges across class and race boundaries, sometimes these organizations offered important social

and cultural capital support that changed the lives of program participants. While staff at organizations based in communities of color were more likely to offer holistic services to program participants with an egalitarian ethos, these organizations did not always have the social capital ties themselves to build bridges into other communities.

If the goals of social service are to support families through services in keeping with their current closed social and cultural capital networks, both types of non-profit organizations in Kenosha achieve this goal quite well, though sometimes in different ways. Both organizations and participants relied on their established closed social capital networks to achieve these goals.

If non-profits also intend to foster bridging social capital, the extra ingredient of social trust between program participant and staff needs to exist in order to make links into different worlds. In many cases, people of color from the same communities as program participants, but who worked in mainstream organizations, provided the important link between closed social capital communities and other opportunities.

Implications for Policy and Programs

• *Making concrete connections between citywide services and core agency services is an important way to build agency use and create bridging social capital.* Given that people using non-profits for citywide services do not pay attention to other services offered by the organization, staff should pay special attention to introducing these people to other agency programs. Since this is best done through social capital networks of participants, introducing people who use the agency in a casual way to people in core programs may achieve this goal.

- *Enhancing the circle of care throughout the community and building bridging social capital through mentoring.* Many people receive strong social supports through agency staff they trust who connect them to goods and services in related organizations. Strengthening this process by drawing on successful people within the community to work more closely with program participants may achieve this goal. Agency board members and church volunteers are important resources in this process.

xvi

Churches and Social Capital

Policy makers and some researchers think of churches as an alternative form of support for families. Some policy makers think that churches can do a better job of providing for poor families than either government or non-profit organizations. These people think that churches have social capital that government and non-profit organizations lack. Others see churches as teaching appropriate values. These people see churches as purveyors of cultural capital.

Instrumental Supports through Churches: Each of the churches offered a variety of social and economic supports to their members and the wider community. For the most part, these ministries took two forms. Formal mission committees of both women and men visited the sick, provided spiritual and emotional support to families facing hard times, and gave away goods and sometimes cash to people in need. People helped through church instrumental support included both parishioners and others in the community.

One hallmark of church instrumental support involved the circle of giving and receiving in the African American congregations. Most families active in helping others through church and their work had received similar support themselves. The circle of care

ranged from social visits when someone was ill to long-term financial or mentoring support.

Church instrumental support took a more formal shape in the Catholic parish. Here, ministry was provided either through the center for the Spanish-speaking population or the St. Vincent de Paul office. Givers and receivers often differed by generation and sometimes race. For example, most of the people receiving aid were newcomer Mexicans or African Americans.

Churches as Training Ground and Developers of Cultural Capital: We found that the churches' role as training ground and spiritual well for people involved in social welfare activities in the community was far more important than direct social service because of the range of social welfare activities provided by congregation members. Most of the African Americans working as teachers, counselors, and social service agency employees, and in other helping roles in Kenosha were active in church and came from religious backgrounds. Churches taught

leadership, values appreciated by mainstream culture, and the patience to work with difficult populations. Churches encouraged both education and work that offered more than financial remuneration.

Faith-based ministries for youth development, education and political activities eclipsed the instrumental ministries in importance for people participating in these activities. Both of the larger African American churches strove to involve their members in several ministries.

We saw the same relationship between faith and works in the Hispanic/Latino Catholic community, though less frequently. Given the formalized nature of social support, church-based activity often involved individuals who either were asked to participate in social welfare activities or volunteered to help others. Examples include nuns or priests asking someone to take on a faith-based social welfare job or Anglos who helped out Hispanic/Latino families through a church-sponsored activity. In both cases, initial participation in church-based service led to a life of work for others through non-sectarian social service venues.

How Do Churches Build Social Capital?:
Kenosha African American and Hispanic/Latino community churches built social capital through a slow and consistent process of developing community and establishing trust among their members. For example, at a meeting at one church committee, parishioners arranged food for a sick person. In addition, Tasha, a newcomer to the church, was offered a combination of emotional, spiritual and instrumental support as she was introduced to the community by her aunt as one in need of prayer as she struggled with a learning disability. Tasha was welcomed into the church community through prayers and caring words. Hugs and encouragement help develop trust in this supporting community. With this trust, Tasha hopefully will feel comfortable asking church members for help if she struggles in school. Church members learn that Tasha has a problem that requires their assistance, understanding her as a member of their community in need rather than a young person who fails at school for an unknown reason. They are more likely to help her because both relationships and trust have been established.

Bridging Churches:
Two churches that participated in this project developed bridging links as organizations and fostered bridging social capital among their members. A number of members of these churches talked about how their church provided a strong sense of self for African Americans. These churches were most likely to have members who went to college, were employed in professional jobs and were involved in social service activity throughout Kenosha. These churches also were most likely to draw members from newcomers to the area.

Implementing a bridging vision included involving church members in active ministries to develop themselves and the community, an active practice of joint worship and advocacy activities with both white and African American churches, and participation in community social service and politics. As a result, African American churches and their members are becoming a visible presence in Kenosha for the first time.

Closed Social Capital:
Members of all churches practiced closed social capital, as was common among most people of color in Kenosha. Closed social capital involves equally strong networks that people rely on for social, economic and emotional supports. However, community boundaries are carefully guarded and social capital networks are maintained within the network. These organizations and their members become invisible to outsiders. As organizations, all of the churches serving people of color practiced closed social capital. The bridging churches exhibited both bridging and closed social capital, while leaders and members of closed communities only went to outsiders when they needed something.

Building Cultural Capital:
Churches built cultural capital in a variety of ways, too. Most mechanisms were subtle encouragement for certain kinds of behavior. For example, one church listed the names of all the college students who belonged to the congregation in the weekly bulletin.

While most of these examples show support for education and advancement, the smaller, working-class and low-skilled worker churches did not always support behaviors valued by mainstream society. For example, one of our fieldworkers, Raymond, was an African American from a low-income community seeking a college education. He reported to me that he felt unwelcome because church members resented him for going to college. Appropriate cultural patterns in this community meant not getting above everyone else through advanced education.

Churches as Providers of Social Welfare Services:
This study suggests that churches provide a wide array of instrumental supports through formal and informal mission activity. Churches also offer spiritual and moral guidance that helps their members develop social and cultural capital appreciated by employers, schools and other aspects of mainstream society.

Churches do not necessarily provide appropriate supports to needy people. Three separate factors can create situations where churches fail to provide the combination of loving support and "appropriate" values that will lead to economic self-sufficiency.

- **The nature of the values taught by the church**
- **The nature of the relationship between the church and people in need receiving service from that church.** For example children in low-income neighborhoods in Kenosha were picked up for church by a bus from one of the larger, white churches. While the church supported middle-class values, the children were not welcomed into the church community as full members like the families where both adults and children attended. The church may have offered new cultural capital, but it did nothing to provide social capital to these children. It is unclear whether or not the children absorbed the cultural capital values taught at church.
- **The nature of relationships within the church.** Some people may attend churches that offer a combination of community, social capital and cultural capital valued by mainstream society. Nevertheless, church members whose lives do not meet the standards common in that church may feel left out due to gossip or more subtle sanctioning in the community.

xvii

Implications for Policy and Programs

xviii

- *Churches offer training in many social support activities.* Volunteer work in churches provides on-the-job training in a variety of social welfare occupations. Organizations seeking new volunteer and paid leaders or employees would do well to strengthen relationships with active churches to locate appropriate people.

- *Churches offer social and cultural capital to their members who meld well with the congregation.* This research found that churches created social and cultural capital supports for their members when they were welcomed into the church community. This means that churches can have a positive influence on their members. At the same time, churches do not necessarily foster bridging social capital or cultural capital valued by "mainstream" society. Nor is everyone who attends a church activity invited to fully participate in the community of care offered by that church. This finding suggests that churches in and of themselves are not an automatic solution to social problems.

- *Bridging social and cultural capital through churches can only be developed when people meet as equals with mutual respect for each other.* This research project found many examples of churches helping low-skilled workers move into the stable working and middle class. Churches that worked together with other churches in trusting relationships can change a community.

- *Church support is limited to the resources of those churches.* Kenosha's African American and Hispanic/Latino churches had much to offer their communities. However, their resources are not limitless. Finances depend on the means and generosity of the congregation. Formal programs

depend on the time and talents of leadership and members, combined with the limits of financial resources. While churches could provide additional formal programs if more financial support is provided, churches are interested in providing supports on their own terms. For example, one pastor offers food or financial assistance only if an individual agrees to church counseling. This finding means that churches cannot take over all social welfare provision or substitute for government or non-profit providers.

Dynamics between Churches, Social Service Agencies and Communities

The various non-profit organization coalitions had little formal connections to the churches. Until very recently, few churches engaged in social activities as a united body. Church coalitions focused on joint worship or educational activities, not creating links to social service organizations. However, during the study period this began to change when the pastor of a key bridging church assumed coalition leadership. The major church

coalition started inviting people involved in various forms of social service to present information on their activities to this organization. More churches became actively involved in social service. Churches also became more involved with politics.

As with non-profit organizations, we found many more connections between churches, non-profits and community through informal ties. This study found multiple connections between churches and non-profits serving the African American and Hispanic/Latino communities in Kenosha. Churches provided the base communities for many of the board, staff and participants in non-profit organizations. Particularly in the smaller organizations, overlapping religious and neighborhood ties became the resource for employees, board and participants. Churches often served as initiators of non-profit activity and training grounds for service. Several of these organizations started out as church missions. Many key staff moved from active church mission work to paid non-profit casework. This was especially true for people lacking professional educational credentials.

Church mission models also pervade service and fundraising strategies for Kenosha organizations. Kenosha egalitarian culture expects most non-profits to rely heavily on church and neighborhood-based volunteer resources. This led to unrealistic expectations for organizations that did not possess similar resources. On the negative side, each of the African American and Hispanic/Latino organizations is expected to fulfill every need for their constituency, just like the church missions would find food, clothing, financial assistance, work and other resources for parishioners and other community members in trouble.

On a more positive note, church models provided creative alternatives to fundraising through grants and other more standard mechanisms. For example, one minority community organization filled the inevitable gaps in operating budgets due to limited government funding with the parish fundraising technique of Bingo games. African American and Hispanic/Latino organizations also turned to churches for volunteers to supplement paid staff.

These strong links among churches, organizations and community show that Kenosha creates a circle of care to support organizations that share the same ethos within that community. It is precisely the three-way links between church, non-profit and caring community that creates the circle of care that people need to develop the skills to bridge across social capital networks in a community like Kenosha. For example, Janice was raised on welfare by a single parent after her mother stopped working to care for a sick grandmother. She grew up in a poor neighborhood and was labeled as learning disabled by the schools. However, she had strong supports through her church, activities from a minority community-based non-profit organization, and youth group activities in another African American community-based organization that provided bridges to

the outside. The encouragement of both closed and bridging social capital connections through church and organizations led her to go to college and become a teacher. She now teaches children labeled "at risk" like she was and actively volunteers for both church and the non-profit organization that provided further support to continue her education.

Janice's story suggests the value of both closed and bridging social capital. Without the support of the financially weak African American non-profit and her closed community church, she would not have developed bridging social capital. However, without the equally strong ties to people who bridged between communities, she would most likely have remained in the closed communities like her peers.

Implications for Policy and Practice:

In recent years, policy makers have debated whether non-profits, churches, for-profit organizations or government can best provide for people in this society. Policy makers also debate whether or not community participation is on the decline. This research study suggests that social capital and community participation is alive and well in communities like Kenosha. However, community and individual development is not a simple thing that happens through one strategy. Instead, communities come out of the dynamics among organized institutions like churches and non-profits, situated with communities of people who share common values and goals. In most communities like Kenosha, society is made up of many smaller communities with closed social and cultural capital.

Strategies to develop more inclusive communities must get beyond simply counting memberships; asserting that church, non-profit or for-profit providers are "better"; or debating the value of minority versus majority controlled organizations. Strong communities need a combination of all

of these things plus people who can bridge between the necessary closed communities.

- *Supporting families involves creating strong partnerships among government, non-profits and churches that recognize the strengths and unique contributions of each type of institution.*

- *Developing partnerships starts with recognizing the assets in communities identified as in need of service.* Many of the books on church involvement in social welfare presume that church members come from economically, spiritually and socially stable communities while the people they aim to help lack spiritual and social supports as well as basic needs. In fact, communities always include a combination of people with different assets and needs. Working with these assets is the first step in building connections among the haves and the have-nots in this society. This means seeking community leaders and drawing on the strengths of the people receiving service.

- *Developing strong individuals involves expanding communities of trust through overlapping networks among non-profits, churches and government.* Programs and policies need to encourage the creation of communities of care like these positive examples in Kenosha through developing staff and volunteer connections among divergent communities and organizations. These connections need to include shared power and respectful interactions. Including partners from targeted communities at all levels of organizations is the first step in fostering these kinds of positive experiences. Providing adequate assets to build bridges across communities is also essential.

Conclusion: Social Capital and Supporting Families through Organizations and Churches

xx The *Kenosha Social Capital Study* shows that social capital is an important ingredient in understanding how families find work, instrumental supports like childcare and education, and social supports. Social capital is equally important for organizations, churches and communities. Formal institutions and groups of people also need trusting connections to survive and grow. This study suggests a number of general implications for policy and programs. While these concluding ideas are focused on Kenosha, they hold for many local communities looking for ways to better support their families and organizations.

Implications for Policy and Programs

- *Developing strong families and communities involves creating equal partnerships among non-profits, government and churches that recognize the different strengths of each type of organization.* The sections on the role of organizations, churches and government in supporting families show that a circle of care involves churches providing basic instrumental, spiritual and social supports; formal organizations offering professional services; and government providing income supports and connections to other services that work best to support families. Sections on organizations show that neither churches, organizations nor government can do the work of the other adequately. Furthermore, the strength of Kenosha's public/private partnership involved adequate funding for all partners. The circle of care fails when one partner relies on the other to provide services due to lack of funding or other resources.

- *Both organizations and communities enable social capital through individual networks.* People obtain work, services, social supports or resources for organizations through connections among individuals. Strengthening ties among communities and organizations in Kenosha involves expanding these individual connections. The challenge for Kenosha and other communities like it involves the fact that these connections are grounded in pre-existing power relations and suspicion of the other. Through mutual activities, organizations and communities need to first break down the negative aspects of closed social capital if they intend to build bridging social capital.

- *Bridging social capital is built through key individuals moving across closed social capital lines.* Individuals or key organizational staff develop links into closed social capital networks. Sometimes this involves a bridging individual creating links for a closed social capital church or organization. In other cases, mainstream leaders insist on diversifying an organization's board and key staff when they are in trouble. As the citywide contracts for organizations show, bridging social capital only develops when people develop trust across networks through personal contacts, not simply by using an organization. The same is true for coalition activities or organizational growth.

- *Community strategies must be grounded in local culture and community practices.* The efforts that succeed in Kenosha draw on community ethos for supporting everyone as equals through work, connections among closed social capital networks, and localized knowledge. Ideas coming from the outside or that do not appeal to all of these elements achieve less success. For example, a church initiative aimed at simply giving things to the needy received limited support while another activity that spoke of helping people find work met with more success. Appeals to programs for all Kenosha residents rather than race-based organizing was more successful. While community culture will necessarily differ in various localities, it is important for planners to identify key cultural traits and understand how the community puts them into action in their organizations and programs.

- *Change comes from drawing on established social and cultural capital to expand into new territory.* The successful programs for individuals drew on the circle of care already established in community churches and organizations to help people find new directions. Positive participation in one activity led to movement into another related activity through individuals trusted in each organization. Without these already established ties, new growth would not occur. The same is true for organizations. The church coalitions that are slowly changing the political and social landscape in Kenosha developed through years of joint worship and participation in activities that drew on older Kenosha cultural forms. The trusting relationships developed in these closed networks provide the foundation for more radical change.

Introduction

The Kenosha Social Capital Study *examined the role of non-profit organizations and churches in the African American and Hispanic/ Latino communities in Kenosha, Wisconsin. Kenosha County is located on the Wisconsin/Illinois border at the Southwest corner of the state. The county has about 135,000 people. Kenosha is located about an hour and a half north of Chicago and about forty-five minutes south of Milwaukee. 1990 U.S. Census figures listed a population of approximately 80,000 people. Ninety percent were white, five percent African American, and another six percent were Hispanic/Latino. Numbers add up to more than one hundred percent because Hispanic origin is a separate question from race in the U.S. census. People choose a racial category (Black, white, Asian/Pacific islander, Native American or other) and then are asked if they are of Hispanic origin. Most of the people of Hispanic/Latino heritage originally came from Mexico.*

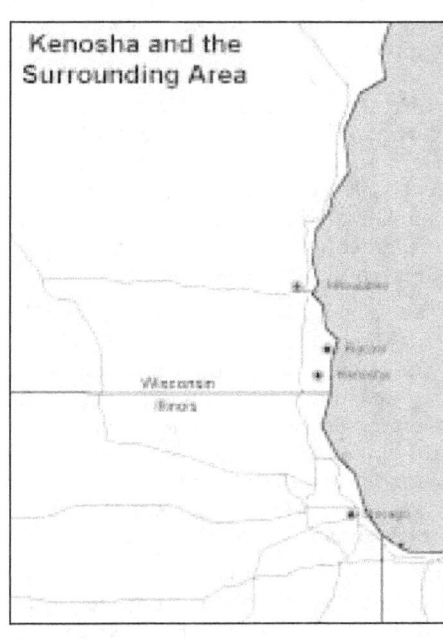

Kenosha and the Surrounding Area

Project History

The *Kenosha Social Capital Study* was an action research project developed and carried out with the guidance of Kenosha community representatives. The research was conducted by a team of faculty, research associates and students from University of Wisconsin-Parks de. Most of the research included observations of activities in organizations, churches

and community events. We also interviewed key leaders throughout Kenosha and typical Hispanic/Latino and African American families. Finally, the project included a survey of Kenosha employers regarding their hiring practices. Some of the research was conducted as class projects by students involved in research methods and social welfare related classes. Leadership Kenosha and the Kenosha Women's Commission also

participated in design and data collection for the *Kenosha Employers Survey.*

The project was one outcome of a community needs assessment conducted in 1997-1998 called the *Kenosha Conversation Project.* The *Kenosha Conversation Project* was a community planning process designed to bring together everyone involved in welfare reform in this locale to discuss the impact of policy changes created by the transition from AFDC to TANF and to suggest ways that the community could best support low-income people transitioning from welfare to work. The *Kenosha Conversation Project* consisted of two components. A research process gathered information on Kenosha residents' experience with welfare reform. People working at the Kenosha County Job Center (the government social welfare agency), government and non-profit social service agency representatives, church representatives, low-income people served by social service programs,

2

employers, government officials and other concerned citizens met to talk about their experience with welfare reform.

The research was used to identify major community concerns, which were addressed at a conference. The conference brought together people from all of these groups in issue-oriented small groups to discuss their experience and strategies for change. The conversation activities were designed to include all participants as equals. The groups developed a number of ideas, which could be implemented by various groups throughout the community.

The *Kenosha Conversation Project* found that the needs of low-income families were largely identical to other working families in Kenosha. For this reason, the *Kenosha Social Capital Study* looked at everyone in Kenosha's African American and Hispanic/Latino communities rather than concentrate solely on low-income families.

One outcome of the *Kenosha Conversation Project* was a concern that African Americans and Hispanic/Latinos were particularly at risk in Kenosha. In addition to high unemployment and low incomes, a greater proportion of people from these two groups used public assistance through the Kenosha County Job Center than their proportion in the Kenosha community. Since implementation of W-2 in 1997, the Kenosha County Job Center welfare client base has shifted from twenty-five percent African American and fifteen percent Hispanic/Latino to forty-one percent African American and thirteen percent Hispanic/Latino. The welfare caseload had also dropped dramatically: only 381 families were on W-2 in Kenosha in 1998 and less than half of these families received cash grants. Half of the eligible population applied for service when the Kenosha County Job Center implemented W-2. Kenosha County Job Center statistics showed that many of these people were

working, but community representatives remain concerned that people are not accessing the needed support services.

The Hispanic/Latino and African American populations were of particular concern for different reasons. The Kenosha County Job Center was concerned that Hispanic/Latinos were not accessing services because they feared that they would be deported or thought that they were no longer eligible for services. Even though the low-income African American community is rapidly becoming a major proportion of the participants served by the Kenosha County Job Center, some African Americans voice confusion over W-2 and suspect that the Kenosha County Job Center does not equally serve them.

Rather than focus simply on the relationship between low-income African Americans and Hispanic/Latinos and the Kenosha County Job Center, the *Kenosha Social Capital Study* chose to concentrate on supports for everyone within these two communities through non-profits and churches for three reasons. First, since welfare reform stressed sending people to community resources for support, the project sought to understand how community-based organizations responded to this shift in government policy. Second, since many families in need relied either solely on private sources or a combination of government and the non-profit sector, we focused on how people used community institutions regardless of the availability of government help. Finally, given the project's wider focus on supports for all African American and Hispanic/Latino Kenosha residents, we studied how non-profits and churches based in these two communities helped or hindered families who thrived in the booming Kenosha economy and families who remained mired in poverty.

Project Goals

Overall, the project focused on 1) how African Americans and Hispanic/Latinos support their families, 2) the role of community organizations and churches in this process, and 3) the dynamic between communities and their organizations. The research project used a social science concept called social capital to understand these issues. Social capital includes two ingredients: relationships based in enforceable trust with people or organizations who have access to resources needed to meet basic necessities and fulfill goals; and knowledge of cultural cues which indicates that an individual is a member of a group and should be given access to those relationships. The purpose of this project was to study how social capital helps or hinders the development of people and organizations in these two minority groups in Kenosha. Through social capital we can also understand the reasons behind people from these two groups utilizing or not utilizing the services provided for them. Research focused on the following questions:

- What are the community dynamics and needs within the Hispanic/Latino and African American communities?

- What roles do community-based organizations and churches play in supporting community residents?

- What is the relationship between these two communities and the Kenosha County Job Center?

- In general, what role do community-based organizations play in facilitating or hindering communication between organizations providing government-funded welfare reform services and the populations served by these programs?

- What role does race and immigration status play in this process?

The project looked at community institutions from two perspectives. First, we studied the ways that families in these two communities used non-profits and churches to meet their needs for basic necessities like food, clothing, money, education, youth activities, to locate work, to find social supports, and as sources of spiritual or moral guidance. This part of the research came out of concerns about the ways that working families in these two Kenosha communities supported themselves in an era of welfare reform.

The 1996 United States federal *Temporary Assistance to Needy Families* (TANF) legislation limited use of government-funded assistance to five years in a lifetime and required people receiving assistance to participate in work-related activities in order to receive assistance. Wisconsin-Works (W-2), Wisconsin's TANF program, relies on a partnership between non-profit organizations, for profit organizations, and government to provide social welfare services. The Kenosha W-2 program also tries to divert families in need to other institutions before providing government assistance. Examining ways that poor families use organizations shows how they adapt to welfare reform.

The *Kenosha Social Capital Study* looked at ways that all working families use organizations and churches as resources. In addition to people who move between work and welfare to support their families, both the African American and Hispanic/Latino communities include families who fall into the middle class and stable working class. However, the unemployment and poverty rates for African Americans and Hispanic/Latinos are much higher than for Kenosha as a whole. Unemployment in Kenosha hovers at about 3.5 percent. Unemployment rates for African Americans and Hispanics/Latinos are much greater than for the general Kenosha population. African American

unemployment is 7.6 percent for men and 11.6 percent for women. Unemployment rates for Hispanic/Latinos are 9.4 percent for men and 15 percent for women.[1] In addition, African Americans and Hispanic/Latinos are much poorer than others in the city. In comparison to a citywide median household income of $30,638, according to 1990 census figures, sixty-four percent of African American households and sixty-five percent of Hispanic/Latino households earn less than $25,000 per year.

Given that many more families in the African American and Hispanic/Latino communities had trouble finding stable, family-supporting jobs in comparison to whites in this community, Kenosha residents were particularly concerned about how these low-income families were faring given welfare reform. Community members and researchers wanted to know how low-income families managed today. The study also sought to understand why some people in these communities found good paying jobs while others remained in poverty.

Since non-profit organizations and churches provide a variety of services to people that can help them meet basic needs and develop successful career paths, the study concentrated on the role of these institutions in this process. We particularly focused on organizations and churches that came out of the Hispanic/Latino and African American communities based on the assumption that people were more likely to turn to help within their own communities before going to other institutions. However, the study also included research in Kenosha's homeless shelter, women's shelter and several youth organizations developed for everyone in Kenosha.

Given that the ability of organizations and churches to help community members depends on the strengths and weaknesses of these institutions, the study also examined the nature of the non-profits and churches serving

these two communities. This part of the study looked at the place of African American and Hispanic/Latino non-profit organizations and churches in their communities and Kenosha as a whole. We focused on ways that community members supported their organizations as employees, volunteers and active members. We also examined the way that citywide resources from individuals, businesses, local foundations and government provided financial support, technical assistance and information to these institutions.

Research on dynamics on the organization level also looked at connections between non-profits and churches based in these two communities and other organizations throughout the city. This aspect of the research also documented the ways that institutions helped or hindered interaction between African Americans and Hispanics/Latinos as groups and the greater Kenosha community. The study asked if organizations served as a conduit between minority communities and majority institutions. Did churches and non-profits represent these two sub-communities to Kenosha as a whole? How did the actions of these institutions promote better inter-group interactions in this community? What was the role of non-profits and churches in encouraging public policy to improve the economic conditions for poorer members of their communities?

By looking more broadly at issues of community supports, we sought not simply to understand how low-income people survive, but to compare the experiences of those who succeed in the present day economy to those who fail. As in the *Kenosha Conversation Project*, we found that low-income families were more similar to working-class and middle-class families than they were different. We also found that many families with stable incomes either had financial troubles themselves in the past, or had members of their extended families

3

4

who were impoverished now. Instead of documenting the differences between the haves and the have-nots, we found a circle of care among everyone in these communities. This circle of care extended to organizations, with many links between churches, non-profits, government and community through both formal coalitions and informal networks. Social capital became the glue cementing families in these communities together. However, we also found families outside of these networks and cases where social capital links between individuals and organizations did not exist because of the closed nature of some social capital networks.

We also found that culture played an important role in fostering different kinds of social capital. Social scientists use the term cultural capital to describe cultural cues that are considered normal behavior in various communities. Cultural capital influenced access to both individual networks and organizations. Social and cultural capital together made a difference in Kenosha.

Plan of the Report

This report describes project findings and discusses their implication for supporting families and organizations. The report first describes the methods used in this project and the social science concepts that guided the research project and analysis. Kenosha history and Kenosha culture are then outlined. The next sections explore the connection between economics and social capital for both employers and people seeking work. Discussion of the role of social capital for government welfare agencies, non-profit social service agencies and churches follows. Final chapters discuss dynamics between non-profits, churches, government and employers in Kenosha and the implications of these findings for policy and practice. Each chapter outlines specific connections between research and practice related to that topic.

A Note on Group Labels

People in Kenosha use several different names to talk about peoples of African descent and people from Spanish-speaking countries. In this report, I use African Americans to mean people whose ancestors migrated from Africa. Most of the Spanish-speaking population in Kenosha and their descendants come from either Mexico or portions of Texas annexed by the United States in the last century; however, this population also includes a group of Central American migrants. Most people in the community call themselves Hispanics. In order to accommodate current preference for the term Latino, I use Hispanic/Latino throughout this document to represent people who migrated from Spanish-speaking countries, peoples in Spanish-speaking countries incorporated into the United States, and their descendants.

Project Description and Methods

The *Kenosha Social Capital Study* was an ethnographic project designed to answer the questions outlined in the introduction by creating a description of the development of social capital through non-profit organizations and churches in this community during the study period. Anthropological ethnography provides a holistic picture of community processes. After discussing the methods used in this research project, this section provides a brief overview of ethnographic methods for those unfamiliar with this kind of research.

In order to address the issues raised in the introduction, the study involved five components:

1. Ethnography of organizations and inter-organizational dynamics in these two communities

This component placed student and faculty researchers from the University of Wisconsin-Parkside into key Hispanic/Latino and African American organizations and churches for eight months to perform ethnographic observation of organization activities and community dynamics. In all, observations were performed in four churches (three African American and one Hispanic/Latino), two church related service organizations (one African American and one Hispanic/Latino), six non-profit organizations (three developed by the African American and Hispanic/Latino communities; three developed by others in Kenosha), one Kenosha city sponsored task force, and two church based community coalitions. We also observed a series of community-wide events related to inter-group relations and citywide elections involving leaders from the Hispanic/Latino and African American communities. In the social service agencies, we observed both daily interactions in the agency and board meetings in order to understand social capital from both the organizational and program participant standpoint. Researchers also attended fundraising events for these organizations.

Ethnography identifies social networks and clarifies intra-community and inter-organizational dynamics through observing behavior patterns over time. This component identified various social capital networks, patterns of network inclusion and exclusion, as well as belief systems regarding the Kenosha County Job Center and other organizations. Observations showed us how behaviors and beliefs play out in every day life in Kenosha. Social and cultural capital are fostered, maintained and changed through these interactions.

2. Open-ended interviews with 25 key organization, church and community leaders

Formal interviews provided the history of organizations, churches and communities in Kenosha. We also used interviews to gather explanations for the things we observed through participant observation in various agencies and churches. Through talking with key leaders, we heard about behind the scenes actions that influenced social capital development in this small city. Finally, interviews allowed us to explore the belief systems of key people in this city.

3. Family study of 26 typical families (15 Hispanic/Latino and 11 African American)

These families were interviewed regarding social resources, life strategies and the role of race and immigration status in accessing resources such as community organizations, churches and the Kenosha County Job Center. These interviews traced perceptions of organizations, the development of social networks, and when and why people use various social resources.

Families were chosen after we had spent time observing these communities and interviewing key leaders. We sought to interview a range of families that represented different economic circumstances, education levels and length of time in Kenosha. Categories for each community were decided after discussion with our community advisory committee. We found families through a combination of our own contacts and recruitment by organizations and churches. The families came from the whole range of institutions that we studied, as well as some individuals who were not associated with any organization or church.

In the African American community, we sought families with different combinations of attributes in the following categories:

- *Work background:* professionals, stable working class, low-skilled workers (for example nursing assistants or salespeople), and welfare-dependent households
- *Length of time in Kenosha:* less than five years, five to ten years, ten to twenty years, greater than twenty years
- *Education:* college, high school and/or post-secondary technical education, less than high school
- *Region of origin:* raised in Kenosha, raised in the South, raised in Illinois or elsewhere in the North, raised in some other part of the country
- *Religion and church participation:* church member, not church member; member of either a denominational church (AME or Baptist) or an independent church

In the Hispanic/Latino community, we sought families with different combinations of attributes in the following categories:

- *Work background:* professionals, stable working class, low-wage workers (for example nursing assistants or salespeople), and people working in the informal economy (landscaping, day labor, cleaning houses)
- *Length of time in Kenosha:* less than five years, five to ten years, ten to twenty years, greater than twenty years
- *Education:* college, high school and/or post-secondary technical education, less than high school
- *Migration and citizenship status:* raised in Kenosha, raised in Texas, raised in Mexico or another foreign country, citizen, legal immigrant, undocumented immigrant
- *Religion and church participation:* Catholic, not Catholic; church member, not church member

In both communities, typical families usually combined several characteristics. For example, established working-class African American families tended to have lived in Kenosha more than twenty years, have migrated from the south, adult members had high school and/or vocational school education or less and families tended to be active in one of the denominational churches. In the Hispanic/Latino families, stable working-class families tended to have similar education backgrounds to African Americans and to have been in Kenosha about the same length of time, their families had migrated from Texas within a generation, and most were nominally Catholic.

4. Analysis of secondary source material such as newspaper articles, agency and church documents, affirmative action reports, and other government reports

We collected reports from participating agencies, government offices or other organizations in Kenosha that compiled general information on Kenosha related to the study. These included reports by the Kenosha Area Business Alliance (KABA), Kenosha County Job Center welfare statistics, and U.S. government census statistics on the area. We also collected annual reports, fliers, histories and other related information from participating agencies and churches. We saved newspaper articles related to our study topic from September, 1999, through July, 2000, and collected older articles in the library archives on participating organizations and the African American and Hispanic/Latino communities in Kenosha. Finally, we also read other studies produced by scholars about Kenosha and these two communities.

5. A survey of 121 Kenosha employers focused on the nature of their labor force, hiring practices and use of the Kenosha County Job Center

The *Kenosha Employers Survey* was a stratified random sample of employers in Kenosha based on the type of business. We developed a list of employers from several available directories of Kenosha businesses and non-profit organizations offered by participating organizations. We then divided the list by type of business (manufacturing, service, retail, non-profit and government) to create our stratification categories. Finally, we randomly selected employers from within each of these categories in order to get fair representation from all employers. The initial sample included three hundred employers, but we found that approximately five

6

percent had gone out of business or were too small to have any employees. University of Wisconsin-Parkside students contacted employers via telephone or in person for an interview. Our final response rate was forty percent. The survey represents approximately five percent of the active businesses in Kenosha who hired people outside of their families.

The *Kenosha Employers Survey* started before the other parts of the project as an initiative of the Kenosha Women's Commission and Leadership Kenosha. Through Guida Brown, these two groups were instrumental in designing the questionnaire and developing the sample. They also participated in the first phase of data collection along with University of Wisconsin-Parkside students. Students collected additional questionnaires and helped with analysis.

A Note on Confidentiality

Kenosha is a small place with few organizations, and where most of the populace know each other well and could easily guess the identity of individuals or organizations. The *Kenosha Social Capital Study* is a community study developed with an advisory committee of organization representatives. These community representatives want the name of the city identified in all publications, but expect that confidentiality and privacy will be respected. Anthropologists normally change the name of the locality as well as disguise the identity of all study participants and their organizations in publications. Informant quotes are never identified by name or date as another mechanism to maintain confidentiality. In order to meet community wishes and maintain privacy, I present most of the organizations serving the
Hispanic/Latino and African American community in aggregate forms. In other cases, names and minor descriptive facts are changed.

UNDERSTANDING   ETHNOGRAPHIC   METHODS:

Data Collection and Problem Statements

Anthropology presumes that the researcher is a student aiming to understand a particular way of life from an insider viewpoint. In practice, anthropologists come to any research site with their own class, race and national biases. However, ethnographers seek to reach outside their own expectations to understand a culture as it emerges through an active dialogue between theory and field data. Present day anthropology is often focused on a particular research question like the role of churches and non-profit organizations in supporting people of color. However, unlike other social scientists, anthropologists do not narrow their research to testing specific hypothesis or narrow research questions. Instead, research questions are defined broadly and the focus of analysis may change as the researcher makes unexpected discoveries through the observation process.

Current practices in anthropological ethnography stress understanding a particular field site such as a community or an organization within both macro-level and micro-level contexts. Macro-level data includes

relevant regional, national, and sometimes international statistical data and policy themes, which influence the local context. For example, for this study I collected data on local, regional and national labor market trends; social welfare policy at the local, state and national levels; and demographic patterns focused on race, nationality and poverty for Kenosha county and city, as well as the region and the nation as a whole. These data are further contexted in terms of international processes such as global economic and policy trends. These macro-level data are used to provide a framework to understand events in a given city like Kenosha.

Present day anthropologists also believe that local events come out of the history of the locality and region. For this reason, this study collected data on the history of labor and inter-group dynamics in Kenosha and southeastern Wisconsin. I also contexted this study by following the history of social welfare policy development in Kenosha, Wisconsin and the nation as a whole. These kinds of data are collected through a combination of secondary sources like the census, local studies or Department of Labor statistics, newspaper articles and interviews with various informants.

These macro-level data are used to understand a micro-level context such as a church, non-profit organization or neighborhood. Patterns in a given context stem from the interaction of macro and micro level processes. For example, the African American and Hispanic/Latino communities developed due to a combination of national migration patterns, local labor recruitment strategies and the evolution of the local culture. Anthropologists define "culture" as the whole way of life of a community or subgroup, not simply their beliefs, artifacts or values.

The primary method of anthropology is participant observation. Participant observation involves regular observation and the recording of events in a particular setting.[2]

Anthropologists are taught that they are students of the culture or community they study, not experts coming in with outside knowledge to be tested. Findings evolve from the process of ongoing observation in a community. Anthropologists seek to understand everyday patterns of behavior, as well as the rhythm of events throughout a cycle. Ideally, anthropologists work in a given setting for a full year to observe an entire annual cycle. While this project lasted the length of a school year, it was combined with another year of research conducted during the earlier *Kenosha Conversation Project* in 1997-1998.

The number of hours spent in a given locality is far less important than the duration and regular observance of events because the objective is to understand the evolution of patterns. For example, I would not consider events at one board meeting indicative of board practice for an organization. However, by watching board meetings over time, particularly when observations are combined with field notes from within the organization and with key informant interviews, I can

develop a reliable picture of board process. By observing half a dozen fundraising events and observing fundraiser development in several organizations, I can see the typical patterns and local variations for this community.

Interviews provide insight into historical patterns and reasons behind the events we observe. Ethnographic interviews are open ended, based on generalized topical guidelines rather than pre-defined questions. The resulting data provides a rich description of a particular topic from the point of view of the individual interviewed. Like most of my studies, this project collected data both from community leaders and average members of the Hispanic/Latino and African American communities.

Since anthropological data relies more heavily on the quality and training of the researcher than quantitative research, ethnographers pay particular attention to the relationship of researcher to researched. Researchers can be insiders to the community such as a Hispanic/Latina student raised in Kenosha or outsiders from racial/ethnic backgrounds either different or similar to the places where they do their research. Examples of outsiders would be a middle-class person of color or a white, working-class student. My own view is that insiders and outsiders have different challenges and advantages in a given research setting. Insiders are more likely to be trusted quickly and understand the basic rules of a community; however, they have blind spots based on their socialization in a similar community. Outsiders need to learn a setting from scratch, but they are likely to see things invisible to an insider. In my experience, the best fieldworkers are either marginal insiders (for example, someone partly raised in a similar community) or a fieldwork team, which combines insiders and outsiders. This project used both of these strategies.

Data Analysis, Writing and Replicability

Ethnography seeks to understand patterns, which inform theoretical questions. Anthropologists regard the research process as a dialogue between theory and on-the-ground observation. Analysis begins after the researcher has been in a setting for a few months and may continue years after the researcher leaves the research site. Research questions are often modified as the study evolves. The point of any project is to test and expand on existing theory. For this reason, research questions are drawn broadly.

Each ethnography concentrates on describing a particular setting in light of theoretical questions. Since theory development comes through observations and interviews in the setting, ethnography relies heavily on description of the setting, events and people the researcher met during the research process. Most ethnographic writing privileges the voices of study participants when possible, rather than rely on secondary analysis by the ethnographer.

Both theory and observation are changed in the data collection and analysis process. Replicability comes when other researchers find similar patterns in their field site. Replicability refers to the ability to do the study again with similar results. For example, this study draws on findings on resistance portrayed by Scott (1985) in Malaysia, as well as research on African American and Hispanic/Latino communities in the United States described by Stack (1976, 1996) and Newman (1999). Sometimes individual researchers will build on their own studies by conducting research on similar theoretical issues in several localities. For example, my welfare research draws on eleven separate projects conducted in Philadelphia and Wisconsin since 1992 (Schneider 1998, 1999a, c, 2000). I found similar patterns in each of these studies. Data

8

collected to address general themes can be used to address a variety of more specific research questions related to those themes.

As a general rule, anthropologists never assume that their studies are generalizable to every community or group, even if the race, ethnicity, class, type of organization or nation remains constant. Since ethnographies focus on understanding a system in process, each setting is expected to have unique characteristics. However, by placing patterns observed in one setting within the context of literature on related topics, the ethnographer can see how and where macro and micro level findings match and differ. Through a dialogue between researchers working on similar topics in different settings, ethnographers produce a rich, nuanced and complicated understanding of a particular topic in a given time and place. Through focus on process rather than a few general rules, ethnographers hope to inform the creation and implementation of theory, policy and practice.

9

Understanding Social and Cultural Capital

Most people are familiar with the idea of "capital": money that people use to start businesses, invest in property, pay for education and training, or save for the future. Capital put to work in any of these ways creates more money that people can use for a variety of purposes. Without capital, people have limited options. Economists and social scientists also use capital to refer to several other kinds of assets that individuals, organizations and communities may have to sustain and improve their way of life. All of these types of capital are intertwined. "Economic capital" refers to money required for an activity. "Human capital" means education and skills needed to fulfill a goal. "Cultural capital" means knowing how to act, dress, talk and otherwise present oneself in order to fit in. "Social capital" provides the means to get access to the other kinds of capital. It refers to social networks that help

people obtain their goals. However, social capital is much more complicated than simply knowing who to contact to get money, obtain skills or learn appropriate cultural habits. This section defines the concepts of social capital and cultural capital that will be used throughout this publication.

Social capital has become a popular topic since the publication of Robert Putnam's 1995 article *Bowling Alone*.[3] Putnam suggested that Americans were less involved in civic life because they no longer participated together in voluntary activities like bowling leagues. Policy makers, scholars and practitioners took social capital to mean engaging in civic activity for the common good. In many circles, the term social capital was used to mean any number of things related to positive civic engagement or the ability to successfully obtain one's goals in today's world. Social capital is often understood as a civic good: people or communities who have social capital

thrive while those who lack it have all kinds of problems. As an ever-wider audience used social capital, the origins and actual meaning of the term became obscured. Here I provide a brief outline of the social science definitions of social capital.

Defining Social Capital

Social scientists see social capital as the social relationships and patterns of trust that enable people to gain access to resources like government services or jobs.[4] The old adage "it's not what you know, but who you know that matters" shows the importance of social capital in any community. For organizations, social capital includes social relationships through both organizations and individuals that help organizations find funding, volunteers, employees, information, program participants and other things that an institution needs to survive. Social capital consists of two ingredients: relationships based in enforceable trust with people or organizations who have access to resources needed to meet basic necessities and fulfill goals; and knowledge of cultural cues which indicate that an individual is a member of a group and should be given access to those relationships. The first half of the definition includes three parts: connections, trust, and networks with appropriate information. The second half of the definition refers to access to cultural capital essential to use social networks. Social and cultural capital are separate concepts, but they work together to help people and organizations fulfill their goals. Using examples, we can see how these elements work together to influence individual and organizational success or failure.

Connections

Most people have social capital networks that help them meet their goals. For example, Jose, a Hispanic/Latino man, recalled learning about possible jobs in government through a social capital contact: "I used to go a lot to the motor vehicles bureau to drop off and get plates, and I met a woman called Maria and she told me that they were giving the exams to recruit for this job, 'why don't you go?' And I went."

Others used the promise of jobs spread through social capital networks to come to Kenosha. Both African Americans and Hispanic/Latinos talked about coming to Kenosha on the advice of relatives or friends who were already here. Luis explained that newcomer Mexicans used the same social capital ties as earlier Mexican-American migrants: "They are coming to Kenosha because mostly they follow families. I do ask them how they ended up in Kenosha and it's 'On ten years ago my aunt moved over here' or 'I got married to a guy that was from Kenosha,' it's like a family tie."

Networks also help organizations gain funding or employees. For example, Chris, an organization board member, recalled that a new executive director was referred by a community contact: "I was approached by [a colleague] who had heard that we were looking for a director. And he had told [me] that he knew [someone] that would be good for your agency and would you like his resume. And I said 'sure' and 'I'll bring it to the board.'"

Trust

While this agency went through a full search to find their executive director, the fact that someone had recommended a candidate meant that this individual received particular attention because the board member trusted the opinion of the person who made the referral. Social capital not only involves connections, but trust based on long term, reciprocal ties. If

the referral had come from an employment agency or another person in the community that the board member did not trust, he would have been less likely to take the candidate seriously.

Trust through established contacts also plays a key role in funding for organizations. For example, a community leader involved in funding decisions talked about how his committee chose among the many good proposals available for funding. Hard choices often relied on knowledge of the agency. Most of the organizations that got high marks in funding decisions had a strong reputation among funders. People making the funding decisions had trusting relationships with key staff and board members. Some had used the services of these agencies themselves. Agencies lacking these social capital contacts only had their proposals to support their requests. Sometimes, information was not enough. When talking about an organization that was turned down for funding, a decision maker commented, "We're just not looking over their shoulder all the time. You hope that they're filling a role in the community that's valid, that's helping people. They can say one thing and maybe it's not all that they're portraying it..."

Networks with Appropriate Information

While all people have social capital, not everyone's networks can help them achieve their goals. For example, Janice was a young African American woman from a strong family that worked together to meet everyone's needs. However, her family could not help her gain access to the resources required to move into professional employment. Other adults also did nothing to provide guidance needed to obtain human capital through education. She explained:

I look back on [this time] and say, I wish someone had been there. Cause I'm the only child, my mother couldn't make me aware. I had older cousins but I think they fell through the same holes and cracks I was experiencing. I had middle school counselors, high school counselors who allowed me to just set myself up for failure because the classes I took in junior high did not prepare me for high school. The classes I took in high school did not prepare me for college. It was like college? Please!

11

Eventually, Janice did find people who offered the advice and support she needed to succeed in college. She recalls that:

When I was in high school, finally it clicked, that's when I did experience some African American mentors. The multicultural Student Office, the Student Support Office they had set up there, that was a wonderful program targeted to first generation students, coming from families and backgrounds like that. It was very good support.

These same mentors suggested courses, helped her choose colleges, and later offered emotional support to continue through college. She chose a career helping others partly based on this kind of trusting support.

Cultural Capital

Janice's story shows that knowing what courses to take was as important as having someone to provide an introduction for an education program or a job. Familiarity with the steps one needs to take to get an education, find a job or obtain funding for an organization is the second part of the definition of social capital. Behaving in ways considered appropriate by the people who are part of social capital networks is as important as having the right contacts. This knowledge about education, employment or organizational development systems and the correct ways to behave and speak in order to succeed is called cultural capital. People need to know how to use the right cultural capital for a given goal like getting an education in order to have access to the trusting relationships of a social capital network.

Anthropologists define *culture* as the whole way of life of a people, including the economic system, government, social service organizations, religious institutions, values, beliefs and ways of behaving. People who study organizations or poverty often use culture to mean values or habits particular to one organization or a

group of people. In this document, I generally use the second definition of culture when talking about cultural capital. However, specific behaviors and beliefs come out of the whole way of life of a people and are influenced by economic structures and other systems in a community.

Many other people we talked to during this study mentioned the importance of gathering information and developing the social capital needed to succeed through growing up in a particular community. Often, not only information but also appropriate ways of behaving came out of cultural capital learned as a child. In comparing himself to low-income families in his community, Marcus, a youth counselor, commented:

Things have changed. When I was coming along, there were expectations on how I was to act and behave. If I didn't meet those then, I was...bringing shame to myself and shame to my family. That was the way it should go and I don't see that with these kids. These kids and their parents. This is interesting because most of the kids I work with are related to one another. Most of their parents I went to school with. I call them on the phone about their child's behavior and they think it's funny. "Oh you're letting my son run all over you?" I'm saying, it's your job at home, but I would never tell them that, to raise them right. They would know how to act in public or when they're not around you. And what I'm getting from these kids is an attitude of "I don't care."

Appropriate ways to behave are specific to local communities. The right way to behave, dress or act can be different for African Americans and Hispanic/Latinos than for whites in the same community. As with Marcus, class background also makes a difference, even within the same community. Marcus' parents were in the stable working class and he is moving into a professional career track. In both cases, families stressed

internal discipline and respect for elders. The low-skilled families that the children in his program come from place less value on these attributes. Instead, taking care of oneself has a higher value. As a result, children behave differently than Marcus' expectations. These families teach their children different behavior patterns or values less appreciated by the middle-class employers.

Karen's experience shows that people develop different cultural habits over time. Karen is an African American woman who grew up in a stable working-class family in a large city. She attended a small, all white college in a smaller city. Finding herself uncomfortable living on campus, she moved into a rough African American community nearby. She explained that she did not fit in anywhere:

It was interesting because in my home neighborhood I was ostracized because I was going to college and thought myself better than them. "Yeah, you're acting white. What's wrong with you? You think you something." In school-"Who is this black girl? She comes here, she acts so weird, she acts hard and harsh and ghetto. Why is she even here? Does she know she sticks out?" So that was the response. It strengthened me, I could effectively cope in any situation I was dropped in. I think that's why I picked up those skills and being able to adapt to any situation and any person I'm talking to. To go from street slang to the King's English in a breath. As the situation call for.

Karen's story demonstrates that cultural capital is often subtle behavior. It involves language, dress styles, and other cues that can be learned over time. Another example from observations describes how these subtle cues provide access to social capital. In this case, the student researcher came from a rough Chicago neighborhood where knowing about gangs and which people one could trust were often matters of personal safety. In a Kenosha organization, Mike recorded the following incident:

I noticed that John had a tattoo on his right hand of a familiar gang symbol; I have seen this symbol in Chicago. I asked him if he belonged to that gang. He responded to me that he used to be but that he didn't do any of that stuff anymore. He felt very self conscientious about the tattoo because then he began to try to hide it with his gold Virgin Mary bracelet. He began to tell me how he used to belong to the gang and we started exchanging names to see who we knew and didn't know.

The cultural symbol of the gang tattoo provided the social trust that helped these two strangers realize that they came from the same community. By comparing social networks, they began to develop a relationship that could have led to network referrals for resources in that community. If Mike was in trouble in Chicago, using John's name and his contacts might provide needed support.

John wanted to change and tried to hide his former life with a new symbol —the Virgin Mary bracelet. The process of changing networks and culture is a slow one. For example, later another person using the social service agency recognized John and tried to talk to him about common experiences from rough neighborhoods. John tried to pretend that he had never met this person.

Often cultural capital is far more subtle than gang symbols. For example, when doing interviews in welfare dependent African American households, I noticed that each family had a glass dinner table set up with full place settings and a centerpiece as if they were expecting guests. In most middle-class households, dishes are only put on the table shortly before a meal. After seeing this pattern several times, I realized that these families were mimicking the displays in African American middle-class home fashion magazines. What they viewed as a statement of middle-class culture in

fact branded them as outsiders who put out their fancy dishes at the "wrong" time.

These subtle mistakes often occur with people trying to cross boundaries. They include dressing slightly wrong, using the wrong phrases or gestures. They signal to people in social capital networks that this person is an outsider. Often, these cultural capital cues are enough to make the difference between getting a job or access to some other resource, or coming in second regardless of credentials.

Links Between Social, Cultural, Human and Economic Capital

Social and cultural capital are linked to human and economic capital. As Janice's story shows, lacking social and cultural capital meant that she did not take the prerequisite courses to succeed in college. Others do not have access to economic capital to meet their goals. Sometimes, coming from environments without access to human or economic capital means that people do not know how to move outside of familiar patterns. In other cases, social capital can help people move into better paying jobs. Tania, a Hispanic/Latina woman told about how social capital networks encouraged her to develop human capital and provided economic capital to obtain higher education. Tania had

started out as a nursing assistant in a hospital. Nurses and other staff befriended her and provided necessary supports. She told this story about how social capital helped her gather human and economic capital:

And I was there for 4 or 5 years and the nurse there said you have to go to school. "I have no money" "I have no money." So I found a program called licensed practical nursing program and I worked part time through that program and I got my LPN license. And again the doctors and the nurses said I did good work but I was not getting credit because I did not have an RN. "I don't have any money" "I don't have any money." "Go to the [local community college]". So I went to [that college] and the hospital picked up my classes for my English, my math, and all that kind of stuff till I got ready to do my practicum and I got my ADN, my associates degree. Then [a four year] college came to [the hospital] to talk about their programs and everything. And I again, "I don't have that kind of money and stuff." So again one of the fellow nurses at the hospital who had graduated with me said: "come on... We will look into it together."

Tania's community networks led her to nursing assistant and practical nurse training. Without additional social and economic capital from her workplace, she may have never gone to college to get the human capital skills she needed to become a professional. As discussed throughout this booklet, both organizations and individuals exhibited the same links between these four types of capital.

Closed and Bridging Social Capital

Social and cultural capital are developed in dense networks often found in family, neighborhoods or churches. There are two kinds of social capital: closed and bridging. Both are equally important for individuals and organizations.

Closed Social Capital

Closed social capital networks develop strong supports for the people in those communities. Everyone belongs to at least one closed social capital network. It may be family, people who graduated from a certain school or simply local community networks. People in these closed networks are familiar with each other, practice the same culture and trust each other. Information is usually spread through word of mouth.

For example, for her class project, Felicia, a University of Wisconsin-Parkside student, attended a church that practiced closed social capital. She came from a similar ethnic background as church members and they considered her a potential member. She spoke to no one on her first visit, but reported on her second that:

> A mature lady stepped forward, leaned towards me and smiled. She was quite friendly, she continued smiling at me and said, "Hi, my name is Sister Mary I am the director of the Women's Ministry and I wasn't here last Sunday when you came but I was told about you. You are a student here involved with a Research Project. Welcome."

Later, Sister Mary and others told Felicia that most members of this church were related to each other. They provided firm material and social support to their church family. For example, baskets for Thanksgiving were handed out to those in need. Families never applied for this kind of help, but others in the church knew they needed help through talk in the community.

Closed social capital networks are suspicious of outsiders. For example, despite the warm welcome she received in church, Felicia's contacts repeatedly stood her up for interviews. Outsiders were not trusted and they did not want to share information.

This suspicion of outsiders hindered the ability of some people in closed social capital networks from moving into new communities. For example, one organization wanted to send a teenager to a youth program in another state. However, the boy was afraid to go because he did not know anyone and it would mean going outside of his community.

Closed social capital exists on all levels in a community, not simply in communities different from the mainstream like an African American or Hispanic/Latino church. For example, one person reported going to a private club and finding most of the members of the school board sitting in one corner talking. In Kenosha, as in many communities, the social capital networks that are considered the community "mainstream" in fact consist of small, closed groups who consider themselves to represent the entire community. The story of social capital in Kenosha involves attempts by those on the outside to build bridges into closed social capital networks of those in power.

Bridging Social Capital

Bridging social capital intentionally tries to create trusting relationships between closed social capital networks. As in Karen's example of negotiating between the white middle class and the African American lower class from her college days, moving between communities involves developing both cultural and social capital. Many African American and Hispanic/Latino community leaders in this study came from working-class backgrounds, but were encouraged to develop links to larger communities by supportive white teachers, counselors or family employers. Building bridges is an intentional and slow process.

One mainstream leader describes his strategy as follows:

> First off, by putting people of color in respectful positions. If someone—no matter what color—is respectful of the person, well naturally the trust issue starts to improve. We have to be aggressive to put people of color in middle and upper senior management positions and have the whites understand that these are human beings and we all have something to offer and just because they may not be the same color they still have something to offer. By having that part of the mission and having people realize there's going to be leaders.

Summary

We have learned that social capital consists of three elements: connections, trust and networks with appropriate information. Social capital is linked to cultural capital—ways of behaving in a particular community or group. There are two kinds of social capital: closed and bridging. Both are equally important. Closed social capital involves strong ties within sub-communities, like a neighborhood or ethnic group. Bridging social capital means that people have developed strong, trusting ties across sub-community groups.

We saw many examples of bridging social capital in Kenosha. We also learned that there is an important relationship between closed and bridging social capital. The rest of this document describes the development of social capital and the role of social capital through organizations and churches in the African American and Hispanic/Latino communities in Kenosha. Helping individuals, communities and organizations thrive includes understanding how social and cultural capital influence both behavior and outcomes. Since social capital comes out of the history of the community and its cultural traditions, I first outline these two dynamics in Kenosha.

14

Kenosha History

Kenosha is best described as an auto manufacturing town, which has rebounded from the loss of its major employer in the 1980s. Rural parts of the county still are agricultural. Founded in the 1830s, Kenosha became a regional manufacturing center between 1890 and 1920. While early manufacturing included a wide variety of establishments, by 1920 the manufacturing base was dominated by Nash Motors, Simmons Manufacturing, and American Brass company. Nash was later bought by American Motors, which eventually merged with Chrysler. By 1960, American Motors was the major employer. The major manufacturers unionized in the 1930s, and by 1963 Kenosha had the eighteenth highest family income in the United States. Education was downplayed as Kenosha residents knew that they could get a good job at the "Motors" without completing highschool.[5] This established employment pattern began to change in the 1980s when

AMC/Chrysler began to shut down production in Kenosha, finally closing everything but the plant making engines in 1988. Kenosha unemployment hit its highest mark of 17.7 percent in 1983 and remained high throughout the 1980s. While a couple of larger manufacturers remain, many of the older large manufacturers moved. Like many U.S. cities, Kenosha experienced deindustrialization as it shifted from a unionized industrial labor base to a small manufacturing and service economy.

However, facing a planned plant closing, Kenosha business and government leaders stepped in early to ensure that Kenosha did not experience high crime and poverty levels. Chrysler offered retraining and relocation packages for unemployed auto workers, government worked with local banks to avoid home loan defaults, and business and government together recruited small manufacturers and service employers to Kenosha.

Around the same time, the outskirts of the city began to develop as a bedroom community for Northern Illinois. This led to an increase in construction employment as well as an influx of more professional residents. By the mid 1990s, unemployment hovered at approximately 3.5 percent. However, many of the good paying, unionized jobs had been replaced by smaller employers offering lower wages and benefits. Only three percent of the employers had over one hundred workers and seventy-one percent of the employers had fewer than ten employees. The company town atmosphere had also been replaced by a larger number of commuting families. Fully 39.5 percent of Kenosha residents commuted outside of the county for work in the 1990s.[6]

The workforce for industry largely came from migration. Kenosha's initial settlers were a combination of Yankees, German, Scandinavian and British immigrants. However, as in the rest of the U.S., the "new" immigration from Southern and Eastern Europe replaced these older settlers at the bottom rungs of industrial employment by the turn of the century. Employers initially recruited these newcomers, but word of mouth through social capital networks quickly took over as friends and family followed earlier migrants in traditional chain migration patterns. These new immigrants and their descendants became the bulk of the unionized workforce.

Kenosha residents report ancestry from many different countries. According to the 1990 census, the largest ethnic groups reported in Kenosha were German (sixteen percent), Irish (two percent), Italian (six percent), Polish (three percent) and English (two percent). Italians

15

have become an increasing presence in business and politics in Kenosha in the twentieth century.

Social capital that recruited immigrants to Kenosha also helped them find jobs. One established Kenosha resident recalled:

16

Because I was an immigrant, we call it connections. We knew a Lithuanian who worked at this place who knew this other Lithuanian who worked at this other place and you could always get in. It was like a buddy system. You get in that way. My ma never spoke English, but she always had work, usually because there was a supervisor in that business who spoke Lithuanian. It was routine, so the person translated and she could do the job forever.

As in other U.S. cities, the new immigrants experienced prejudice in housing, employment and all other aspects of life. As a result, they developed tight communities focused on church, fraternal and benevolent societies to provide social support. Immigrant neighborhoods and churches developed strong closed social capital networks that helped people in each group to find jobs, housing, social support and recreation. This developed a strong history of distrust to people outside of each closed network.

As unions developed, social life also began to focus on the union hall. The combination of working together in the manufacturing plants and solidarity built in the union hall created bridging social capital among union members and their families. By the 1990s, the initial ethnic enclaves had broken down, but social capital and community still focused on the small group of known people developed through church, union, family, neighborhood and school ties.

Given economic prosperity through union employment, Kenosha was slow to develop non-profit and government supports for low-income people. Most

people had plenty of money to take care of themselves and their families. People who had grown up in poor families recalled getting support from others in their ethnic community or through the churches.

The one homeless shelter began in the 1980s during the plant closings as a church based initiative. Two community women drew together people from churches and the union to help those in need. While this organization now has a building and paid staff, the bulk of its budget and services come from wide spread community volunteer efforts with churches and community organizations like the union and Boy Scouts, each taking a regular turn to provide food and serve at the soup kitchen. The homeless shelter also offers a small family shelter funded largely through government funds, but most housing is offered in church basements on a regular rotation schedule.

The domestic violence shelter developed in 1976. It offers a thirty-three bed shelter along with a combination of economic, social and counseling assistance to help women and children escape abusive situations. Both of these organizations receive consistent government support, but also rely on the community for funds.

As one community leader stated, "in terms of social service, I guess I would categorized Kenosha as very, very benevolent to populations that they classify as deserving poor." He explained:

Pretty much individuals who had suffered a hardship not of their doing or individuals or families who had certain physical handicaps. Individuals who were construed as being on some form of assistance were seen as being undeserving.

This philosophy led to the creation of creative public/private partnerships offering welfare services combining work and social supports that became a model for U.S. welfare reform. Kenosha policies consistently try to

"mainstream" people in need. For example, Kenosha has no public housing complexes, offering only a small number of scattered site "section 8" vouchers for housing assistance.

Kenosha's history created a community with a strong history of economic prosperity through blue-collar employment. It also meant that people were used to relying on resources in local ethnic communities, not on government or non-profit organizations in times of need. Most people were expected to earn their own living, as jobs were plentiful. At the same time, when economic conditions became difficult, the close-knit ties created through closed social capital in immigrant communities and the union hall meant that everyone in the community helped out until people could get back on their feet. The same belief that the old and sick who need support *deserve* support fostered community assistance for the needy. Government was not seen as the appropriate or only provider for these kinds of services. Non-profit organizations also were late to develop in Kenosha. Instead, churches, family and local community became the first place people turned for support.

Kenosha's history also created strong segregation among different groups. While segregation was significant for everyone in the early parts of the century, it was particularly important for African Americans and Hispanic/Latinos when they started settling in the city of Kenosha. One long-term white community member recalled:

In terms of race, it was very low focus for me except for what might have been a typical blacks and whites not trusting each other, only whites with whites and blacks vice versa. There wasn't any real—I didn't have any reason for integration with people of color at that time and I was not aware of a big Hispanic population. When I was growing up there was nothing but a segregated environment.

Every white Kenosha resident we spoke to said the same thing. They simply did not know about populations different from themselves until more recently. People in their forties had more recollection of integration and were much more likely to have friends from many groups because schools and desegregated union employment in the 1960s and 1970s began to break down these barriers. However, racism and social segregation are still a big issue in Kenosha for communities of color. We next look at the development of the African American and Hispanic/Latino communities in Kenosha.

population and Hispanic/Latinos at 5.5 percent (1990 Census). These two groups have been labeled "invisible people" due to their small numbers and the tendency to maintain passive, closed communities.[7] This characterization was just beginning to change during the study period.

African Americans

In the early 1940s, Nash began hiring African Americans in the foundry, the least desirable part of the plant. Word of mouth through social capital networks in several communities in the South led small groups of family and friends to migrate to Kenosha for good

with ties through already established networks can find good paying jobs.

African Americans experienced extreme discrimination in housing and public accommodation in Kenosha until after the passage of the 1964 U.S. Civil Rights Act. Many landlords refused to rent to African Americans and local banks refused to loan mortgage or building money. As a result, many African Americans lived in the relatively friendlier communities of Racine, Wisconsin and Waukegan, Illinois or found loans and imported building materials from Racine or Milwaukee. Others lived in a run down public housing complex called Bonnie Hame until it was closed in the 1960s. One person described Bonnie Hame as follows:

It looked like the buildings were made out of roof tar paper. It was built during the war for temporary workers to help out. That was all a community. They had their own school there and everything. I was warned as a kid not to cut through there. I'd get beat up. There were a lot of minorities there. There were also whites who lived there. But the, quote, "poor trash." That was the impression we were given.

Several African Americans reported receiving threats when they sought to buy or build houses in all white areas as Bonnie Hame began to close. However, once they moved into new housing, they universally found their white neighbors friendly. Kenosha residents focus on individuals, and once they got to know their new African American neighbors, fear of the "other" disappeared. Today there are few segregated neighborhoods in Kenosha, and newcomer African Americans generally report few problems with near neighbors.

African American and Hispanic/Latino Community History

The history of the African American and Hispanic/Latino communities mirrors the experience of the new immigrants. However, people of color experienced even more extreme prejudice than the white immigrants and still face discrimination in education, employment and other daily life experiences today. Current estimates place African Americans at 4.4 percent of the Kenosha county

paying factory work. A few other African Americans had come to Kenosha before this post-war migration and others later followed from Chicago, Detroit and other communities in addition to initial southern feeder sources. African Americans remained restricted to the foundry until a few people broke these barriers with the help of sympathetic white union representatives. Both African Americans and Hispanic/Latinos still experience discrimination in hiring and promotion. However, like most social capital resources in Kenosha, people

Racism in restaurants and other public places was overt until the late 1960s. Both published accounts and research interviews report bar owners breaking glasses used by African Americans. Besides the African American-owned bar, few restaurants would serve people of color. Sam, a retired African American American Motors employee recalled:

When I first started at American Motors, the only place you could get your check cashed on Friday was one bar. He was the only one would cash your check. Those other bars around the plant, you couldn't go in there to get a sandwich when I first started. This was around '59.

As a result, African Americans socialized in their churches and in the few African American bars. This re-emphasized closed social capital developed through common employment in the foundry, segregated housing and discrimination in public places.

The story of how African Americans began to be allowed into the mainstream restaurants and bars shows a classic example of bridging social capital. A sympathetic union leader found out about this problem and decided to change it through example. This same leader helped African Americans break into better jobs as skilled workers in the manufacturing plants. One union member recalls:

I got to talking to him about how the taverns weren't serving people or cashing their checks, anything like that. I didn't think anything more about it and about two or three weeks later, this is probably in about '62 or '63, he says I want to meet you over at [a white bar]. I say, I can't go in there. He says I just want to meet you there. So we went over there and he's in there and I looked in there. He motions me to come in and I motion to him to come out. He comes out and I say, I can't go in there. He says, I want to tell you something, don't you say anything but we're going to visit every one of these taverns and see what goes on. I have done talked to those people and we're going to see if those changes have been made. So I went in and of course, they give—everybody in there give a look. People I had worked for, they probably thought, "What's he

doing in here?" Then they seen [the union leader] and didn't say anything. We did that all around the block and next thing you know, everything opened up.

Despite the end of overt discrimination, both African Americans and Hispanic/Latinos today report being followed in stores and other forms of subtle discrimination. There are widespread reports within the community of racial profiling by police. However, since people of color in Kenosha hesitate to openly report problems, public officials routinely fail to substantiate reports.

Community institutions include half a dozen African American churches (two Baptist, one AME congregation and several independent churches). One of these churches had a mission project to their local community attached to it. The primary Baptist congregation started as a mission project in 1919. For most of the first twenty-four years of its existence, this church used space in a white Baptist church. In 1943 they bought their own storefront building, later moving to their current church site. The large Baptist congregation has grown from a small, older congregation of fifty to seventy-five people to a vibrant congregation of approximately six hundred people. A small group split off from this church in the 1970s and is still trying to build its own congregation.

The AME church also started as a mission church in 1932. After a few years in rented halls and storefronts it also built its own building near the Baptist church. The AME congregation remains relatively small—perhaps forty families. Unlike the larger Baptist church, they recruit primarily through established members.

Until recently, there were three social service/advocacy organizations developed by these two communities. Two of these organizations are local chapters of national organizations for African Americans. One of these organizations is a satellite office of a

national organization chapter located in nearby Racine. The third was a community center started in a changing neighborhood after a racial incident at one of the high schools. This organization recently merged with a mainstream organization after a long period of financial and leadership instability.

Hispanic/Latino Community Development

Latino migration took a different form. Through the 1960s most Kenosha Mexican Americans came to Wisconsin as migrant workers from Texas or the Texas-Mexico border towns. One older Hispanic/Latina explained that:

We traveled back and forth between there and Crystal City every year and in 1943 my parents decided to come to Wisconsin, they heard lotta work, that's when we started migrant. So we commute in to Wisconsin and every year we went back in November/ October and return in late March/ early April to work in the fields.

For migrant workers, their permanent homes were in the Texas towns where they resided in the winter. In Wisconsin they lived on the farms and developed close communities among themselves. Priests came to the farms to celebrate Mass for the mostly Catholic population. One lady recalls:

It was very happy times for us. Because at that time we all traveled together. I remember my mother, my grandmother, my great-grandmother and my aunts and all my cousins. We grew up together. All the time it was very hard for my parents because they had to work in the fields but it compensated because we were together, living together and keeping an eye on each other.

As automation increased on the farms and AMC and a few other companies started recruiting minority workers, Hispanic/Latinos began to move into factory employment. In some cases this was a deliberate placement through the local branch of a migrant social service organization which developed the social capital ties and training programs to move migrant workers into factory work. This social service organization was a branch of a national migrant organization. In Kenosha it was founded by nuns from Illinois. Most of the original workers were recruited from among women working in the fields. In this way, the agency organizers drew on established closed social capital networks to help the community transition from migrant farm work into factory employment. Others found jobs because they heard about opportunities in the factories from their friends and family. One man observed, "during that time American Motors was recruiting workers from the farms, from the fields. And my older brothers and my brother-in-law were recruited to come work in American Motors and that's how we ended up in Kenosha in '69."

These Hispanic/Latino factory workers have become stable working-class like their African American and white counterparts. A small group of professional class Hispanic/Latinos also migrated to Kenosha separately. Since the 1980s, migrants increasingly come directly from Mexico to work in the small factories and service establishments. An unknown number of these newcomers are undocumented immigrants. Like others, they follow social capital networks to Kenosha and use them to find work, housing and social supports.

Hispanic/Latinos are generally scattered throughout Kenosha neighborhoods. They are even more invisible than the African American population as far as "white" Kenosha is concerned. While African Americans report individual friendships with Hispanic/Latinos developed through school, work or neighborhood, the two communities do not really interact as groups.

Two organizations associated with this

community exist in Kenosha today. The national migrant organization still has a small office in Kenosha, but it only has one employee now since most newcomers are not migrant workers. Another Hispanic/Latino based non-profit organization also exists in Kenosha, developed originally as a satellite for a Racine-based organization. However, when the Racine operation ran into problems, the organization shut down operation in Racine and moved all remaining programs to Kenosha.

Most Hispanic/Latinos are Catholic or Catholic by tradition. Some of the more established residents attend neighborhood Catholic churches. There is one Spanish Mass hosted by a large Catholic church. The Catholic Hispanic/Latino congregation started as a mission to the migrant workers. Until Hispanic/Latinos started settling in Kenosha in large numbers, priests came to the farms to celebrate Mass. As the population moved into the city of Kenosha and neighboring Racine, the Hispanic/Latino Mass moved into established community Catholic churches. In Kenosha, the Hispanic/Latino Mass was first hosted by a parish near where most newcomers lived. However, about five years prior to this research project, the original host church requested that the congregation be moved elsewhere, citing other needs for their space. Another church with a liberal priest friendly to a Hispanic/Latino mission, but outside of the population center, became the congregation's new home.

This Catholic church also hosts a social service mission to the Spanish-speaking population that is overseen by people from the Hispanic/Latino congregation. Funding for this mission project comes from all the Catholic churches in Kenosha. Like the Hispanic/Latino community, these organizations also practice closed social capital, working closely together to meet community needs. However, since the non-profit organization moved to Kenosha, it has developed more bridges into other

communities in Kenosha.

Like the new immigrants before them, Kenosha African Americans and Hispanic/Latinos developed closed, close knit communities in reaction to discrimination. Until recently, these two communities remained extremely passive and quiet. As organized entities, the white and African American communities connect through a few bridging leaders while the Hispanic/Latinos today remain largely an invisible community. Only a few of the Hispanic/Latinos have become spokespeople for their community in the Kenosha mainstream. There are further divisions within both of the communities between long-term Kenosha residents and newcomers. In the African American community, newcomers include professionals, some stable working class, and low-income people who come to Kenosha to escape danger and poverty in larger cities. Hispanic/Latinos are largely Mexicans coming to Kenosha to find work. As in earlier days, Mexicans are recruited through word of mouth and direct recruitment postings. Several people reported seeing signs in the border towns advertising jobs in Kenosha.

Summary

The history of Kenosha and its communities of color show this small city to be a place where people migrate to find work, first in factories and now in a combination of factories and service businesses. It is a place where people are expected to support themselves, but where strong communities based on closed social capital networks provide resources to find work, housing, to socialize, worship and find other supports when needed. Churches remain a source of support and community in the 1990s. The non-profit sector is relatively new and reflects community history and values. This report next looks at Kenosha culture and the way it affects social capital and community development in this locale.

Kenosha Culture

seeking factory work. Much of Kenosha's unique way of life stems from close, supportive networks of people working together to meet their needs through churches, neighborhoods and factory employment. Kenosha culture also reflects blue-collar lifestyles and community economic structures.

People working with other communities may find much in common between the culture in their locale and that of Kenosha. Preference for known insiders is typical in most localities, particularly smaller cities or towns. Highlighting parochial knowledge over education is familiar in many working-class communities. Patterns of individualism

are influenced by economic structures and other systems in a community.

Every culture has both positive and negative traits. In many cases, cultural habits that are helpful to many people within a community can cause trouble for people who do not understand community rules. This is particularly true for communities made up of multiple closed social capital networks like Kenosha. Each cultural trait discussed below was mentioned by many people as impacting on the lives of people living in Kenosha, especially African Americans and Hispanic/Latinos.

Kenosha culture is a tension among several seemingly contradictory elements. People negotiate these contradictions in everyday life, learning them as they are socialized into the culture. Newcomers learn Kenosha culture through trial and error, sometimes getting help from established insiders. These next sections explore several of these more important contradictory parts of Kenosha culture.

Kenosha is a study in contrasts. Widely described as a blue-collar, conservative town, it also developed internationally known models for social welfare. Understood as twenty to thirty years behind most areas in the U.S. in developing affirmative action and anti-racism initiatives, this community also offered good paying factory jobs to many African Americans and Hispanic/Latinos. While some people of color still are harassed when moving into all white neighborhoods, there are few segregated neighborhoods and most people of color report positive relationships with whites.

Kenosha culture comes out of its history as a migration point for people from many different backgrounds

and expectations that others are available as needed come from wider Midwestern cultural traits. These traits come together to form unique patterns for Kenosha. Understanding how local culture is similar and different to that in other communities becomes essential in developing programs in any locality.

Anthropologists define *culture* as the whole way of life of a people, including patterns of work, ideas and behavior. People who study organizations or poverty often use *culture* to mean values or habits particular to one organization or a group of people. This section describes unique aspects of Kenosha culture as in the second definition of culture. However, specific behaviors and beliefs come out of the whole way of life of a people and

Rules and Allowances for Insiders

The first contradiction involves a balance between a wide variety of rules known only by insiders and the ways that the community makes allowances for known people who break those rules. This pattern shows how the community sets boundaries and tells people about how things work in Kenosha. As with many parts of Kenosha culture, these traits come from wider regional patterns.

Rules and Community Knowledge: the Wisconsin Germanic Heritage

Kenosha adheres to cultural patterns common throughout Wisconsin including a strong sense of community rules enforced through a combination of word of mouth knowledge, unofficial sanctioning and official rules. Community culture develops from a combination of local socio-economic systems and the history of that locality and its surrounding region. National patterns also influence local culture. In the United States, community culture usually blends patterns from the initial places that residents emigrated from and conditions in the place of settlement. Culture patterns continually change over time as the community evolves.

As newcomers enter the country from other regions or countries, local culture may change to include traits from the newcomers. However, research on ethnicity and local culture in the United States suggests that newcomers are required to adjust their external behaviors to existing patterns more than the base community changes to meet newcomers. This was particularly true in earlier parts of the century. Immigrant communities frequently developed bi-cultural habits where they practiced their own lifeways at home and conformed to community-wide patterns in public places. Over time, ethnic identity became a symbolic and variable part of self as U.S.-born descendants of the initial immigrants mostly followed the same patterns as other established residents in their daily lives. Being Italian, Irish or Lithuanian became important in parts of one's life but not everywhere. Kenosha's pattern of closed social capital networks particularly support this kind of ethnic identity development for second and third generation descendants of earlier immigrants.

Kenosha community standards can have positive advantages. For example, many newcomers to Kenosha and other Wisconsin cities noticed that there was very little graffiti in comparison to other U.S. cities. Respect for community property came from several places. First, since Kenosha provided a relatively high level of basic community services and an ethos of people working together, community residents were less likely to deface property.

Equally important, Kenosha residents, like others throughout Wisconsin, learned early and often that people followed set patterns to accomplish their goals. Children were to sit quietly and do what the teacher said. Given community fears toward danger for their children, Halloween was restricted to a two-hour period on a weekend afternoon near October 31. People learned when Halloween would occur through their schools, word of mouth or the local newspaper.

Official permission was required for many activities. For example, teenagers were required to get work permits in order to obtain part-time jobs. The non-profit agency issuing these permits required that children show up during set hours with a series of documents proving their age and permission to work. Anyone showing up without one of the required pieces of documentation or outside of the specified hours would be turned away. As with much in Kenosha, there was little deviance from the rules allowed.

In addition to knowing the right rules, people needed to know exactly how to present information in order to obtain information or achieve a goal. Many people in Kenosha became uncomfortable if things were presented in a form outside of the set pattern that they had learned. This trend stemmed from a combination of Wisconsin's rigid patterning and its manufacturing culture where people learn rote tasks as part of an assembly line process. Surviving in factories meant learning to follow rules without question.

When transitioning to a service economy, rote patterns became problematic. For example, I once watched as someone tried to ask for a substitution on a menu item at a restaurant. The waitress politely said that the item was not listed that way on the menu. As the patron persisted, the waitress looked increasingly pained and repeated that the item was only available in the way listed in the menu. Eventually, another guest stepped in to tell the newcomer to give up.

Humorous events like this restaurant incident become more important when they involve job applications, government benefits and other necessary parts of daily life. People who did not ask questions in exactly the wording expected by staff, or name a form correctly, would not be given the information they required. Furthermore, the forms needed to be filled out in specified ways, be presented on the appropriate color paper and so forth.

More important, front line staff presumed that anything that they did not know simply did not exist. For example, on several occasions in this research project, people called office supply stores asking for paper that the store did not stock. Rather than respond that the store does not carry the item, the clerk responded that nobody made that kind of paper. Similar statements were reported by many people regarding anything from welfare benefits to non-profit organization activities.

Localized Knowledge

Declaring that anything unknown to the individual does not exist comes from a pattern of localized knowledge. People learn set patterns through personal knowledge. Information is not readily shared with outsiders and established Kenosha residents assume that others already know the expected patterns. This became particularly problematic when related to quality of life rules regarding parking, traffic and other related matters.

One example from the field research illustrates the magnitude of this problem. Hispanic/Latino representatives came to my research methods class to talk about designing a questionnaire for a needs assessment for this community. Knowing how to handle parking tickets was one major problem they identified. Kenosha only allows parking on one side of the street during the winter, but switches which side one is allowed to park on each day. While this information is posted in the newspaper, information on parking rules is not widely distributed to newcomers or Latinos. Newcomers may miss this information because homeowners or landlords may not distribute it or it is not available in their language. People new to Kenosha who do not speak English are particularly likely to unknowingly park on the wrong side of the street.

For established Kenosians, these rules are a way of life. For example, one student commented "everyone knows that" when community representatives raised this issue. Since everyone supposedly understands the many unspoken rules, people who break them are considered worthy of punishment.

Parking tickets become a major problem in Kenosha because breaking the rules in Wisconsin leads to severe consequences. Fines are large and the state takes away driver's licenses in a period of months from anyone who fails to pay fines for a wide variety of minor community infractions. More important, the tickets only list where people can pay fines, not any information on responding to a ticket. Several people reported calling multiple offices trying to gain basic information related to parking tickets or related matters without success. Losing one's license means having no way to get to work or achieve other goals. Kenosha County Job Center staff reported that many welfare recipients lacked driver's licenses because they had been revoked, creating a barrier to making a living.

Conformity

Community rules worked well for those familiar with them and who could live within them, but caused large problems for those who did not follow them. Many people reported that Kenosha is resistant to change, and following community cultural patterns is one aspect of fearing change. Since cultural patterns are transmitted through informal socialization rather than readily available written information or widespread education, newcomers are judged on whether or not they fit existing patterns. People who look and act differently are expected to learn to conform.

Support for Insiders

The positive side of Kenosha culture is that people within the known social capital circle are provided with every kind of support. Rules are bent when the person breaking the rules belongs to the same group. Despite rigid and often arbitrary rules, many people considered Kenosha a safe, supportive place to live. People especially valued Kenosha as a place to raise children, and many people reported happy childhood experiences that developed long-term friendships. Even those in need within the community were given every support to get on their feet. For example, one African American woman reported how her often welfare-dependent family survived through the support of a white storeowner who would provide food and other necessities on credit. Overdue bills were sometimes forgiven.

When many Kenosha residents fell on hard times due to Chrysler plant closings, city and county government rallied together to make sure that people would not lose their homes or other basic necessities. Government worked closely with local banks and other businesses to circumvent mortgage foreclosures and other negative consequences of job loss. The soup kitchen founders were able to draw on every voluntary element of the community to create basic commodities support for people in need. The same support continues today.

Both political patronage and social service are extremely individualistic, based on the face-to-face ties among known individuals characteristic of most social capital. On the plus side, political and social service leaders conceive of social supports as necessary and strive to treat people in need as the deserving poor who will quickly return to the mainstream. However, most political and social service leaders have limited understanding of reasons why some people would have trouble prospering in Kenosha, attributing consistent poverty to individual failings. Both interviews and fieldwork revealed numerous instances of social service personnel who viewed their clients as outsiders who needed to learn the local culture of work and follow community rules.

In day-to-day interactions, members of the insider community are supported through social contact, friendly talk in public places and informal supports. Often, insiders and outsiders are clearly designated through behavior in public places. For example, one African American couple reported:

> There was one time in the stores where we checked through with four or five items and this gentleman behind us started talking to the cashier and the cashier never put our stuff in the bag. They're going on in the conversation and she's getting ready to start checking his stuff. We're like, "You want to put our stuff in the bag?" She was like, "I'll just finish—" I said, "No, you're going to stop, just like you did and put the stuff in the bag."

As this example shows, outsiders can be ignored in favor of serving insiders. This kind of closed social capital has many consequences—both positive and negative—for Kenosha residents.

Kenosha residents viewed anyone from outside of their community with suspicion. Both whites and some people of color would not venture into adjacent Racine. Illinois was particularly considered the enemy. For example, one newcomer to Kenosha, active in city activities, commented that even though he had been in the community for many years, people still reminded him that he was not "from" Kenosha.

Localized Knowledge and Many Equal Truths

Another aspect of Kenosha culture involves the way that rules are enforced. People in Kenosha strongly believe that individual opinion developed through socialization within the community is far more important than knowledge from outside sources. As Katherine Dudley states in her book on Kenosha, suspicion of outsider knowledge comes from shop-floor culture developed in auto manufacturing employment. Here, the solidarity of the line workers is pitted against the actions of management. Authority figures are perceived as arbitrary and enforcing rules only known to them. Interactions among people from different groups or in different power roles involve denying the truths of others. Those who successfully enforce their view or who can rally their community around them get the resources they need. Outsiders are left out in the process.

Reputations were made and broken by often-distorted word of mouth reports. For example, one professional reported during one hiring experience: "The workers came to me and they had heard through the grapevine that this person had applied for this job. And his ex-wife worked in our environment and he was such a terrible person... And so, don't pick him, don't pick him." Here, we see that ability to get along in the closed social capital network is more important than qualifications. The workers presumed that the ex-wife's

report of this individual's character was correct. Localized knowledge superseded any outside information. Truth was established within the network, and reset depending on the views of insiders. In fact, the manager hired this person and he turned out to be a good employee. However, in most cases, localized truths would have ruled this individual out from serious consideration for the job.

Arbitrary truths are understood by many people of color as deliberate racism against them. Many people reported tickets for violation of unknown or arbitrarily enforced rules. After reviewing many motor vehicle incidents, I came to the conclusion that police were targeting people with out-of-state license plates. Sanctioning outsiders who do not follow community rules combined with widespread racial profiling in Kenosha. For example, one person reported that a local police officer told him that "he had a ticket waiting" for his son that looked Hispanic/Latino. This young man was repeatedly stopped by police, influencing his expectations of himself and others around him.

In another example, one interracial couple was stopped and ticketed for driving through a park after dark. These people were newcomers, with out-of-state plates, and were attempting to drive through the park to another main road. When they tried to explain this to the officer, each of them was given a ticket for over one hundred dollars. No information was provided to fight the ticket. This couple interpreted the incident as racism.

Americans from different class and race backgrounds define racism in various ways. Many whites think of racism as deliberate acts against people of color. African Americans and Hispanic/Latinos are more likely to interpret subtle behaviors like excessive parking tickets as examples of racism. Even though whites also receive tickets, they note that people of

color get ticketed more often than others in the community. A wide variety of actions by whites create a pattern of disparate treatment that people of color understand as racism. Subtle racism does not require that the person responsible for the action intend to discriminate against people of color. For example, the officer may claim that he is simply enforcing the law when ticketing the inter-racial couple. However, patterns of more tickets for people of color and the fact that he gave two high tickets to this couple show subtle discrimination prevalent in many aspects of life in Kenosha. This adds up to a sense of generalized racism in the community.

These examples show little-known rules used to sanction outsiders who do not fit community patterns. The fact of supporting behavior toward some people combined with unfriendly behavior to outsiders reinforces the view of supervisors or insiders to the community that individuals who complain are just presenting their own view of the truth. They presume that the people complaining are lying in order to uphold the view of their small group against an outsider from another group. The supervisor or insider then supports the person they know. The following story came from an established Kenosha African American woman who called a manager after being ignored by a store clerk who instead waited on a white customer:

So she says to me, "You called for me?" I said, "Yes, I did." She said, "What's the matter?" I said, "The young lady over at the jewelry counter, she asked me to wait and I waited my turn and then this other lady came and she left me to go to her. I'm not a person hard to get along with but that was so unfair to me." She said to me, "She's not like that." I said, "You say she's not like that. Didn't I just say she was like something?" She says, "She's not like that." So I said, "Who's your boss?" I was kind of perplexed. Because I could see and I could see what was going on. So she told [me], her boss would not be free till after 3:00.

The department manager supported her employee against this outsider with the statement that "She's not like that." When the customer persisted, she created another barrier—waiting until after 3:00 for a manager. Established community patterns through individualized truths were supported and change was limited by creating barriers to speaking to someone higher up in the organization.

Even public organizations practiced localized communication patterns. For example, during one event an African American community resident reported a racist attack on her son by a storeowner. The newspaper story the next day included six factual errors. When I asked the woman how she felt about the story, she commented that the reporter had put words in her mouth. The incident involved a child misbehaving in a store. The newspaper reporter had said the child was African American, but the boy's mother said he was white. "We aren't like that, we have friends of all colors." In fact, the mother had not mentioned the race of the child during the event. The reporter relied on his own presumptions about race based on historic patterns of closed social capital networks based on race or nationality. He shared his own truth when writing this article. As with the other examples, personal truth was far more important than outside knowledge.

Support for Various Views
In order to meet community expectations regarding following rules within a structure where truth varied, Kenosha residents developed ways to negotiate these patterns. Since insiders understood these patterns, they made allowances for variable practices for people that they knew and trusted. For example, even the correct time was open to individual interpretation. People would often set

their clocks anywhere from five to twenty minutes ahead of time in order to avoid being late. They would then forget that the clocks were set ahead, expecting people to abide by their version of local time. Given the prevalence of time variability, known individuals were expected to appear whenever they chose, but outsiders were expected to intuit the time used by a particular individual or establishment. This could lead to structural consequences as an outsider arriving late for school, work or an appointment could be shut out of opportunities based on inability to play by unspoken rules.

Insider Status Comes from Social Contact, Not Simply Racial Background
While this study documented many cases of negative behaviors toward people of color, the research consistently also found that individual ties developed through going to the same school or working in the same place were far more important than race or other group identity. Often, people had friends and social supports exclusively within one community because most of their social contacts were developed within the migrant community neighborhoods, churches and work connections. Even today,

newcomer African Americans recalled not being able to locate African American churches or other community institutions simply because they were not visible and insiders did not share information with outsiders.

At the same time, people who developed networks across race or ethnic boundaries found that trust developed through individual contacts was far more important than their background. This was reported throughout the research. For example, one long-term Kenosha resident reported:

All I knew was I saw a mixture of individuals. I saw—my friends were white, they were black. I had maybe two Hispanic families that I hung around with.

These primary networks formed the basis for interracial closed social capital networks throughout a lifetime. This pattern of closed social networks based on individual trust was strongly held by most people in Kenosha. For example, several white leaders could not think of distributing community resources in terms of groups. Instead, they talked about serving individuals—regardless of their background—through community institutions that they trusted. Trust, in both organizations and individuals, was developed by individual contacts. These cultural patterns had an important effect on all aspects of life in Kenosha.

Individual Attention and Boundaries through Rules

Another tension in Kenosha culture involves the conflict between attention for the individual versus the need for boundaries. The many rules in an office establish those boundaries. These rules are negotiated around the expectations of individual support.

Individual Attention

The incident with the cashier who forgets to bag the outsider's purchases illustrates another way that individualized networks and emphasis on the individual's perspective influences interactions with others. Part of supporting insiders involves being available to help them whenever they are in need. This plays out in a variety of ways. Workers put family needs before the expectations of an employer. Within a work context, supervisors are expected to respond to an employee whenever they have a problem. This comes from shop floor culture where foremen are expected to be available to solve worker concerns. The same is true for program participants asking for service. A "good" service person turns full attention to a client whenever they show up for service.

This expectation of constant availability often creates time issues for people providing service. Individuals focused on their own concerns show limited consideration of others. For example, at the beginning of one interview the social service agency director locked his office door, explaining, "I have an open door policy and sometimes my staff forgets to knock." Needs are expected to be met as they arise, regardless of closed doors, ongoing appointments or other commitments. Just like the forgotten

purchases, previous obligations fall by the wayside as the staff person seeks to please the next request. This results in people failing to respond in a timely manner to less present requests as they always focus on the person standing at their desk at that moment. Slow response led to people developing strategies to make sure that their requests were honored, often evoking expressions that they were as important as others. In other cases, people used social capital ties to make sure that their needs were met.

Boundaries through Rules and Egalitarian Ethos

The many rules of Wisconsin culture serve as a buffer from these expectations of always available support. Always available support is only available to those who follow approved community patterns. Since people also choose between multiple demands by favoring people within their social networks, patterns of support may appear arbitrary. In fact, the individual is trying to fulfill their obligations and evaluate who deserves primary attention by using established community culture patterns of first helping those in their closed social capital networks.

Southeastern Wisconsin has a strong egalitarian ethos and will often resort to lotteries or other first-come-first-served strategies to get around accusations of favoritism. People developed insider knowledge in order to make sure that they got resources. For example, tickets for a Martin Luther King event offered through the union sold out quickly. Insiders knew when the tickets would go on sale and were sure to ask for them promptly. Here we see how attempts to maintain equality exist hand-in-hand with closed community knowledge. The result is that insiders still get privileged access to resources even though everyone theoretically has an equal chance for the tickets.

Presentation Patterns

Another aspect of Kenosha culture involves approved ways of interacting with others. People are calm and polite. On the surface they appear friendly. To people within their networks, friendliness is genuine— insiders receive every consideration. Outsiders, on the other hand, may be politely ignored. For example, one woman reported that people she knew would not talk to her on the street. This kind of observation was common. Others reported that people would say "Hello," but not take the conversation further:

> Just walking out there and meeting someone black and talking to them, you'll get a response, you'll get a smile and a "hi." But if you want conversation, you get, "What you asking me that for?" Or somebody's been brainwashing them that everything's a secret.

Communication patterns combine with communication styles. In addition to only talking with known individuals, insiders and outsiders are distinguished by their ability to maintain a calm, surface-friendly demeanor. People who exhibit emotions, talk more loudly than expected, move more quickly than locals or use hand gestures are potentially considered violent or crazy. For example, at one community forum a person of color who works in law enforcement reported that he rapidly discovered that he needs to put his hands in his pockets otherwise people here consider him threatening for using hand gestures.

Minor differences in cultural patterns get exaggerated given Kenosha expectations. Kenosha residents were very concerned with safety, expressing concerns about violence on many different occasions. Disagreements were also considered violations of community expectations of niceness. An African American professional reported an incident where he said that he had gone out while dressed professionally and had acted professionally collecting data in a case related to his job. He said that before he had even gotten back to his office, his boss and the Kenosha newspaper had received a call saying that he had intimidated the person he interviewed and he was banned from public buildings in this small town outside of Kenosha.

Insider and outsider status are reinforced by community rules about correct behavior. People are quiet and nice. They keep to themselves and help others within their group. They support people who behave in the same way. They sanction others who behave differently.

Education and the Egalitarian Ethos

As a community in transition, Kenosha residents had to address the need for more education against a history of factory work. Shop-floor culture privileged the camaraderie of line workers against educated or skilled outsiders. This played out in Kenosha as a suspicion of people with advanced education or who actively sought status through credentials.

Valuing Workers over Educated People

Privileging individual opinion from people within established social networks also combines with preference for workers and subtle hostility among many Kenosha residents toward people with college education. Part of this comes from the value of manual labor in the community. For example, several people commented that union factory workers often made more than teachers.

Suspicion of education also came from still open wounds related to the plant closures. For some in Kenosha, plant closings were interpreted as encouraging a new way of life through education to change resistant factory workers. Since jobs in the new

economy required more preparation often for less money, workers viewed people promoting education as falsely thinking of themselves as "better than" the Kenosha working-class.

Anti-intellectualism led to discounting suggestions based on expert testimony or models from other communities. Instead, Kenosha leaders focused on using ideas from known people. Good ideas from locally recognized people received strong support. Often, as a way to mesh outsider ideas with Kenosha expectations, community leaders may have obtained education elsewhere, but stressed their blue-collar Kenosha roots when presenting their ideas.

Egalitarian Ethos Among the Educated Middle Class

Kenosha's egalitarian and anti-intellectual ethos played out differently among the educated middle class. Here, education and credentials were played down in favor of a low key, casual approach to others with similar ideas. The educated middle class were careful to ground conversations in the local milieu, sharing with the working class a sense that Kenosha was different from other places. We saw open reception to people offering good ideas to support the community. This meant that community leaders sought input from a wider variety of sources than in localities that only paid attention to a small, insular elite. While being established in Kenosha mattered, the educated middle class was more open to newcomers who made a commitment to the area. Much of the creative social service activities came from the educated middle class melding ideas to fit the local community.

Reactions of Kenosha African American and Hispanic/Latino Communities to Kenosha

People of color responded to Kenosha culture in three ways: 1) developing passive, invisible closed social capital networks within the Kenosha community, 2) blending into existing community patterns by adopting Kenosha culture and establishing cross-group networks, and 3) maintaining alternative cultural styles and fighting for group rights in Kenosha. The first two strategies were most welcomed by established Kenosha culture and most prevalent until recently. Leaders were beginning to practice the third strategy shortly before this research project. Kenosha responded through resistance and slow change.

Invisible Communities

Until recently, most people of color in this community kept to themselves, as with the African American newcomer who felt that established community residents did not want to share information because they "feared they would steal their jobs." Information was passed through word of mouth contact, organizations were not known outside of the closed social capital network and people stayed as quiet and passive as they could. Given the slow, hard-won gains in employment and other basic rights, many Kenosha African Americans were cautious about behaving in any way visible to outsiders. They knew that any display of anger or loudness would be interpreted as violence, leading to the development of self-depreciating patterns in public expected by many whites.

Part of this pattern involved simply not responding to communications with outsiders. Phone calls were not returned. Newcomers were viewed with suspicion and not given key information to learn about community events. Social life was restricted to the small network of known individuals.

Inside these invisible communities, people developed strong social life and support networks. We heard about small social clubs that offered both instrumental support and recreation. Churches often became the foundation for these activities. While invisible to others in Kenosha, these communities maintained their own culture, often connected to other places in the South, Texas or Mexico. However, newcomers had no way to become part of these communities without a direct invitation from an insider. This kind of invisibility still exists in Kenosha today.

Blending In Across Lines

At the same time that African American and Hispanic/Latino culture remained largely invisible to the mainstream, individuals developed strong links across racial groups based on other social capital ties developed through school, work and union involvement. These patterns often existed simultaneously with participation in closed social capital networks. Blending in meant learning Kenosha rules through socialization into the local culture. It also meant developing strong links across race boundaries. This resulted in many interracial friendships, dating and bi-racial unions.

While people crossed race boundaries, they seldom crossed class boundaries. The working class developed strong links among others of the same class background. Educated people, particularly newcomers, developed social ties among people they met at work, organizations and in the new, more upscale neighborhoods. Again, people followed the prevalent local culture practices for people from similar backgrounds.

Stressing Racial Identity

One strategy for racial justice involves people of color focusing on their differences from the mainstream as a group. In this practice, articulate people become spokespeople for their communities, intentionally setting themselves apart from whites. Using language highlighting discrimination and the achievements of people of color as separate groups, they seek resources as a group through people and organizations that are based in these minority communities. This strategy was new to Kenosha and only practiced by a few people.

Strategies to highlight racial identity came from established patterns that evolved as part of the United States civil rights movement and later movements for group identity. Group solidarity provides opportunities for people considered different from the mainstream to develop positive self-identity and draw on strength through working together as a group to seek equal rights in situations where they are treated unfairly. The leaders who asserted group identity brought national organizing practices to Kenosha either as newcomers or as long term Kenosha residents with strong ties to equal rights movements in other parts of the country. Most started slowly within their own communities, and by working with sympathetic whites, to create a more multicultural atmosphere in Kenosha.

During the research project, these activities began to draw city-wide attention through a bi-racial coalition to address racism in Kenosha. Coalition members primarily came from several liberal churches and one of the bridging African American churches. Activities included a series of community-wide forums on race related issues as well as study circles to discuss race. The community-wide events were widely attended by African Americans and whites, drawing from church congregations and other interested people in the area. Few Hispanic/Latinos attended these events.

Stressing racial identity also included banding together as a group to claim that others were discriminating against people from that group. For example, at one meeting an African American professional loudly demanded to know if "anyone who understood the community" was involved in the research. This was code for questions about whether African Americans were conducting the research. These statements were often a performance to assert the importance of understanding minority viewpoints. On several occasions, people who made loud, public statements on behalf of their groups later apologized for it, saying that this was expected in order to show racial solidarity. These leaders were concerned that they would damage carefully built bridging social capital by appearing to draw into race based closed social capital networks.

At the same time, many in the African American and Hispanic/Latino communities felt that they would do best to assert racial identity in order to claim resources unfairly distributed in the past. People from one minority community interacted with others in the same way. For example, at a Martin Luther King day celebration, a Hispanic/Latino representative commented that she understood this African American public figure because of links to Caesar Chaves. The Hispanic/Latina appeared as representing one community in solidarity with another oppressed group. Identity came from the racial community, not other sources.

Most Kenosha residents did not know how to respond to people who stressed racial identity. This pattern violated most Kenosha cultural norms of egalitarian behavior, surface friendliness and localized knowledge. Racial identity politics by definition connected local people to groups of outsiders associated with the same race. Stressing racial identity only slowly began to lead to change during the study period.

Conclusion

Community cultural patterns go hand-in-hand with social capital networks, reinforcing each other. Cultural patterns influence community life in many other ways. These range from public assistance program development, to employment, to social service and church activities. The rest of this publication explores the ways that social and cultural capital plays out in Kenosha.

Economic and Social Capital: Employers

I can tell you that if the job pays between seven and nine dollars [per hour], I'd be willing to bet it's probably two-thirds minority there. So there's a network for the lower paying jobs. There's not necessarily a network [for minorities to get into] the higher paying jobs (government employee).

Successfully implementing W-2 involves moving low-income families into stable jobs that pay enough so they can survive without government assistance. Particularly for single parent households, jobs need to pay enough to cover the costs of childcare, transportation and other expenses related to working. In order to be completely free from government supports, employment also needs to provide health insurance and leave to address such family events as childbirth and illness of a family member.

Moving low-income families permanently out of poverty through work requires three essential ingredients. First, jobs that provide family supporting wages and benefits must be available in the area. Second, the people looking for work must have the skills (human capital), knowledge of appropriate behaviors to be a successful employee (cultural capital) and access to childcare and transportation to both qualify for these jobs and be able to keep them. Third, employers and employees have to connect to each other. This third ingredient involves social capital links between employer and employee.

This section explores the first ingredient in this mix: available employment in Kenosha. Relying primarily on findings from the employer survey and secondary sources, I first discuss the types of companies currently in Kenosha and the kinds of jobs they offer. Next, ways that employers recruit employees are outlined. Finally, using data from the employer survey, interviews and ethnographic data, I show how social and cultural capital plays a role in employer decisions in Kenosha.

Size of and Types of Employers in Kenosha

Before the large, unionized factories left Kenosha, jobs paid enough to support a family and offered benefits to take care of workers and their families when things went wrong. The new Kenosha eco65015178030001nomy is far more diverse. Most of the unionized factory jobs have left the area and many of the smaller firms pay lower wages and offer fewer benefits.

TABLE 1: TYPES OF BUSINESSES IN KENOSHA

Primary Business Purpose	Kenosha Employer Survey	KABA (1998)	U.S. Census Business Survey
RETAIL	29%	20.8%	24%
SERVICE	42%	22.8%	49%
MANUFACTURING	11%	24.2%	9%
GOVERNMENT	6%	14.9%	NA
WHOLESALE DISTRIBUTOR	3%	4.5%	6%
NON-PROFIT	9%	N/A	5%
OTHER	N/A	0.1%	NA

Table 1 compares the types of businesses in Kenosha from the U.S. Census Bureau and two recent surveys: the Kenosha Area Business Alliance (KABA) survey of its members and the *Kenosha Employer Survey* (KES). Differences in the percentages from the two surveys comes from the fact that the two studies drew from distinct lists to collect information. The KABA study sent questionnaires to their members, which included a greater percentage of manufacturing enterprises. The *Kenosha Employers Survey* selected businesses that appeared on either the KABA list, the Chamber of Commerce directory or the directory of social services in Kenosha. For this reason, the KES has more retail and service businesses than the KABA study. The KABA study has more manufacturing firms for the same reason. The KABA study combined government and non-profits in the government category. Adding the government and non-profit categories from the *Kenosha Employer Survey* yields fifteen percent, roughly the same percentage as in the KABA study.

The *U.S. Census Business Survey* is usually considered the most accurate accounting of the number and types of companies in a community. The census survey only collects data on companies that pay employees. The census survey found 2,273 firms in Kenosha County that fit this description. In comparison to the census figures, the *Kenosha Employer Survey* is closer to the census breakdown of types of business than the KABA study. KES interviewers talked to a few more retail store owners and non-profit owners than is representative of the city as a whole. We reached half as many wholesale distributors and a few less service sector employers than the census reports for the city as a whole. Overall, the employers who responded to the KES represent similar percentages to the census survey and can be considered reasonably representative of the whole county.

All studies show that Kenosha has a diverse employment base. Together, retail and service sector firms are the majority in Kenosha, but manufacturing, non-profit and government jobs are also available. Retail includes any type of store. The service sector includes a wide variety of businesses that supply a service. Service sector firms include construction (seven percent of all employers responding to the KES), trucking (three percent, KES), auto repair (six percent), personal services like drycleaners and hair salons (thirteen percent), professional services like lawyers and doctors (nine percent) and business services like duplicating and accounting (three

percent).[8]   Government employers include schools, the Kenosha County Job Center and other city and county offices. Non-profits include a wide range of organizations too: nursing homes, youth recreation organizations, poverty related agencies and many other kinds of not-for-profit organizations. The KES did not include churches or all volunteer organizations like the girl scouts or AAUW in its sample of non-profits.

This range of employers means that many types of employment are now available in Kenosha. This diversity is good news in many ways: people with varying skill levels and interests can all find work in Kenosha. However, if much of the older workforce consists of people formerly employed in factories, the new Kenosha economy means that a lot of people have had to retrain in order to qualify for the new jobs. Fewer younger workers can follow the same path as their parents and neighbors into good paying unionized manufacturing jobs. Since many of the new jobs require more education than previous employment, workers also need to obtain more education than before. In a community that values manual labor over educated people, the new economy requires changes in the education system and community culture in order to meet the needs of Kenosha's current employment base.

The current unemployment rate of 3.5 percent suggests that employers are eager to find workers that meet their qualifications.

Conversations with employers during the *Kenosha Conversation Project* and the *Kenosha Social Capital Study* suggest that employers can easily find workers, but that the growing retail and service sector businesses have a harder time locating people with the communication skills and education levels they need. Given the low unemployment rate, many employers say that they have a hard time keeping workers. Employees dissatisfied with their wages or working conditions will simply move on to something better. The impact of the labor market in Kenosha on wages and working conditions will be discussed later in this section.

The size of business also influences the types of jobs available in Kenosha, wages and working conditions, and who is likely to be hired for these jobs. Table 2 compares findings on the size of Kenosha companies from the KABA study and *Kenosha Employers Survey* (KES). Differences in the two sets of statistics come from the way that employers were selected for each study. KABA sent questionnaires to everyone on their list, regardless of the number of employees. They found that fifty-two percent of the employers who responded employed zero to four people. For the most part, these were individual or family businesses like an electrician or someone who ran a computer business out of his or her home. These businesses often had no employees outside of the immediate family. Since the *Kenosha Employer Survey* deliberately left out companies that had not hired anyone outside of their family recently, the KES has fewer small employers. The *Kenosha Employer Survey* has greater percentages of larger businesses for this reason.

While the U.S. Census Business Survey does not collect information from small employers with no payroll, it does note the number of these types of businesses in a community. The census survey found 812 companies with no payroll in Kenosha County. When added to the firms who do pay wages to employees, these self-employed individuals account for one-third of Kenosha companies. It is important to note that some small family businesses do create formal salaries like larger businesses; these firms would be included in the census survey. Since the census survey does not report information on size of company at the local level, it is not possible to tell whether the KABA or KES figures are more comparable to the census breakdowns for size of business.

for themselves. Many retail stores and service establishments have bulletin boards where self-employed people can advertise their services. Other contractors use their informal contacts to find customers. Since many people find service businesses like contractors or house cleaners through word of mouth referrals, the strong closed capital social networks available in Kenosha may help these small businesses thrive.

31

TABLE 2: SIZE OF BUSINESS		
Number of Employees	KABA (1997)	Kenosha Employer Survey
0-9 (KABA)/UNDER 10 (KES)	71%	52%
10-19	13%	----
11-34	----	25%
20-49	10%	----
50-99 (KABA)/35-99 (KES)	3%	8%
100 AND OVER	3%	15%

Both studies suggest that many of the new employers in Kenosha are very small businesses. Since a majority of these small employers really represent self-employed individuals, this means that there are fewer options for people who are not interested in becoming entrepreneurs.

On the other hand, the prevalence of self-employed individuals in Kenosha suggests that the community strongly supports people who go into business

TABLE 3: KENOSHA EMPLOYER SURVEY, BUSINESS PURPOSE BY SIZE

Business Purpose by Size	10 or less	11-34	35-99	100 or More
RETAIL	39%	30%	31%	----
SERVICE	55%	31%	14%	----
MANUFACTURING	39%	7%	39%	15%
GOVERNMENT	----	----	43%	57%
WHOLESALE	----	100%	----	----
NON-PROFIT	64%	27%	9%	----

32

The remainder of the tables in this section only use data from the *Kenosha Employers Survey*. Table three compares business size to the type of business. Retail businesses show the most variation in terms of size. Nearly forty percent of these businesses have ten employees and less, but approximately one-third are larger stores with eleven to thirty-five or thirty-five to ninety-nine employees. No stores had one hundred employees or more. Examples of a small retail business might be a gas station with three employees. The middle size business range includes drug stores, grocery stores, discount stores and a variety of businesses that have several shifts of sales staff.

Service sector businesses tend to be very small. Over half have less than ten employees and eighty-six percent have less than thirty-five employees. Examples of very small service sector businesses include beauty parlors, doctors' offices and travel agencies with fewer than ten employees. Examples of middle size service sector businesses include larger health care clinics or real estate offices with several agents and clerical staff.

The study also found a large range in size of business for manufacturing firms. Thirty-nine percent had ten employees or less and another thirty-nine percent had between thirty-five

and ninety-nine employees. These smaller firms include packaging companies and companies that make a wide range of products. Fifteen percent of Kenosha area manufacturing firms have more than one hundred employees. The majority of these firms are similar to the small and middle size firms. Only three percent of the employers who responded to the Kenosha Employers Survey had five hundred employees or more. These large employers include firms like Snap-On Tools and the small Chrysler plant still functioning in Kenosha.

Government businesses tended to be larger than most other types of companies. Forty-three percent of the government offices were middle size operations with between thirty-five and ninety-nine employees. Examples included fire stations and smaller schools. The majority, fifty-seven percent, had more than one hundred employees. Larger government offices would include schools and government social welfare offices.

All of the wholesale businesses in the Kenosha Employers Survey had between eleven and thirty-four employees. Most were small-scale warehouse operations.

The majority of non-profits had small offices. Sixty-four percent had less

than ten employees and ninety-one percent had less than thirty-five employees. Only nine percent had between thirty-five and ninety-nine employees. Examples of a small non-profit would include the mission projects attached to churches in the African American and Hispanic/Latino community or the social service agency with one employee. In fact, all of the non-profit organizations associated with the African American and Hispanic/Latino communities, except one, had less than ten employees. Middle range non-profits would include most of the anti-poverty agencies like the homeless shelter, some of the youth serving organizations and nursing homes.

The *Kenosha Employers Survey* found that the size of the company and the type of business combined to influence wages, types of jobs available and working conditions in these companies. The next section looks at the size and type of business together in discussing working conditions in the new Kenosha economy.

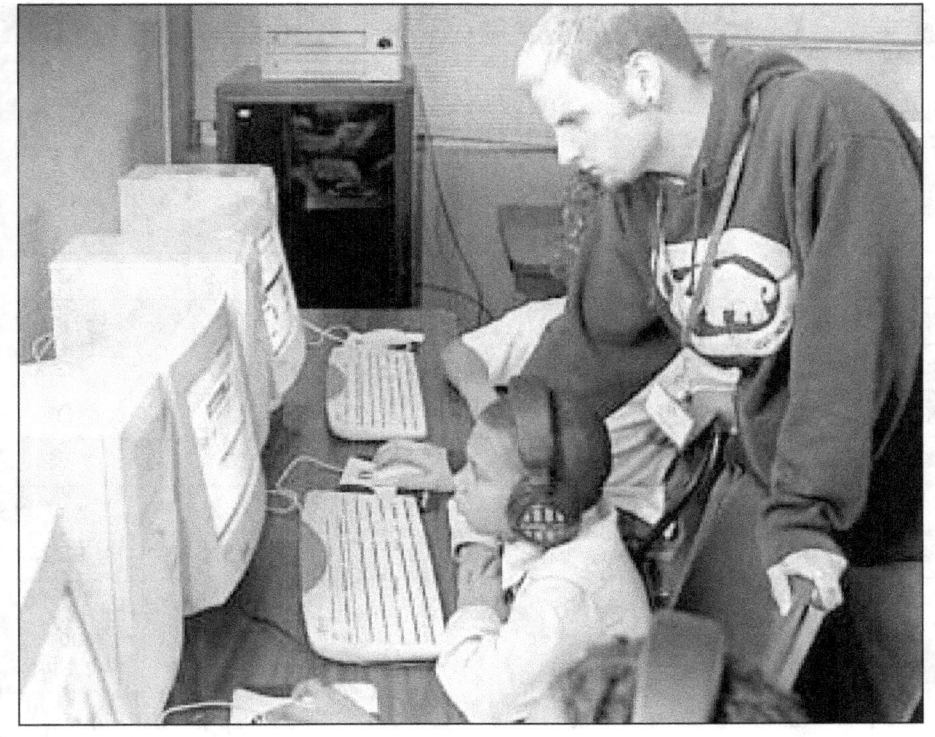

Wages and Working Conditions in Kenosha

Labor market scholars divide the U.S. labor force into two sectors that offer very different wages and working conditions. Hiring practices in these two sectors differ dramatically too. Primary sector firms are large manufacturing firms like Chrysler. Large government offices tend to behave in ways similar to primary sector for-profit firms. These companies tend to have unions, offering high wages and good benefits. These firms also have formal hiring structures including personnel offices that follow government anti-discrimination and affirmative action hiring practices. Since primary sector firms have unions and formal promotion practices, advancement in these companies is more likely to follow seniority, or a combination of seniority and other factors, in determining career paths for people employed in these firms. Traditionally, primary sector plants hired mainly white men. After civil rights changes in the 1960s and 1970s these firms

were more likely to hire African Americans and Hispanic/Latinos in order to meet government guidelines. For example, several people reported that AMC/Chrysler started hiring people of color after they received government contracts to build jeeps.

Many people concerned about poverty in the United States look for primary sector employment as the preferred type of work. However, just as Chrysler shut down most of its operations in Kenosha, most primary sector employment has left the area. This means that a smaller pool of these desirable jobs are available to people looking for work in this area.

Smaller companies, like those common in the new Kenosha economy, are part of the secondary sector. Secondary sector firms are smaller and more likely to be owned by one family or individual. They tend to have less capital when they start and are more likely to go out of business when times are difficult. They also tend to pay lower wages and offer fewer benefits than primary sector firms. More jobs are temporary or part time. Secondary sector firms are less likely to have

unions. They also tend to be more flexible in their hiring and promotion practices. On the plus side, it is easier for a new employee to advance in a secondary sector firm because seniority rules are less likely to be followed. On a negative note, secondary sector firms are less likely to follow affirmative action or anti-discrimination laws. They are more likely to hire people they know and promote people that the owner likes than in a primary sector firm.[10]

Table four describes selected characteristics of the labor force for each of the major types of companies. These percentages represent the median for each type of firm for each characteristic.[11] Taken together with the information comparing type of company to firm size, these figures show that Kenosha employers fit in to the model of primary and secondary sector common throughout the United States. As discussed later in this section, this pattern became clearer when companies were grouped on several characteristics. Primary sector manufacturing firms are more likely to pay better wages than the secondary sector in Kenosha. They are also more likely to hire men than women. Primary sector firms are more likely to offer full-time employment.

33

TABLE 4: KENOSHA EMPLOYER SURVEY, SELECTED EMPLOYMENT

(Percentages represent the average number of employees in these types of companies for each category. Since numbers within firms vary, the wage averages do not add to one hundred percent)

Employee Characteristics	Retail	Service	Non-Profit	Government	Manufacturing	Wholesale
PART TIME EMPLOYEES	45%	16%	42%	0%	0%	0%
FEMALE	52%	65%	95%	28%	29%	25%
% PAID LESS THAN $7/HOUR	20%	0%	0%	14%	0%	2%
% PAID $7 -$9/HOUR	25%	0%	20%	24%	2%	0%
% PAID $9-11/HOUR	10%	10%	20%	20%	25%	4%
% PAID >$11/HOUR	10%	23%	15%	5%	20%	41%
% SKILLED	44%	61%	46%	31%	71%	97%

34

Wages and benefits in Kenosha reflect the tight labor market in the area during the study. In an economy with a 3.5 percent unemployment rate, employers tend to offer better wages and benefits. We found this to be true in Kenosha. On average, Kenosha employers paid less than $7 an hour to only sixteen percent of their labor force. Most employers paid everyone more than seven dollars an hour. As shown in Table 4, twenty percent of the retail labor force earned seven dollars an hour or less and fourteen percent of government employees earned this same low wage. In the late 1990s, "low wages" in Kenosha meant between seven and nine dollars an hour.

Comparisons show that each type of employer offers different wage and working conditions. The percentage of women employed varies across the type of business, too.[13] Retail and non-profit sector businesses were most similar to each other. These two types of businesses had the largest percentage of part-time employees and, on average, paid lower wages. More women were employed in retail and non-profit organizations. On average, more than half of the retail employees were women and almost all of the non-profit employees were women. Retail and non-profit sector

employers were most likely to offer jobs for unskilled or semi-skilled people. On average, less than half of the jobs available in each of these firms required specific skills. This means that people who have less human capital are more likely to find jobs available in companies that offer lower wages and part-time hours. This is particularly true for women.

Manufacturing, wholesale and service sector employers offered better wages and more full-time jobs. They also hired fewer women and required a higher level of skill from their employees. While the service sector employed an average of sixty-five percent women, less than a third of the employees in manufacturing and wholesaling businesses were women. On average, service sector businesses had specific skill requirements for sixty-one percent of their employees. Over seventy percent of manufacturing employees were skilled and nearly all wholesale jobs required specific skills. Examples of skilled, full-time jobs varied widely. They included computer programmers, accountants, nurses, doctors, teachers and skilled trades people like electricians or plumbers.

Government offered a variety of types of jobs at a wide range of wages.

Nearly forty percent of the government workforce earned less than nine dollars an hour. Only one third of government jobs required specific skills. Examples of low paid, unskilled or semi-skilled government jobs included clerical work, garbage collectors, janitorial staff, nursing assistants and teacher's aides. Examples of jobs paying better and requiring more skills included teachers, social workers and human service program managers.

Benefits
The tight labor market also affected the kinds of benefits offered by employers. Health insurance was a key concern of Kenosha employees. As a result, eighty-five percent of Kenosha employers offered health insurance to their employees. However, most companies asked their employees to contribute to the cost of their health insurance. Seventy-one percent of the employers expected employees to contribute something to the cost of their health insurance. Forty-three percent expected their employees to contribute less than twenty percent of the cost of health insurance, thirty-seven percent expected employees to pay for between twenty and fifty percent of health insurance costs, and twenty percent asked employees to pay

more than fifty percent. Only half of the companies responded to a question about whether they paid for insurance for the entire family rather than just the employee. Seventy-two percent of these employers offered health insurance for the entire family.

Eighty percent of Kenosha employers had some sort of family leave policy to support their workers when a relative was sick, after the birth of a child or when a family member died. However, reporting a family leave policy did not necessarily mean that employees could count on this kind of support when they had a problem. Thirty percent of the employers who had a family leave policy said that leave was based on the boss's discretion. In other words, if the boss liked the employee or believed in their need for time off, the worker would get time off without losing his or her job. If the supervisor and employee did not get along well, a worker with a valid excuse may be fired for missing work.

Sixteen percent of the companies reported that they followed the Family and Medical Leave Act (FMLA) provisions in allowing time off for their employees. FMLA policy allows twelve weeks unpaid time off for a new child or a sick family member. Most of the employers who followed FMLA were large companies required by federal law to offer time off.

Another twenty-seven percent of the companies had a formal sick leave policy. Most of these policies allowed workers to take time off when family members were sick as well as recuperating from illness themselves. Employees in these firms had more formal rights than people who were dependent on the bosses' discretion.

Despite reports of different kinds of leave policies in various companies, survey data, interviews and observations revealed that not everyone in a company followed the policy reported by an owner or personnel manager responsible for creating such policies. For example, the *Kenosha Employers Survey* received

questionnaires for all Kenosha branches of one chain store. When we interviewed the district manager, he told us that the company had a formal leave policy that was taught to all store managers during their initial training. However, the student processing these questionnaires for the chain discovered that half of the stores reported that sick and family leave was at the "boss's discretion." In keeping with the Kenosha cultural practice of individualized knowledge, employees were still at the mercy of their supervisor's whims despite corporate policy. Many supervisors ignored standardized policy.

Variable policies combined with closed social and cultural capital to impact on the employment experience of people from different backgrounds. Low-income African Americans, in particular, were more likely to lose jobs due to failure to fit in with a company policy. This was particularly true for people transitioning from community service employment into paid work. For example, one caseworker spoke about a woman who missed several weeks of her community service due to an illness, but was excused because she had a doctor's note. The caseworker was concerned because the community service worker did not call in when she was sick, angering the agency hosting her community service placement. The caseworker commented that she would have lost the job if it were regular employment.

Real world employers confirm the caseworker's observation. We heard many complaints from employers about employees who were unreliable. For example, one nursing home supervisor complained about two nurses' aids that went home to the south for several weeks after a relative died without telling the employer. She commented that while they were good workers, she could not keep them after this behavior. However, if an employee had come to her to report family problems and ask for time off, she would have been more lenient. We

found many cases where employees who had good relationships with their supervisor, particularly those practicing the same cultural capital behaviors, received very different treatment than employees who followed different patterns. One of the challenges to both employers and employees involved matching social and cultural capital in the workplace so that everyone understood the rules and received equal treatment.

Employer Clusters

Since the *Kenosha Employers Survey* found a wide range of wages and working conditions within each general type of employer, businesses were grouped by similar characteristics. Grouping employers by similar characteristics revealed several very different kinds of employment opportunities for people seeking work in Kenosha. We found the following five clusters of business:

1. *Small retail and service sector businesses, sixty-two percent skilled labor force, moderate to high wages* Twenty-one percent of the companies fell into this group. They included small doctor's offices and high-end retail employers like a shop that makes and sells computers. Only twenty percent of the employees in these firms were part-time workers. Sixty-four percent of these companies had less than ten employees. Forty percent of their employees were female. All paid wages of over nine dollars an hour to their employees. Eighty-six percent of these businesses offered health insurance benefits to their employees.

2. *Small service and manufacturing firms offering high wages and requiring skilled employees* Twenty-six percent of the Kenosha employers in this study offered good wages and benefits, but required primarily skilled workers. Firms in this group included professional service organizations

like lawyers and doctors' offices and small manufacturing firms hiring skilled craftsmen. On average, seventy-seven percent of their labor force are skilled workers. Eighty-nine percent of the workers earned more than eleven dollars an hour. Ninety-seven percent of these companies offered health insurance and only fifty-three percent expected employees to contribute to the costs of their health insurance. Most of the people employed in these firms (sixty-one percent) were men.

3. *Service sector and manufacturing firms paying moderate wages, fifty-three percent skilled labor force, one-third labor force part-time*
Thirty-five percent of the companies clustered into this group. Firms in this category included beauty parlors and small manufacturers. Most jobs paid between seven and eleven dollars an hour. These employers offered an even mix of skilled and unskilled jobs. Seventy percent of these employers offered health insurance to their workers.

4. *Middle to large size retail and non-profit firms paying low to moderate wages, over fifty percent part-time workers*
Examples of companies in group four were large chain stores, nursing homes and large youth serving agencies. Ten percent of the employers in the survey fell into this category. These employers offered the most "entry-level" jobs that unskilled or semi-skilled low-wage workers were most likely to find. On average, forty-seven percent of their workforce was paid less than seven dollars an hour and the rest of the workers earned less than eleven dollars an hour. Only twenty-eight percent of the workers in these companies were skilled. Seventy-one percent of the workers in these organizations were women. Seventy percent of these organizations offered health insurance.

5. *Small to middle size retail and service companies paying low wages and offering part-time hours* These organizations were very similar to group four, but were smaller operations. Examples include small restaurants, house cleaning services and small stores. Wages and working conditions were worse in these companies. Eight percent of the employers fell into this group. On average, half of their employees were part-time.
Eighty-five percent of their workers earned less than seven dollars an hour. Sixty percent of the labor force was female. Only half of the employers in this group offered health insurance. Even when employees could get insurance through their work, they were expected to pay for the insurance themselves.

The clusters show two largely divergent types of employers. On the one hand, firms in clusters one and two offer family supporting wages and health insurance benefits. For the remainder of this report, I will call these companies *family supporting, education-required firms*. Nearly half of the firms in Kenosha fell into this category. Companies in these two clusters included a mix of manufacturing, service and high-end retail employment. In both categories, over sixty percent of the employees were skilled workers. Sixty percent or more of the workers were men.

The other half of the employers offered lower wages, a larger percent of part-time jobs and fewer benefits. For the remainder of this report, I will call these companies *lower wages, wider range of opportunity firms*. While most of these companies offer health insurance, seventy percent of them expect employees to contribute to the costs of insurance. Paying for health insurance becomes more difficult at these lower wages. Over sixty percent of the workers in these companies are women. Most of the jobs in these companies do not require specific skills.

Cluster three, which includes a mix of manufacturing and service sector employment, offers wages that may support a family but do not offer much security or money to save. However, one-third of the employees in these companies are part time, meaning that fewer of them will earn family supporting wages.

Wages and working conditions get worse for people employed in the last two types of companies. The majority of people working in these firms earn wages that will hardly support a family. Since many jobs are part-time, it is even less likely that employees will bring home a living wage. While many of these employers offer health insurance, employees need to pay for it themselves. Low-wage workers struggling to make ends meet are more likely to go without insurance rather than see large portions of their paychecks go toward health care. Most of the employees in these companies are women.

Most people hope for jobs in companies like those in the first two groups. However, not everyone can find work in these firms. As the quote at the beginning of this section suggests, just as there are two divergent types of employers in Kenosha, employees are tracked into either low-wage or high-wage employment. This tracking partly comes from the human capital and cultural capital characteristics of employees themselves. Ways that jobs are advertised and employer hiring practices also influence who finds jobs in different kinds of firms.

Advertising and Hiring Practices

On average, employers reported that one-third of their referrals came from friends and family, thirty-one percent came from newspaper advertising, sixteen percent from walk-ins, eight percent from training programs, two percent from unemployment, and nine percent from other means.[14] The nine percent "other" category included hiring through temporary agencies. Temporary agency employment is a particular concern to some ant-poverty agencies because temporary employees rarely receive benefits and often do not graduate to full time, permanent jobs. On the other hand, employers like temporary agencies because they screen their employees for them and allow them a flexible workforce.

The types of advertising used to garner applicants varied depending on the size of the company. Small companies were more likely to get referrals from friends and family while larger firms were more likely to advertise in the newspaper or use the unemployment office.

Referral sources also varied by the type of business. Retail, service, manufacturing and wholesale businesses each got approximately one-third of their referrals from friends and family. Eighteen percent or less of the referrals for government and non-profit employers came from personal contacts.

These social network referrals become a powerful source of employees. As discussed further in the next section, people are more likely to actually get a job through a personal referral than through any other source. For example, while I was interviewing someone active in the union, our interviewee received several phone calls from people looking for work in the new plant that Chrysler was building during the study. After the second call, I asked if this happens often. He responded that he gets several calls a week from people asking him to help them find a job. Most of these calls were from people from the same race and class background. Individuals were using their closed social capital networks to help find work.

Service, government and non-profits were more likely to get a small percentage of their applicants from a training program. Between eleven and thirteen percent of the applicants for

these types of organizations came from training programs. Other types of businesses got two percent or less of their applicants through training. This difference is probably due to the nature of the jobs in these types of organizations and connections to government programs. For example, a nursing home may recruit employees from a certified nursing assistant training program.

Non-profits and government may hire interns first referred through their college or vocational training program. For example, Janice, the young woman described earlier in the discussion of social capital, was placed in an internship while in college at the school that eventually hired her. Her employer noticed her good work while she served as an intern and hired her after she completed her education. She would count as a referral from a training program. Government and non-profit agencies have also reported hiring community service workers who do well in their volunteer positions.

Non-profits, government and manufacturing firms were more likely to advertise in the newspaper for applicants. Forty percent of non-profit applicants, forty-one percent of manufacturing applicants and sixty percent of government applicants came from newspaper advertising. Organizations that use this method to gather applicants tend to follow civil rights and affirmative action policy either due to agency philosophy or because they are large enough to fall under government regulations. For example, a small non-profit may not need to advertise through the newspaper to find applicants, but may feel that they will get the widest and most representative pool of candidates through advertisements. If the agency believes in equal opportunity employment, they are more likely to advertise in the newspaper so that everyone will know that they are hiring. Government agencies, large employers and particularly employers who work with government are

required by federal law to post job openings regardless of the philosophy of the organization.

Twenty-nine percent of the applicants for retail businesses and twenty-six percent each of the service and wholesale establishments' applicants came from the newspaper. Chain stores and larger businesses in each of these categories were more likely to use newspaper advertising.

Only retail businesses and wholesale distributors got a significant percentage of their applicants from people walking in off the street. Retail businesses got twenty-seven percent of their applicants from these sources while wholesale distributors got thirty-three percent of their applicants from walk-ins. It is not surprising that stores would get large percentages of walk-in applicants. They are visible businesses that often advertise for new workers by putting signs in their windows. The wholesale warehouses appear at first glance as potential employers for men with limited skills. In fact, one of these companies did offer many semi-skilled jobs. However, wages and benefits at this company were very low. Most firms that used walk-in applications for a major referral source paid low wages, offered part-time work and few benefits.

While we found no statistically significant differences among the five groups of employers in the ways that they advertised for employees, observation data suggests that employers fitting into clusters four and five are most likely to get more walk-in referrals. At the same time, firms in all the categories received large numbers of referrals through friends and family or formal advertising.

Hiring in Kenosha is usually done by one individual. Employers reported that the owner or chief executive was responsible for hiring decisions thirty-nine percent of the time. A manager or department head made hiring decisions forty-three percent of the time. Four percent of the hiring decisions were made by a human resources department head. Only nine percent of the companies used team hiring to decide on workers. Owners and executives primarily did the hiring in small companies while managers and department heads were responsible in chains and large firms. Team hiring primarily occurred in small, professional service establishments where people need to work together.

38

Individualized decision-making meant that employees may have little say in who worked with them. On the other hand, like the situation described in *Kenosha Culture* where employees tried to influence the manager to not hire another employee's ex-husband, employers might rely on employee referrals in deciding among applicants. Combined with the fact that managers and owners often had a lot of say regarding benefits, this meant that the employer had a lot of power in employment relationships. As discussed in detail in the next section, in small firms where most employees come from similar cultural capital backgrounds and share social capital connections, the power dynamics between employee and employer may not become cause for concern.

However, in companies hiring people different from themselves, individualized hiring and employment decisions meant that the employer set the tone for employment decisions. For example, we noticed several employers who would not consider an applicant from a different racial and ethnic group. Others in the community noted the same hiring practices. During a skit at a racial awareness event, church members played out a scene where a white employer tells a highly qualified applicant that a position is filled after learning that the applicant is a person of color. After the event, a number of

African American audience members commented that they had first hand experience with this kind of behavior.

Employers who made an effort to hire people from diverse backgrounds consciously set the tone in their organizations. For example, one employer reported:

Well, I—first off by putting people of color in respectful positions. By having that part of the mission and having people realize [people of color are] going to be leaders. Hopefully that will make it easy for a person to enter the company. And we do, we try to make a gender mix as well, women as well as men.

This employer's strong reputation for offering good jobs to people of color meant that he received many applications from people in that community. By creating trusting, social capital relationships with African Americans and Hispanic/Latinos, he had no need to advertise for workers. He reported:

We do have a lot of walk-in applications because of some perceptions that this is a respectful place to work for. So we don't usually have a problem—we have enough of an applicant base that [we] don't usually have to reach out to the job center or placement firms. We normally have a pretty good applicant base of people of

color....We've started going out and making sure that we diversified this work base and employment base and by that—word of mouth—to some degree of involvement with the nonprofits. I can go through McDonalds and have someone say, "Can my daughter come and apply for a job?" And it's usually someone who's not Caucasian. Its just part of the exposure, people know you've got it in your mission.

As discussed in more detail in the section on employees, most employers found that they could use social capital networks to help find workers. As this

example suggests, the tone set by the employer influenced who chose to come in the door. As with the union representative described earlier, race-based social capital networks profoundly influence who chooses to apply for a position and their chances of getting hired.

Retention

The tone of the workplace also influenced the ability of employers to keep employees. Employees leave an organization for two reasons: 1) they seek better pay and working conditions or 2) they quit or are fired because they do not fit into the workplace. Often these two reasons go together. In a tight labor market like Kenosha, churning—or quick turnover of employees—is a real concern for both employers and people hoping to place low-income workers into stable employment. The value of a supportive workplace is particularly important in a community with closed social capital networks relying on individualized knowledge and cultural practices. The *Kenosha Employers Survey* sought to understand this process by asking about mentoring available for new employees on the job. Sixty-eight percent of the employers reported that they think mentoring is important and assign a mentor to newcomers. However, mentoring largely turned out to mean orientation by a supervisor or more established employee. Sixty-two percent of the firms only assigned a mentor for less than thirty days. Only twenty-six percent assigned a mentor for over forty-five days. Companies with longer mentoring periods tended to have skilled crafts apprenticeships or professional employment.

Limited mentoring means that employees need to learn quickly the rules of the workplace. If they fit into the unspoken culture because they come with appropriate cultural capital or they already have friends in the workplace due to social capital networks that encouraged them to apply, adjusting to a new workplace may be easy. Those lacking either appropriate social or cultural capital may have a harder time. For example, one woman was hired as a manager in an organization where most employees and program participants came from closed social capital networks in one neighborhood. She reported that she had a hard time fitting in and was "never accepted" by established people associated with the organization. The job ended badly.

On the other hand, another newcomer found that he got a hostile response from unionized workers he supervised, but that friendly managers made every effort to explain the local culture. This individual thrived in Kenosha and has been promoted through the organization.

Taken together, hiring and support on the job largely depend on the individual actions of managers and owners in Kenosha workplaces. Other employees in the organization may support these actions, particularly if they share the same social and cultural capital as newcomers.

The Role of the Kenosha County Job Center

The Kenosha Employers Survey and the observation data suggest that few employers need to use a government service to find employees. In fact, the Kenosha Employers Survey found that only thirty-four percent of the organizations in the study used the job center in any way. These employers fell into three types: sixty-nine percent of the manufacturers; seventy-one percent of the government agencies; and sixty-four percent of the non-profits used government referrals. Interviews and observations revealed that these three types of organizations used the job center due to social capital networks. Government and non-profit organizations have strong ties to the job center due to

contracting and information-sharing networks. Manufacturers are tied to the job center because KABA, their professional organization, works closely with the job center to recruit employers to Kenosha and facilitate employment in the area.

These ties are even more important when it comes to hiring W-2 workers. Only eight percent of the Kenosha Employers Survey organizations reported that they actively recruited W-2 applicants, and only government (thirty-three percent) and non-profits (thirty percent) recruited them regularly.

Why don't employers use the Kenosha County Job Center to find workers? Primarily, employers have no need of the job center. Like the employer quoted above, thirty percent responded that they had enough applicants through other means. Only seven percent each responded that they needed employees with skills not offered by the job center or that the job center had sent them inappropriate applicants. The rest of the organizations had not thought about using the job center.

The survey also found that most employers did not know about benefits available to help low-income people find and keep jobs. Only thirty-six percent were aware of the transportation and childcare co-pay programs. These tended to be organizations already working with the job center. On the other hand, twenty-seven percent were interested in learning more about tax credits for hiring W-2 eligible employees.

This lack of knowledge about the job center suggests that employers rely on individualized knowledge passed through their social capital networks to find out about benefits available to

workers just as others in Kenosha rely on the same Kenosha cultural habits and social capital ties to share information and interact with others. While the job center does advertise its activities, information is not readily available to employers outside of the social service networks. More importantly, employers are likely to ignore information from government or any other source beyond those they know and trust. This is particularly true of small employers who make up the bulk of firms in Kenosha.

Implications for Policy and Programs

This picture of employment in Kenosha suggests the following concerns for people intent on finding stable employment for families:

- *Employment and support practices need to be targeted toward small, secondary sector firms.* The prevalence of small companies in Kenosha suggests that many of the strategies to support working families developed for large companies, such as good employer based health insurance, on site day care, and employer-sponsored transportation, will not work in this community. Instead, local government and agencies need to design childcare, health insurance benefits, and transportation strategies that do not assume that the employer should take responsibility for these supports. Ideas like small business health insurance pools, neighborhood based childcare, and car donation and repair services may work better in this type of community.

- *Employment development strategies need to address the needs of two divergent types of employers in Kenosha.* Kenosha employers fall into two categories: service and manufacturing firms that require specific skills and offer good wages and benefits; and service sector,

39

manufacturing, retail and non-profit firms that offer lower wages, poorer benefits and more part-time jobs. More women work in this second type of firm than the first. Both types of employers are needed in the Kenosha economy. Since the tight labor market has already increased wages and benefits, simply calling for improving basic wage levels will not improve conditions for Kenosha families. Given the small size of these firms, many cannot remain in business if solutions simply focus on employer driven strategies. Given the strong sense of individuality common in Kenosha culture, mandates are not likely to be well received. Therefore, more individualized strategies to improve wages, working conditions and employment prospects are important in Kenosha.

- *Targeted training combined with links between employer and potential employee will work best for some Kenosha firms.* This research suggests that half of the employers offer good benefits and wages to a skilled workforce. Developing targeted training initiatives to help Kenosha residents develop the skills needed for these jobs will improve working and training conditions for half of the employers and employees in Kenosha. However, given the limited number of jobs of this nature in Kenosha, trying to move everyone into these jobs will not succeed in fulfilling the needs of

either employees or employers in this community. While some companies may be drawn to Kenosha if it had a more educated workforce, it is equally possible to saturate the market with employees. As already occurs in Kenosha, people with skills that do not match available jobs may need to find work elsewhere. Simultaneously, producing too many employees in one category may lower wages and benefits. Education and training for higher skilled jobs is important, but must be combined with initiatives for low-skilled workers.

- *Community support strategies need to be developed for people in low-wage sectors of the economy.* The other half of the jobs in Kenosha are in service, retail, non-profit and government firms that offer low wages, limited benefits and part-time hours due to available funding and common business practices in these sectors. Given that many of these firms cannot or will not be able to improve wages and working conditions due to circumstances largely beyond their control, strategies for these firms should include supplements for childcare, wages, benefits and transportation through government and non-profits. Issues related to this observation will be addressed in more detail in the section on non-profit organizations.

- *Supports for entrepreneurs could provide additional family-supporting jobs in Kenosha.* Given the trend toward self-employment already evident in Kenosha, providing supports for these kinds of initiatives through small loans, technical support, pooled insurance plans and community-based marketing assistance could provide employment opportunities for some people struggling to find family-supporting work. These kinds of supports would also benefit existing small employers.

- *Social and cultural capital play a role in employment decisions in Kenosha.* Most employers in Kenosha are secondary sector firms that use a combination of friends and family and word-of-mouth referrals to find applicants. Hiring decisions, benefits and supports on the job depend on the good will of the individual in charge of the organization. This means that employees need to develop ties to these organizations and develop the cultural capital appropriate to sustain employment.

The next section focuses on this last observation by talking about employment from the individual perspective. Individual career paths show more clearly the links between social capital, cultural capital and employment in Kenosha.

Economic and Social Capital: Family Survival Strategies

The portrait of employment in Kenosha reveals a community that large y consists of a diverse, secondary sector employment base. Currently, firms fall into two general categories. Half of the companies, *family supporting, educction required firms,* offer family supporting wages and benefits primarily to well-educated male workers. The other half of the firms, *lower wages, wider range of opportunity firms,* offer lower wages, more part-time work and less benefits to people with varying educational backgrounds. This second group of firms offers more opportunities for people with limited education and semi-skilled or unskilled work experience. More women are employed in this sector.

Until the mid-1980s, Kenosha offered many primary sector jobs through AMC/Chrysler, Snap-On Tools and other large companies. A few of these firms still exist today and offer jobs to some workers in Kenosha. However, the majority of Kenosha workers have either had to leave the community to stay in unionized factory employment or transition into jobs in the new

economy.

This section explores ways that families meet their needs in Kenosha in the past and present. We begin by outlining some general statistics about income, education and work in Kenosha from the U.S. Census Bureau. Next, work strategies and other supports to maintain a family

are outlined using information from observations and interviews. Information on connections to churches and social service agencies will be explored in more detail later in this report. The study found that human, social and cultural capital combine to influence the amount of economic capital available for families to meet their needs.

Family Economic Patterns in Kenosha

Poverty and Income

Overall, the *Kenosha Social Capital Study* found three types of families in Kenosha: *Rising educated middle class, stable working-class,* and *low-skilled workers.* Rising educated middle class families consisted of wage earners with some college education who worked in professional or managerial occupations. In some cases, where there were two adult workers in the family, both adults had some advanced education, but one may have worked primarily in stable factory or working-class employment. For example, in the Jansen family, the wife

had a college degree and worked as a social service worker. The husband had some college education and yet had spent most of his career in a combination of factory work, military and protective services.

Stable working-class families consisted of people with long term good paying jobs in either factory or clerical employment. These individuals may have had some specific vocational training like a union apprenticeship or clerical training, but did not have a college education. In families with two adult wage earners, men frequently worked in factories while women worked either in factory work, clerical work or social service work.

Low-skilled workers spent most of their work life in jobs that required limited skills and education. They alternated between spells on welfare and working in low-wage jobs. Examples included people who worked in low-wage secondary sector factories or service sector occupations like gardening, nursing assistant or cleaning houses. While most of the people in this group did not have a college education, some had completed high school. People in this group were most likely to use welfare when times became difficult because they lacked the savings or on-the-job wages and benefits to survive without government support.

We also saw families that moved between these three categories. In many cases, African American and Hispanic/Latino extended families included people in all three groups. The role of churches and social service organizations in supporting families and encouraging low-skilled workers to find family supporting work will be discussed in more detail in later sections of this report.

TABLE 5: RACE OF HOUSEHOLDER BY HOUSEHOLD INCOME IN 1989 (SOURCE 1990 U.S. CENSUS)

Income per Household	Number of Households	Percent of Total Households	Percent of Households Within Racial Group
Universe: Households	46483		
WHITE:	44568		
LESS THAN $9,999	5063	10.9%	11.4%
$10,000 TO $24,999	11876	25.5%	26.6%
$25,000 TO $49,999	17611	37.9%	39.5%
$50,000 TO $99,999	9127	19.6%	20.5%
$100,000 OR MORE	891	1.9%	2.0%
BLACK:	1527		
LESS THAN $9,999	462	1.0%	30.3%
$10,000 TO $24,999	514	1.1%	33.7%
$25,000 TO $49,999	431	0.9%	28.2%
$50,000 TO $99,999	117	0.3%	7.7%
$100,000 OR MORE	3	0.0%	0.2%
AMERICAN INDIAN, ESKIMO, OR ALEUT:	205		
LESS THAN $9,999	21	0.0%	10.2%
$10,000 TO $24,999	78	0.2%	38.0%
$25,000 TO $49,999	66	0.1%	32.2%
$50,000 TO $99,999	40	0.1%	19.5%
$100,000 OR MORE	0	0.0%	0.0%
ASIAN OR PACIFIC ISLANDER:	183		
LESS THAN $9,999	27	0.1%	14.8%
$10,000 TO $24,999	60	0.1%	32.8%
$25,000 TO $49,999	58	0.1%	31.7%
$50,000 TO $99,999	30	0.1%	16.4%
$100,000 OR MORE	8	0.0%	4.4%

TABLE 6: HOUSEHOLD INCOME IN 1989 FOR HISPANICS/LATINOS (SOURCE 1990 U.S. CENSUS)		
	Number of Households	Percent of Households
Universe: Households with householder of Hispanic origin	1281	
LESS THAN $9,999	192	15%
$10,000 TO $24,999	539	42%
$25,000 TO $49,999	389	30%
$50,000 TO $99,999	161	13%
$100,000 OR MORE	0	0%

Tables 5 and 6 show household income data by race and Hispanic origin from the 1990 census. Comparing whites to African Americans and Hispanic/Latinos shows that people in each group fall into each of the three types of families based on income. However, more African Americans and Hispanic/Latinos have low incomes than whites. Thirty-seven percent of whites had household incomes of less than $25,000 per year in comparison to sixty-three percent of African American households and fifty-seven percent of Hispanic/Latino households. Some of these low-income households represent retired people on a fixed income while others consist of low-skilled workers.

More whites appear in the middle and upper income ranges than African Americans and Hispanic/Latinos, but there are still significant percentages of people in the stable working class and educated middle class in both of these communities. Given the wide salary ranges for professional workers, it is not possible to determine middle- or working-class status by income. A family with two union factory workers could easily make more than two teachers or social service agency personnel.

Thirty-nine percent of whites had household incomes between $25,000 and $49,999 while twenty-eight percent of African Americans and thirty percent of Hispanic/Latinos fell into this category. More whites also had household incomes greater than $50,000. Twenty-one percent of the white population, compared to roughly eight percent of the African American and thirteen percent of the Hispanic/Latino population earned above $50,000. This means that both the African American and Hispanic/Latino communities have middle-income families, but this group with stable incomes is smaller than the number of white middle-income households in Kenosha.

TABLE 7: BELOW POVERTY: STATUS IN 1989 BY RACE AND FAMILY TYPE (SOURCE 1990 U.S. CENSUS)

	Number of Households	Percent of Total Households	Percent of Households within Racial Group
Universe: Families below the poverty level in 1989	2448		
WHITE	1944		
MARRIED-COUPLE FAMILY	725	29.6%	37.3%
MALE HOUSEHOLDER, NO WIFE PRESENT	95	3.9%	4.9%
FEMALE HOUSEHOLDER, NO HUSBAND PRESENT	1124	45.9%	57.8%
BLACK	462		
MARRIED-COUPLE FAMILY	59	2.4%	12.8%
MALE HOUSEHOLDER, NO WIFE PRESENT	13	0.5%	2.8%
FEMALE HOUSEHOLDER, NO HUSBAND PRESENT	390	15.9%	84.4%
AMERICAN INDIAN, ESKIMO, OR ALEUT	21		
MARRIED-COUPLE FAMILY	2	0.1%	9.5%
MALE HOUSEHOLDER, NO WIFE PRESENT	5	0.2%	23.8%
FEMALE HOUSEHOLDER, NO HUSBAND PRESENT	14	0.6%	66.7%
ASIAN OR PACIFIC ISLANDER	21		
MARRIED-COUPLE FAMILY	15	0.6%	71.4%
MALE HOUSEHOLDER, NO WIFE PRESENT	6	0.2%	28.6%
FEMALE HOUSEHOLDER, NO HUSBAND PRESENT	0	0.0%	0.0%

TABLE 8: POVERTY STATUS IN 1989 BY RACE BY AGE (SOURCE: 1990 U.S. CENSUS)

	Number of Total People	Percent of Persons	Percent of People within Racial Group
Universe: Persons for whom poverty status is determined	124062		
INCOME IN 1989 ABOVE POVERTY LEVEL			
WHITE	107314		
UNDER 18 YEARS	26673	21.5%	24.9%
18 YEARS AND OVER	80640	65.0%	75.1%
BLACK			2853
UNDER 18 YEARS	992	0.8%	34.8%
18 YEARS AND OVER	1861	1.5%	65.2%
AMERICAN INDIAN, ESKIMO, OR ALEUT	496		
UNDER 5 YEARS	124	0.1%	25.0%
18 YEARS AND OVER	372	0.3%	75.0%
ASIAN OR PACIFIC ISLANDER	496		
UNDER 5 YEARS	248	0.2%	50.0%
18 AND OVER	248	0.2%	50.0%
INCOME IN 1989 BELOW POVERTY LEVEL			
WHITE	9429		
UNDER 18 YEARS	3350	2.7%	35.5%
18 YEARS AND OVER	6079	4.9%	64.5%
BLACK	2233		
UNDER 18 YEARS	1365	1.1%	61.1%
18 YEARS AND OVER	868	0.7%	38.9%
AMERICAN INDIAN, ESKIMO, OR ALEUT	0		
UNDER 18 YEARS	0	0.0%	0.0%
18 YEARS AND OVER	0	0.0%	0.0%
ASIAN OR PACIFIC ISLANDER	124		
UNDER 18 YEARS	124	0.1%	10000.0%
18 YEARS AND OVER	0	0.0%	0.0%
OTHER RACE	992		
UNDER 18 YEARS	620	0.5%	62.5%
18 YEARS AND OVER	372	0.3%	37.5%

45

TABLE 9: ABOVE POVERTY: STATUS IN 1989 BY RACE AND FAMILY TYPE (SOURCE: 1990 U.S. CENSUS)			
	Number of Households	Percent of Total Households	Percent of Households within Racial Group
Universe: Families above the poverty level in 1989	31254		
WHITE	30291		
MARRIED-COUPLE FAMILY	25826	82.6%	85.3%
MALE HOUSEHOLDER, NO WIFE PRESENT	1322	4.2%	4.4%
FEMALE HOUSEHOLDER, NO HUSBAND PRESENT	3143	10.1%	10.4%
BLACK	718		
MARRIED-COUPLE FAMILY	499	1.6%	69.5%
MALE HOUSEHOLDER, NO WIFE PRESENT	22	0.1%	3.1%
FEMALE HOUSEHOLDER, NO HUSBAND PRESENT	197	0.6%	27.4%
AMERICAN INDIAN, ESKIMO, OR ALEUT	124		
MARRIED-COUPLE FAMILY	93	0.3%	75.0%
MALE HOUSEHOLDER, NO WIFE PRESENT	17	0.1%	13.7%
FEMALE HOUSEHOLDER, NO HUSBAND PRESENT	14	0.0%	11.3%
ASIAN OR PACIFIC ISLANDER	121		
MARRIED-COUPLE FAMILY	101	0.3%	83.5%
MALE HOUSEHOLDER, NO WIFE PRESENT	6	0.0%	5.0%
FEMALE HOUSEHOLDER, NO HUSBAND PRESENT	14	0.0%	11.6%

TABLE 10: HISPANIC/LATINO POVERTY STATUS IN 1989 BY FAMILY TYPE (SOURCE: 1990 U.S. CENSUS)		
	Number of Households	Percent of Households
Universe: Families with householder of Hispanic origin	1103	
INCOME IN 1989 ABOVE POVERTY LEVEL		
MARRIED-COUPLE FAMILY	710	64.4%
MALE HOUSEHOLDER, NO WIFE PRESENT	53	4.8%
FEMALE HOUSEHOLDER, NO HUSBAND PRESENT	105	9.5%
INCOME IN 1989 BELOW POVERTY LEVEL		
MARRIED-COUPLE FAMILY	61	5.5%
MALE HOUSEHOLDER, NO WIFE PRESENT	35	3.2%
FEMALE HOUSEHOLDER, NO HUSBAND PRESENT	139	12.6%

Tables 7, 8, 9 and 10 show poverty status by race and household type. It is important to note that low incomes do not necessarily mean that families are on public assistance. In fact, in 1990 only eight percent of Kenosha families had some public assistance income. Most of these families are the working poor who either live entirely by low-wage work or combine work with government and private support to survive.

As is true in the rest of the United States, single parent, female-headed households are more likely to be poor than two-parent families or male-headed households regardless of race. This pattern occurs because many jobs that employ women pay less than jobs that typically employ men.

Women with small children to care for may need more flexible hours and more supports than two-parent households, thus also influencing their wages and working conditions. However, we found a number of single parents who maintained stable working-class and middle-class households. Being a single parent alone did not condemn a family to poverty.

Tables 7 and 10 show that a higher percentage of African Americans and Hispanic/Latinos live in poverty than their four percent of the population. Thirty-nine percent of the African American community and twenty-one percent of the Hispanic/Latino population lived in households below the federal poverty level in 1989.[15]

Looking closely at these figures shows that a larger percentage of Hispanic/Latino two-parent families are in poverty than either whites or African Americans. This suggests that more families in these two communities are low-skilled workers than in the white community.

Factors that contribute to family income include human capital through education and work experience, and social capital through networks that help people find and maintain family supporting employment. These same factors also influence occupations. Next the occupational and educational breakdown for Kenosha county residents is described.

TABLE 11: RACE BY OCCUPATION, KENOSHA COUNTY (1990 CENSUS)[16]

Occupation	White	Black	Hispanic
EXECUTIVES, ADMINISTRATORS, MGRS	8%	3%	2%
PROFESSIONAL	12%	10%	3%
TECHNICIANS	3%	1%	2%
SALES	11%	9%	11%
ADMIN. SUPPORT AND CLERICAL	16%	12%	10%
PROTECTIVE SERVICE WORKERS	2%	2%	0%
SERVICE WORKERS	12%	29%	19%
SKILLED PRODUCTION, CRAFT AND REPAIR	15%	6%	9%
PRECISION PRODUCTION WORKERS	6%	3%	2%
MACHINE OPERATORS, ASSEMBLERS	10%	15%	24%
HANDLERS, HELPERS AND LABORERS	5%	10%	13%
TOTAL	100%	100%	95%

Occupation

Table 11 shows racial breakdowns for different occupations in Kenosha. More whites are managers than either African Americans or Hispanic/Latinos. Roughly the same percentage of whites and African Americans are professionals, but only three percent of Hispanic/Latinos hold professional positions. These percentages suggest that Kenosha has not reached racial parity in the middle-class professions for either group, but African Americans are much closer to whites than Hispanic/Latinos. Reasons for these differences will be discussed below.

About the same percentage of whites and Hispanic/Latinos work in sales positions, and slightly fewer African Americans work in sales. While fewer Hispanic/Latinos and African Americans work in administrative support and clerical positions than whites, the percentages are not large enough to make a significant difference. These figures show fairly close percentages in white-collar jobs, but limited-education jobs like sales and clerical work are more common in the new Kenosha economy.

The largest differences in occupations occur in the manual labor and low-skilled service sector categories. At twenty-nine percent, a much greater percentage of African Americans work in service jobs such as nursing assistant or food service than Hispanic/Latinos (nineteen percent) or whites (twelve percent). Whites (fifteen percent) hold many more of the good paying skilled factory jobs than African Americans (six percent) and Hispanic/Latinos (nine percent). The same is true for good paying precision production jobs.

Hispanic/Latinos (twenty-four percent) are most likely to work in lower paying machine operator jobs like meat packing or small assembly work than African Americans (fifteen percent) and whites (ten percent).

Taken together, the occupation breakdowns show a small middle class for both the African American and Hispanic/Latino populations. The Hispanic/Latino professional and white-collar class is very small in comparison to either the African Americans and whites. Both African Americans and Hispanic/Latinos hold more working-class and low-skilled jobs than whites. However, these two groups are clustered in different kinds of jobs. African Americans currently work more in service occupations while Hispanic/Latinos hold more low-paid factory jobs.

48

TABLE 12: OCCUPATION (SOURCE: 1990 U.S. CENSUS)		
Occupation	Number of Individuals	Percent of Individuals
Universe: Employed persons 16 years and over:	57896	
MANAGERIAL AND PROFESSIONAL SPECIALTY	12245	21.1%
SALES OCCUPATIONS	6600	11.4%
TECHNICIANS	2032	3.5%
ADMINISTRATIVE SUPPORT	9486	16.4%
SERVICE	18115	31.3%
FARMING, FORESTRY, AND FISHING	874	1.5%
PRECISION PRODUCTION, CRAFT, AND REPAIR	8544	14.8%
OPERATORS, FABRICATORS, AND LABORERS	11350	19.6%

TABLE 13: RACE BY EDUCATIONAL ATTAINMENT

	Number of People	Percent of Total	Percent of People Within Racial Group
Universe: Persons 25 years and over	83246		
WHITE:	76781		
NO DIPLOMA:	18374	0.23	0.24
HIGH SCHOOL GRADUATE:	28358	0.35	0.37
SOME COLLEGE, NO DEGREE:	14144	0.18	0.18
ASSOCIATE, BACHELOR'S:	12749	0.16	0.17
GRADUATE DEGREE:	3156	0.04	0.04
BLACK:	2302		
NO DIPLOMA:	961	0.01	0.42
HIGH SCHOOL GRADUATE:	709	0.01	0.31
SOME COLLEGE, NO DEGREE:	384	0.00	0.17
ASSOCIATE, BACHELOR'S:	202	0.00	0.09
GRADUATE DEGREE:	46	0.00	0.02
OTHER RACE:	1025		
NO DIPLOMA:	618	0.01	0.60
HIGH SCHOOL GRADUATE:	218	0.00	0.21
SOME COLLEGE, NO DEGREE:	115	0.00	0.11
ASSOCIATE, BACHELOR'S:	60	0.00	0.06
GRADUATE DEGREE:	14	0.00	0.01

49

TABLE 14: EDUCATIONAL ATTAINMENT (SOURCE: 1990 U.S. CENSUS)

	Number of Individuals	Percent of Individuals
Universe: Hispanic origin 25 years and over	2383	
NO DIPLOMA	1231	51.7%
HIGH SCHOOL GRADUATE	622	26.1%
SOME COLLEGE, NO DEGREE	331	13.9%
ASSOCIATE, BACHELOR'S	199	8.4%
GRADUATE DEGREE	27	1.1%

Education

Tables 13 and 14 show 1990 census figures for adult educational attainment by race. As a community with a high number of well-paid factory jobs that did not require a high school diploma until recently, it is no surprise that high percentages of people from all races have less than a high school diploma. However, much higher percentages of African Americans (forty-two percent) and Hispanic/Latinos (sixty percent) than whites (twenty-four percent) did not complete high school. These people have trouble finding family-supporting jobs in the new Kenosha economy. The high percentage of Hispanic/Latinos without a high school diploma is partly due to the fact that there are many Mexican immigrants in Kenosha who have lower education levels than many native-born people. However, immigrants are not universally less educated. For example, we interviewed several immigrant families where adults had college degrees from Mexico.

50 Similar percentages of whites (eighteen percent) and African Americans (seventeen percent) have completed some college, while fewer Hispanic/Latinos (eleven percent) have attended college. These people may have more success getting jobs in companies in the *family-supporting wage, education-required* category than people lacking any credentials. But individuals who do not complete college are more likely to find work in *lower wages, wider range of opportunity firms.* Fewer African Americans (eleven percent) than whites (twenty-one percent) have completed college or graduate school. In comparison to whites, only one-third of Hispanic/Latinos (seven percent) have completed college. These educational disparities account in large measure for the small percentage of African Americans and Hispanic/Latinos in professional and managerial positions.

Reasons for Differences in Occupation, Education and Income

Several factors contribute to the current occupation, education and income differences among whites, African Americans and Hispanic/Latinos in Kenosha. First, the history of migration of these two communities to Kenosha plays a role. People in both the African American and Hispanic/Latino communities initially came to Kenosha for manual labor jobs and subsequent generations also focused on work that only required a high school education. Community leaders acknowledge that only a small percentage of Kenosha-born African Americans and

Hispanic/Latinos have completed college and stayed in the community. Most of the African Americans and Hispanic/Latinos we met during this project who had completed college and worked as professionals had obtained their education and much of their work experience before moving to Kenosha as adults.

As migrant workers, the first generation of Hispanic/Latinos moved back and forth between Texas and Wisconsin farms for work. Children's education was secondary to earning enough money through farm labor to support the family and many young people did not complete high school. When the second generation moved into the factories in the 1960s and 1970s, families again focused on good paying work that did not require education. Education was downplayed until very recently in these families. Newer migrants also came directly for work, but stressed education for their children. We found many families that came to the U.S. seeking better educational opportunities for the next generation.

African Americans migrated to Kenosha to take factory jobs and newer African Americans still come to Kenosha seeking work opportunities today. Focused on factory work, the second generation intended to follow their parents into good paying jobs at AMC/Chrysler and other plants. Even though many third generation African Americans did not want to work in heavy, dirty factory jobs like their parents—like Janice profiled in chapter three—most had little family or school guidance to complete college or locate good paying work in the new economy.

Nearly identical patterns are reported for newcomer Hispanic/Latinos by some community activists. First generation college students have the most problems because they are caught between poorly educated parents and counselors who steer students toward vocational education or fail to provide guidance for college. In other cases, more middle class

Hispanic/Latinos make an extra effort to disassociate themselves from people of color, particularly African Americans, in order to receive more equal treatment from teachers and counselors.

For example when talking about his career path, Marcus—son and grandson of people in stable working-class factory jobs—commented, "I knew that was a type of work I did not want to do. I knew it was hard work. I saw the effects it had on my father and grandfather." However, in high school he did not realize the need for a college education and checked "no" on a form asking if he planned to go to college. This led to him being tracked into non-academic classes. He recalled:

So I'd say I was tracked in school because of that one question. Which was interesting to me—parents were not brought into this discussion. Students and the counselor. So I thought my dad didn't go to college, my mom didn't go to college. I really didn't think we had enough money to send me to college. So I said, "no," I don't think I'll be going.

The failure of school counselors to bring parents into education discussions or share information on various opportunities with younger generations comes from the Kenosha cultural tendency to only share information with people within one's closed social capital networks. This cultural tendency combined with strong racism among whites in gate-keeping positions like counselors, some teachers and even front-line clerical workers. Some of these tendencies continue in Kenosha today. For example, one newcomer professional of color recalled how lower-level workers used passive resistance to keep him from obtaining a job. Even though this candidate had a test needed for a position scheduled early in the day due to other commitments, he was not called for the exam for many hours and had to leave. If upper level management had not

interceded to make sure that he took the exam, he would not have been employed in Kenosha. Another college-educated professional recalls being told by front-line workers that "no jobs in the kitchen" were available when asking for an application.

Another recently arrived African American family reported discrimination in schools that required constant vigilance on the part of the parents. They reported:

Like last week at school, my son, she told him he couldn't be in a program, advanced marketing. But he has an A in marketing and she told him, no, you're not articulate enough. They make us work for everything harder because that is a program he should have automatically. He had to fight for it. And why they did this? They don't have an answer for it. My other son is a three-time honor student and there's a file on his grades. Once we go up and demand to open up the book, he's been getting all A's. He had a counselor and then it comes out to a mistake.

We observed a number of examples of whites steering African Americans and

Hispanic/Latinos away from good jobs and educational opportunities. Children considered disruptive were not included in placement tests. Adult apprenticeship applicants who had no ties to union members were disqualified on technicalities. People of color who were not persistent or did not fit in had a hard time succeeding in Kenosha.

In keeping with the Kenosha cultural tendency to judge people on personal connections rather than simply race or nationality, we found an equal number of instances where people were helped by others outside of their racial group when a personal connection had been made by someone trusted by closed social capital networks. For example, one woman moved to a Kenosha homeless shelter with several school-aged children. The shelter found a school for her children to attend. Her children were welcomed in this integrated Kenosha school by the teachers. The mother commented on how the children had accepted her daughter, inviting her to parties and other events.

Mark, an African American newcomer, found a veterans affairs liaison very supportive in referring him to work

opportunities. Given this initial contact, front-line workers went out of their way to tell him about work opportunities.

Social capital universally served as the entry point for jobs, education and other social supports in Kenosha. Almost everyone encountered in this study found work through family, friends and occasionally church or formal social service contacts. Both African Americans and Hispanic/Latinos initially found work in the AMC/Chrysler foundry because people they knew had already started working there. Large numbers of newcomer Hispanic/Latinos found their way into low-level manufacturing jobs, gardening jobs and other service positions because friends and family had already paved the way into these occupations. African Americans are heavily involved in service work for the same reasons. Educational decisions were made in the same way. Often, work and education decisions were influenced by cultural capital too. Social and cultural capital also influence strategies to deal with childcare, health care, transportation and other social supports.

Families in the three categories of *rising educated middle class*, *stable working-class* and *low-skilled workers* each have access to different kinds of social and cultural capital. The remainder of this section looks carefully at ways that families in each of these categories found jobs, education and other supports.

Work Patterns

Everyone we met in Kenosha used social capital networks to find work. However, networks had different resources for people in each of these three groups. We also found different levels of trust within both closed social capital networks and among bridging networks for people in each of these three categories. I begin with a profile of families in each category to illustrate the differences between them. Given that most Kenosha African American and Hispanic/Latino families came

51

from low-skilled or stable working-class roots, most family histories for middle-class and stable working-class families reveal movement from low-skilled or working-class beginnings into the middle class.

Rising Educated
52 *Middle Class*

Tania and Roberto are examples of educated middle-class Hispanic/Latinos in Kenosha. They moved to Kenosha as adults twenty years ago. This family is a rising educated middle-class family because one of the two adults has a college degree and professional employment and their children have either attended college or are in school now. They moved to Kenosha because Roberto got a job at American Motors. Tania and Roberto participate in strong friendship social capital networks within the Hispanic/Latino community and through their church. They also have active social capital networks through their jobs.

Tania was first introduced in the chapter on *Understanding Social and Cultural Capital* (see page 13). While she started off as a nursing assistant in a job found through friends, she went to college and found additional jobs through the support of workplace social capital contacts. At one point, she applied for a job in government along with a friend. Although she did not have any contacts in this agency, they hired her because they needed bilingual workers. She has been able to move between jobs using both professional and personal contacts.

Tania's husband worked for American Motors for most of his career. He has not gone to college, but his stable income from factory employment helped maintain his family's lifestyle and facilitated his wife and children's educational goals.

Like Tania, most educated middle-class African American and Hispanic/Latino families have found links to college and middle-class employment through supportive

teachers, co-workers, supervisors or church members. These supports provided both the cultural and social capital to move into professional employment.

People in this category also were able to use their credentials to find jobs even without strong social networks. Just like Tania got the government job because they were looking for bilingual workers, other professionals in Kenosha found work because they brought strong work and educational experience with them when they moved to Kenosha. However, like Tania, many of the professionals of color who lived in Kenosha actually worked in Illinois. These included people who worked at Abbot laboratories, teachers, health care workers and social welfare workers. Kenosha was a good place to live and raise children but did not always offer work opportunities for professionals. Our research suggests that African American and Hispanic/Latino professionals are just beginning to find work in Kenosha because of the closed social capital networks in many Kenosha companies combined with lingering racism.

Just as these educated middle-class people were comfortable applying for

jobs without a personal connection, the study found that people in this group were more comfortable using citywide resources or professional organizations where they may not have a personal contact to find resources. For example, these people were more likely to report looking for childcare centers through the Kenosha County Job Center referral service. They relied on the Internet and published documents to find education as well as personal networks. While all of them said that they would use personal contacts to find jobs, they were equally likely to network through professional organizations and apply for jobs posted in agencies and through the newspaper.

This comfort with published sources and professional guidebooks came from familiarity and trust of "mainstream" white resources. Unlike people in the stable working-class category, these people moved beyond the individualized knowledge common in Kenosha. They also felt competent to judge among resources found through formal systems like a listing of doctors or childcare facilities. This comfort reflected cultural capital that these families had developed through education and middle-class work

Most of their other resources for childcare, transportation and other needs come from friend, family, and neighborhood and church networks. Many of the children of stable working-class families tend to develop similar career paths using the same kinds of networks. Given changes in the economy, the next generation also either moves down into the low-skilled worker category or moves into the educated middle class if they receive appropriate supports.

Low-Skilled Workers

General patterns for Hispanic/Latinos and African Americans were largely identical. However, we found different patterns for low-skilled workers in the African American and Hispanic/Latino communities due to differences in migration patterns to Kenosha and citizenship status. Two cases are profiled here for that reason.

Juan is a legal Mexican migrant who has been in Kenosha for about seven years. His wife, Anna, is also in Kenosha but is undocumented. Neither of them speaks English. Anna recalls:

When I had my child, he left his job because there was nobody to take care of me. Then, he decided to take off for one week and be with me. But I was not well and he asked for another week and they did not want to give it to him. So, he decided to leave the job. He began to work with a man laying roofs, but that was not secure. There were three, four days per week, or one day yes, one day no. So, we decided to come here. Here I had a first cousin who was working in gardening. That is how we came here and my husband began working here.

When he also found gardening work low paying and unsteady, Juan went to a temporary agency to find another job. Many low-skilled workers in both the Hispanic/Latino and African American communities use temporary agencies to find jobs and will recommend them to each other. The agency placed Juan in a small,

experience that allowed them to trust materials created by people in different social capital networks. In the same way, educated middle-class people were also more easily able to bridge into other social capital networks among people with similar education and work experience backgrounds. For example, educated African Americans and Hispanic/Latinos were more likely to participate in organizations outside of their ethnic and racial communities.

Stable Working-class

Mary and John Hughes are part of an African American family that has been in Kenosha for over thirty years. While living in Chicago, John's brother heard about jobs at American Motors and moved to Kenosha to take one of those jobs. John followed and also started working at American Motors based on his brother's reference. He spent his entire career at that plant.

Mary had gone to a clerical training program beyond high school, but could not find clerical jobs initially. She found a cleaning job through a government job service program. She recalled,

They needed somebody to clean. And I had experience in cleaning because I used to work for a nurse. I knew how to clean, so that's how I got that job. When I joined church these ladies were telling me about [a government facility] and we started studying and that's when I went to [the government facility] and took the test.

Mary was successful on the government civil service test and began a long-term career working as a government clerical worker. Most of her social resources still came through her friends, family and African American church. She remains active in the church today.

Most of Mary and John's children and grandchildren are also factory or service workers. Some are in stable working-class jobs, while others are in low-skilled jobs in the new economy in Kenosha and the surrounding area.

Like the Hughes family, most stable working-class families rely primarily on friends and family to find work. Closed social capital networks also come from churches, as with Mary finding her clerical job through church friends who studied together and applied for the same kinds of jobs.

low-wage factory where he has worked ever since.

Anna has worked on and off in service jobs, usually in restaurants, found through friends. At other times, she stays at home with her small children. She sometimes helps watch her friends' and family members' children as well.

54 Margaret is a divorced, middle-aged African American woman with a high school diploma. She is also a certified nursing assistant. At the time of the interview, she was living on a combination of support from her ex-husband, informal childcare and some government benefits. She has used welfare on a couple of occasions as an adult when her husband was out of work or family wages were too low to survive. She describes her work history as follows:

> [My first job] was through my sister, she was telling me about the VA hospital. She worked at the naval base and she was telling me that they was needing some nurse's assistants there. So I went down there and got a job. I stayed there for a year because in the wintertime I didn't like driving. It was third shift so I didn't like driving.

After she had left that job, she moved on to several other nursing homes through ads in the newspaper or referrals from friends. She recently quit working as a nursing assistant after working in several private nursing homes for a number of years. She explains:

> Like I said, that's the only job I ever worked was as a nursing assistant and I love working with older people, I really do. But it would get to me, I would have patients and I would get so close to them and they would die. Then too, my back started bothering me with the lifting the patient out of bed. I just felt like I needed to get away for a while, so that's what I did.

As with families in the first two categories, low-skilled workers also had strong social capital networks that helped them find work. The same networks helped with childcare, transportation, housing and a variety of basic needs. Just as Margaret babysat other people's children, low-skilled workers often turned to other family members, friends or neighbors for support. The same was true when cars broke down, people were evicted or they ran out of food. The difference between low-skilled workers and the families with more stable incomes is that these people do not have networks that can get them into more stable work.

Like the educated middle class, low-skilled workers are not afraid to go to outsiders familiar with the community when they need help. Just like Juan found a job through a temporary agency and Margaret turned to welfare when times got tough, many people in the low-skilled worker category use both government and private supports to find help.

Low-skilled workers lack private resources to fall back on when they have health problems like Margaret's back injury. Government or non-profit services provide an important safety net for these families. Another example was a whole network of people who shared information on the Kenosha homeless shelter with people who lived elsewhere. Knowing that Kenosha had a safer environment and more jobs than their home communities from friends who had moved to the area and had used shelter services, they referred their friends and family members to the same resources.

Formal social service agencies are part of the social capital resources of low-skilled workers. Church social services are known in the same way. Through word-of-mouth knowledge within closed friend and family social networks, people learn which agencies to contact and, often, which services may be most helpful. Knowledge about how to use these services is also part of the cultural capital of these communities. Unlike the stable working class, who are often ashamed to use government supports, the culture of communities that uses social services by necessity involves understanding how formal services can provide help when family, church and community networks cannot offer enough help. While many low-skilled workers dislike using formal services because they are sometimes treated badly by agency staff, they do not feel shame when turning to an outside agency for help.

Low-skilled workers are also more likely to simply walk in and fill out applications for jobs than people in the stable working class, because they lack direct connections to many jobs. For example, Margaret found one nursing assistant job through the newspaper. Since people in the low-skilled worker category often lack the requisite work history to get jobs beyond their previous low-skilled employment, filling out applications for better jobs often leads nowhere.

Just like the government job service sent Mary Hughes to a cleaning job even though she had clerical training and Juan was sent to a low-paying factory by a temporary agency, these formal services most often place low-skilled workers back into low-paid, unstable and low-benefit jobs.[17]

Using Networks and Organizations To Move Within and Between Categories

Comparing families in these three categories suggests that everyone uses personal contacts through family and friends in order to gain information to meet family needs. However, the type of information available for people within these different categories varies dramatically. Like Janice (profiled earlier in this booklet), suggested people without appropriate guidance can "fall through the cracks" into the low-skilled worker category.

People like Tania and Janice, who received support to gather education, can move up into professional careers. Using these word-of-mouth networks, people currently employed in an industry will help people they consider promising to advance. Teachers and pastors often play the same role in the life of someone currently in a low-skilled or stable working-class family. These bridging connections recognize in these individuals potential human capital often combined with appropriate cultural capital. If Tania and Janice had not shared similar values with their mentors, they probably would not have been singled out for advancement.

The stable working class is least likely to turn to outsiders to find work or other supports. These families have succeeded in creating and maintaining a stable life style through closed social capital networks. When times become difficult, they are most likely to trust only people in their communities or those closely associated with them rather than expand their networks to outsiders. For this reason, even though most auto manufacturing jobs have left the area, the union hall still remains a major place to socialize and to turn to for support. The remainder of this section briefly outlines ways that families use different kinds of supports in Kenosha.

Personal Contacts

Most often, social capital came through connections from friends and family. For example, like John Hughes, many people reported that they came to Kenosha because friends told them that there were jobs available at American Motors. Personal networks can also help people change career paths. Cathy cleaned houses for a number of years before she became a teacher's aid. While being a teacher's aid is still a low-skilled, low-paid position, it is more stable than the work she had earlier. Cathy explained how she got her jobs as follows:

I got jobs through relatives too. My aunt would tell me someone needed housework. Or I would take one of the jobs she had and from that word got around, that she's a good housekeeper and people like good housekeepers. So I was one of the best. So from there they would have friends and I would go to them.

[I got the school district job through a friend] I was talking to her one day. She was already in the classroom as an aid. She was telling me, I had been off work, I had been sick. She said, "Why not apply. Fill out an application to be a lunchroom supervisor." I said, "I guess I will." And they hired me and that's how I got in the school system. Also, my son had gone to these schools. I was like a member of the PTA so I knew about these schools and everything.

Cathy's story shows that social capital through personal contacts involves trust on both sides. Cathy would not have applied for a teacher's aid position if her friend was not working there already and she did not already know the schools. Cathy's application was received favorably because people at the school knew her already as an active parent who participated in the PTA. While Cathy has remained in the working class, her children have gone on to professional careers with support from teachers and other people the family had met.

Childcare was also most often obtained through personal networks for both low-skilled workers and the stable working class. People turned to family members when they could. Next, they looked for local providers known through their social capital networks. The educated middle class was most comfortable using childcare centers because they felt that they could afford appropriate care and could adequately evaluate a center. Stable working-class, and particularly low-skilled workers, felt less trusting of formal day care centers. Often, these families could not afford licensed childcare even with government help.

Government Supports

Families in both the low-skilled and educated middle-class categories would turn to government agencies for supports when in need. Low-skilled workers were most likely to be familiar with government supports and use them when necessary. Educated middle-class people were more likely to use government job service and childcare lists. However, we found a number of families who used unemployment and, in a few instances, medical assistance and food stamps when times were difficult. Public assistance use will be discussed in more detail in a later section.

Stable working-class families were least likely to use government assistance in times of trouble because they felt ashamed to turn to the government for help. However, given the current history of widespread unemployment in Kenosha, more of these families had used government unemployment and even welfare benefits. A number of stable working-class African American families had knowledge of public assistance because a family member needed assistance. For instance, one stable working-class family got food stamps for grandchildren who lived with them. Others had relatives in low-skilled worker categories that turned to the government for aid and were familiar with government programs for this reason.

Social Service Agencies

As with government supports, this study found that people in the educated middle class and low-skilled workers were more likely to go to a formal agency for assistance for basic needs, job search or other supports like childcare. People in all groups used non-profit organizations for recreational activities for their children. The types of agencies used depended on the social and cultural capital within each group. Educated middle-class people would use professional organizations or create self-help networks. For example, the African American professionals had created several semi-formal organizations that met regularly. We discovered no formal organizations for professionals among Hispanic/Latinos, but professionals in this community would participate in citywide professional organizations like AAUW or citywide politics.

56

The stable working class was most likely to restrict organization use to recreational activities, union participation and church based activities. They avoided social service agencies that they perceived as serving the needy in most cases, fearing the stigma of people thinking that they were needy. However, stable working-class people were active volunteers in all types of social service agencies.

Low-skilled workers used private non-profits that they trusted because of good reports within their social capital networks. Since Kenosha had strict rules about how often families could receive commodities based on a combination of national guidelines and collaboration among agencies, families also knew when and where they could turn for support.

Churches

Families from all three groups relied on churches for basic needs, social support, work referrals, recreation, and moral and spiritual support. Church help will be discussed in more detail in a later section. Just as Mary Hughes found work through church contacts, we witnessed many cases of people being told about work and educational opportunities through church. The same was true for childcare, recreation and other basic needs. For example, one stable working-class family reported that they were given a new car by someone associated with their church when their vehicle broke down suddenly. Other examples of instrumental supports through churches were reported.

Implications for Programs and Policy

- *Formal supports are best advertised through informal networks.* People found resources through their closed social capital networks of friends, family, neighborhood and church. They learned about formal services like jobs, educational opportunities and other resources through the same channels. The best way to spread information given this tendency is to develop bridging contacts in closed social capital networks.

- *Supports are based on trust and cultural capital, not just information.* Throughout this study, we found that people evaluated both organizations and individuals based on the good report of people or organizations that they trusted already. Much of that trust came from shared cultural capital. For organizations offering services or trying to develop workers, contact needs to go beyond simply sharing information. Agencies need to develop strong relationships with the people they work with and be prepared to modify cultural expectations to reach across communities.

- *Moving between communities involves developing both cultural and social capital.* The families who were most successful and resilient in this study could move between several closed social capital networks. These skills come from trusted, long-term, positive involvement with people in different communities. While the mechanisms to improve bridging social capital will be discussed in more detail later, at this point it is important to note that bridging social capital means more than connections or short-term interactions among people from different closed social capital networks.

The Kenosha Welfare System

To empower the Kenosha County residents who are eligible for Wisconsin Works Program services to attain and sustain economic self-sufficiency.

—Kenosha W-2 program mission statement

The Kenosha welfare system experienced rapid change during the study period. Wisconsin's new welfare reform program, W-2, had just been implemented during the earlier Kenosha Conversation Project. As discussed below, W-2 requires low-income families receiving government assistance to participate in work-related activities in an effort to rapidly move them into the labor force. Kenosha succeeded in achieving W-2 goals of reducing the welfare caseload. The Kenosha Conversation Project Education Booklet reported that by 1998 Kenosha had reduced the number of people receiving cash assistance to 140 families, with another 190 families receiving case management or other services related to W-2. This change was due to a combination of Kenosha's booming economy and W-2's emphasis on

moving welfare recipients rapidly into the workforce.

The number of families on W-2 in Kenosha has not changed much in the following two years: in September 2000, 176 families were receiving cash assistance and another 126 were enrolled in case management or related services.[18] With so few families participating in W-2, welfare programs became a minor concern for most Kenosha residents. For this reason, the Kenosha Social Capital Study chose to focus on the community institutions that provided supports to families regardless of their use of government aid.

While few families are involved in W-2, many more receive supports from government in the form of food stamps, medical assistance and subsidized childcare. W-2 emphasizes

supporting working poor families through these kinds of supplements. Given that many of the jobs in Kenosha's new economy are service sector or small factory employment offering low wages and limited benefits, these kinds of supports are particularly important. In September, 2000, food stamps, Medicaid or a combination of the two were received by 4,901 families. The majority of these families (3,080) only used government supports for medical assistance through Badger Care, Wisconsin's Medicaid managed care program. A small proportion of Kenosha families (818) were enrolled in subsidized childcare in Kenosha.[19]

Given the need for these ancillary supports, the Kenosha Social Capital Study looked at the ways that African Americans and Hispanic/Latinos used public assistance through the Kenosha County Job Center. The study also asked about connections between the organizations that were the focus of this research project and the Kenosha County Job Center.

Kenosha differed from most of the United States in its approach to providing assistance to families in need through government. In keeping with Kenosha's egalitarian ethos of helping everyone in its community to become self-supporting, the Kenosha County Job Center did not distinguish between public assistance recipients and other community residents when offering job search and other related services. The Kenosha County Job Center was available to everyone looking for work in this community. The Kenosha County Job Center also developed close links to organizations offering housing, energy assistance, childcare, parenting, education and other services needed to support a working family. Through contracts and well-developed coalitions, the Kenosha County Job Center epitomized the one-stop-shop system that has become the ideal for social supports in the United States in recent years.

Despite goals of serving all Kenosha residents, funding for the Kenosha County Job Center largely came from state welfare funds. During the *Kenosha Conversation Project,* roughly seventy percent of the Kenosha County Job Center budget came from W-2 and related contracts. Given the sharp reduction of people on public assistance after W-2 started, new state contracts implemented halfway through the *Kenosha Social Capital Study* reduced funding for W-2 programs by forty-four percent. Fortunately, Kenosha also received community reinvestment funds from the state as a reward for their good performance in implementing W-2.[20] Still, the Kenosha County Job Center lost $6,084,231 in the W-2 contract that began in January, 2000, providing around thirty-seven percent less money than the previous W-2 contract.[21] As a result, Kenosha is now trying to offer the same universal program to its residents with less money, resulting in some staff and program cuts.

About the same time as the Kenosha County Job Center lost significant funding for its programs, the management structure of the agency shifted due to changes in county government. Until January, 2000, the Kenosha County Job Center was a combined non-profit/for-profit/ government partnership providing services under an "umbrella" management structure. Since January, 2000, the Kenosha County Job Center has become a government facility that contracts some services to other organizations. Kenosha County also intends to move other human service activities into the Kenosha County Job Center building, making it easier for families in need to access government services. It is unclear how the changes

in management structure will affect activities at the center.

Given the rapid changes in welfare related services in Kenosha and the focus of this study, this report does not examine government assistance at the present time in Kenosha. However, the project did note use of government programs over time by members of the communities that we studied. This section of the report outlines the public assistance system in Kenosha in the late 1990s. Focusing on the role of social capital through agencies and individuals in Kenosha, this section also describes the use of the Kenosha County Job Center and related government assistance as reported in our interviews and observations. We find that government assistance is part of a package of services sometimes used by low-income families to survive. However, access to these services depends on knowledge within closed social capital networks, cultural capital expectations of assistance, and dynamics between individuals, organizations and government workers.

Welfare Reform in Wisconsin

Wisconsin Works (W-2) is one of the most radical welfare reform programs implemented under the 1996 U.S. federal welfare reform legislation. The *Personal Responsibility, Work Opportunity and Medicaid Restructuring Act of 1996* ended entitlements for public assistance, replacing the *Aid for Families with Dependent Children* program with block grants to the States under the title *Temporary Assistance to Needy Families* (TANF). States had much flexibility in designing welfare reform strategies, as long as local programs rapidly moved low-income people into work related activities. Federal legislation restricted government aid for low-income families to five years in a lifetime. In order to help people move from welfare to work, the legislation increased support for childcare assistance. The food stamp

and medical assistance programs were left alone. This meant that people could still qualify for food stamps or Medicaid outside of welfare reform, but they needed to meet the income eligibility requirements.

Wisconsin Works replaced cash assistance based on limited income and the number of minor children in the household with a system designed to help people find work and provide supports to keep them employed. Each person requesting assistance was supposed to meet with a Financial and Employment Counselor (FEP) who would evaluate their employment prospects and develop a self-sufficiency plan. W-2 created a four-level employment ladder with the following steps:

1. **Unsubsidized Employment:** People were first guided to jobs. Those who found work became eligible for food stamps, Medicaid, childcare assistance and the earned income tax credit (EITC) depending on their income. Employed people on W-2 also received some case management assistance.

2. **Trial Jobs:** People who had trouble finding work could be placed in regular jobs subsidized by the government during a three to six month training period. These people were also eligible for food stamps, Medicaid, childcare, EITC and case management. This employment strategy is rarely used.

3. **Community Service Jobs (CSJ):** People who were not likely to find employment quickly were placed in community service positions. The CSJ positions were expected to develop work experience for participants, which would lead to regular employment. People in this category worked at their CSJ placement for thirty hours a week and attended training for another ten. They received a cash grant of $673 per month. However, this cash grant could be docked if they

missed hours without good reason. CSJs were also eligible for food stamps, Medicaid, childcare, EITC and case management.

4. W-2 Transition: People with major problems, which kept them from performing independent, self-sustaining work, were placed in this last category. In Kenosha, W-2 transition included people with developmental disabilities, those caring for disabled children, and others with similar problems. These people received cash grants of $628 per month and were eligible for food stamps, Medicaid, childcare, EITC and case management. They were expected to participate in work or developmental activities for twenty-eight hours per week and education and training for twelve hours per week. The program assumed that people would eventually transition to CSJs and then unsubsidized employment.

In order to assist people in gaining employment, W-2 also provided several forms of additional assistance. Case management changed from determining if someone was eligible for assistance to a social service system designed to help participants solve problems which stood in the way of work. Transportation assistance was available to get to required programs or job interviews. The program required local agencies to provide drop-in childcare for participants. Job access loans were available to cover the costs of such items as clothing, work related tools or money to buy a car to get to work.

As required by federal mandates, W-2 also increased enforcement of child support. W-2 applicants were required to name the father of their children so that the state could ensure that they provided cash support. People who were working received all the money that the state collected while those in the cash grant program got forty-one percent of child support payments. Local agencies complain

that child support enforcement is significantly under funded.

While the W-2 program carefully outlined the various kinds of assistance available to people once they were placed in the system, it was less clear about support while they looked for work. AFDC supplemented income with cash assistance for people working in low paying or part-time work. It also provided income to people while they looked for work. These benefits disappeared under W-2. During the study period, people working in part-time or low-wage jobs could receive more in food stamps, but no additional cash assistance. The W-2 program began offering pro-rated cash grants to people working part-time in the 1999-2000 TANF plan. These individuals received some cash assistance in exchange for participation in community work or education programs. W-2 program applicants deemed job-ready were offered workshops and other assistance to find work, but no cash support during their job search.

As a work-first program, W-2 focused on work rather than educational benefits. CSJ participants can take GED or other educational programs. Until the federal *Workforce Attachment and Advancement* (WAA) program started in 2000, the amount of time that people could participate in training was limited. The new program still emphasizes work, but also provides funding for qualified people to attend technical or vocational training that will help them obtain a job or advance in their career path.

W-2 blurred the line between low-income working people and welfare recipients. In the first state plan, people earning up to 200 percent of the federal poverty level were eligible for W-2 assistance for children and other related services. The current TANF plan allows any family earning up to 250 percent of the federal poverty level to use W-2 related services. This policy decision

attempted to reduce the stigma of government support and provide benefits to low-income workers often ineligible for any benefits under AFDC. Childcare support was available to anyone earning 165 percent of the federal poverty level or below from 1997-1999. In 2000, the cut-off limit was raised to anyone earning 185 percent of the federal poverty level. However, recipients must co-pay for this aid. Related legislation made Medicaid available to more children.

W-2 shifted the focus from providing income to support children to seeking work for the adult responsible for a family. Under AFDC, relatives caring for their family member's children received cash benefits. W-2 replaced this system with Kinship care, which provided $215 per month for each child. This amount was often less than AFDC. Kinship care also required extensive background checks for relatives caring for children. No additional funding was given to local child welfare agencies to perform this work.

AFDC provided aid through government. W-2 allowed government, non-profit and for-profit organizations to bid for W-2 services. The W-2 contracts cover administrative and staffing costs. Each agency is also allocated money to pay for cash grants or other payments to program recipients based on an estimate of the number of people who will use the system in that area. Agencies who place more of their participants into jobs can keep a portion of the cash in this account as a "profit" to put toward new programs. The community reinvestment funds that Kenosha received to supplement lower W-2 contract funding came from this "profit" account. However, if more people than expected need CSJ or W-2 transition assistance, the agencies can lose money. This system encourages local administrators to concentrate on moving people into paid work quickly.

59

Welfare Reform in Kenosha

Kenosha's W-2 program was largely in place before implementation of recent welfare reform initiatives. Kenosha participated in an early work experience and job training program in 1987. In 1990, Kenosha opened a one-stop job center that became a national model. Kenosha contributed to the formulation of W-2. The Kenosha County Job Center has successfully run a work-first program since the early 1990s. Implementing W-2 meant few initial changes in their program design.

Located in a remodeled one-story department store, the center offers completely integrated services for employment and training. The management configuration in effect until January, 2000, evolved during the early 1990s, including twenty-three different programs run by a collaboration of nineteen different agencies. The Kenosha County Job Center was a unique public/private partnership run by a combination of non-profit organizations, for-profit consulting services and government.

In 2000, changes in funding and government philosophy led to dismantling the public/private partnership in favor of a government-run entity. As a Kenosha County facility, the Kenosha County Job Center now has government employees managing the organization. Most of the case management services and other direct service programs are transitioning from non-profit to government employees. Due to budget cuts, twenty-two people lost their jobs at the end of December, 1999. Given fewer staff and less funding, some services were offered less frequently. The adult education program offered through the Kenosha County Job Center was eliminated and replaced by Gateway technical college classes offered at the Job Center. Parenting

classes were also eliminated; people needing this service were referred to programs offered on an occasional basis by local non-profits.

Kenosha's program is unique in two respects:

- **The integrated services model does not distinguish between W-2 eligible people and other county residents needing employment services.** Kenosha provides the same general range of services for all residents. Part of the Kenosha County Job Center model involves treating low-income people the same as everyone else. W-2 eligible people use the same job resource room as others seeking work in the county. Job development and assessment workshops include both W-2 recipients and other community residents. Job placement services do not distinguish between low-income and other workers in recruitment, interviewing or placement activities. All programs in the center are available to any county resident equally. This strategy is meant to combat the stigma attached to welfare recipients.

- **Case management and employment services are provided by a team.** Rather than one FEP who is responsible for decision making and referral for a W-2 case, the Kenosha program includes a team of economic support specialists, case managers, job placement specialists, and employment support specialists. The initial employability plan is developed through a team discussion. Any additional needed services involve a wide range of people throughout the organization.

In keeping with this model, the Kenosha W-2 program offers newcomers several options when they enter the building. People can go directly to the job resource room, where a job placement specialist will

guide them toward job listings, résumé development tools and other resources. The facility includes a phone and fax machine to help participants apply for work. Employers also interview potential workers on site.

People also can start with the general reception area across from the job resource room. Like many W-2 programs, Kenosha attempts to divert people from cash assistance whenever possible. The receptionist first refers people to a community service representative who offers information on job related workshops and other employment services, food pantries, housing and rental assistance, and family services. This same person also provides information on food stamps, medical assistance and childcare support. Besides providing information to the general public seeking help, this customer service representative tries to resolve low-income people's needs without enrolling them in W-2.

These entry points can either help or hinder people attempting to access government services, depending on the quality of interactions with the staff person handling initial questions. If the staff person at the desk when someone comes in has both knowledge and an inclination to help the person seeking assistance, the interaction can provide needed aid. However, if the person initially encountered by the community resident seeking assistance is hostile to people outside of his or her social networks or simply uninformed of the nuances of government assistance, people eligible for services can be sent away without help.

Two examples illustrate this tendency in Kenosha. In one case, a newcomer to Kenosha received good service when using the job center to find work. Mark was a stable working-class veteran moving toward professional middle-class employment. Guided to the Kenosha County Job Center by a friend, he easily gained access to the postings in the employment section of the job center and had no trouble using the available computers. A veteran's representative told him about job openings.

Others have had less positive experiences. Another example illustrates a Kenosha County Job Center employee relying on individualized understandings of W-2 program rules and following rigid guidelines to deny services to a potentially eligible applicant. In order to test the Kenosha system, I sent an African American college student, Kinesha, to the Kenosha County Job Center to apply for childcare. Kinesha worked part-time and was probably eligible for subsidized day care. She asked the person at the first desk how to apply for this benefit.

The staff person immediately told her that she had to name the father of her child and enroll in government child support enforcement in order to apply for the childcare benefit. While W-2 applicants must name the father of their children in order to apply for cash assistance, these rules should not apply to government-subsidized childcare. Kinesha had an informal agreement with the father of her child, another college student. Government child support enforcement would require him to work in order to make regular cash payments, making it harder to complete his education. Rather than jeopardize her boyfriend's future, Kinesha decided not to apply for government assistance with childcare. Through the worker erroneously following the rote process for W-2 enrollment, Kinesha lost access to a benefit that may have provided additional support to complete her own education as well as enrichment for her child through quality day care she could not afford on her part-time wages.

These kinds of negative experiences rapidly spread through the community of low-skill workers by word of mouth reports, leading them to limit their use of the Kenosha County Job Center. People presumed that they could not get government aid unless they were part of the W-2 program and complied with all its regulations. For example, one low-skilled worker with several children told us, "There's no childcare available unless you're in the KCJC programs. Since I'm going to school and sometimes working, there's nothing available to fit my financial needs."

The initial entry process became more haphazard with budget cuts related to the new W-2 contract. Fewer people were available to provide initial guidance to people looking for assistance. In addition, the person handling the phones and reception desk became a volunteer through W-2 Community Service Jobs or a related program. On several occasions, I watched these volunteers mishandle people asking for information because they were unfamiliar with the center. The potential for unprofessional behavior at this important entry point increased due to the fact that volunteers were responsible for first contact with the public.

The Kenosha social support program showed a dynamic tension between creative public service and limited funds. For example, realizing that many of their potential customers worked during their hours, Kenosha county started sending employees out to hospitals, businesses that employed people at low-wages with limited benefits, and other places used by low-income families in order to facilitate signing them up for services like food stamps and medical assistance. In the *Kenosha Conversation Project*, we found that most people using childcare assistance were also on W-2; other community

residents remained unaware of this benefit. Rather than simply attempt to advertise their services in order to increase wider community use of the job center, Kenosha went to the places where people needing those services congregated in order to tap into closed social capital networks. This innovative program made government services more accessible for low-income people, particularly given the limited public transportation in Kenosha. This initiative facilitated use of government benefits. For example, eighty-four percent of the families now using childcare assistance have no connection to the W-2 program.[22] However, some community advocates complained that the Kenosha County Job Center was slow responding to requests for on-site service or other information. This slow communication was probably due to limited staff.

KENOSHA COUNTY JOB CENTER FLOW

62

NON W-2, OPTION 1
↓
RECEPTIONIST
↓ COMMUNITY
SERVICE REP
↓
COMMUNITY
RESOURCES ↓

JOB SEARCH RESOURCE
ROOM

NON W-2, OPTION 2
↓
RECEPTIONIST
↓ COMMUNITY SERVICE
REP
↓
PRE-SCREENER
↓ CHILD SUPPORT SERVICE
REP ↓
NEW APPLICANT

REGISTRATION

W-2, OPTION 3
↓
RECEPTIONIST
↓ COMMUNITY SERVICE
REP
↓ JOB SEARCH RESOURCE
ROOM ↓ COMMUNITY
SERVICE REP
↓
PRE-SCREENER
↓ CHILD SUPPORT SERVICE
REP ↓
NEW APPLICANT

REGISTRATION

People requesting government services go through a screening process to determine a plan of action based on the W-2 program ladder. Depending on their employability plan, they then participate in job search, job development workshops and other activities.

As with all W-2 programs, participants receiving food stamps, childcare and Medicaid are required to meet with a case manager every three months to continue eligibility. People involved in active job search, CSJ or transition programs may meet with case managers or other job center staff more frequently.

Kenosha's program offers comprehensive services to people enrolled in W-2. CSJ and W-2 transition participants take part in a series of workshops and assessment activities before placement. Given the size of the caseload and linkages within the community, individual problems can be resolved through a concerted team effort. Community size also means that service providers often know details of individual cases. More

importantly, the Kenosha system incorporates links to non-profits in the community. In cases where non-profits and government work together, this can lead to holistic services for families in need.

For example, Marisha was a homeless shelter resident. The homeless shelter required her to apply for W-2 shortly after she entered that facility since she had no job. The non-profit agency gave her explicit guidance on how to apply so that she would not be denied services. This became important as the front-line worker at the Kenosha County Job Center initially told her that she was not eligible for cash assistance even though she qualified as a shelter resident. A homeless shelter employee also called Marisha's government caseworker when calls were not being returned, solving communication problems. The non-profit agency staff helped Marisha find schools for her children and obtain documentation on schooling and other matters required to qualify for W-2.

Caseworkers at the Kenosha County Job Center, in turn, linked

into a range of government and non-profit services. In addition to an employment specialist and other members of the FEP team, Marisha was linked to a family support worker to help her with family problems. This family support caseworker was also part of the Kenosha County Job Center, and was mandated to provide additional supports to particularly at-risk families. The W-2 caseworkers sent Marisha to apply for rental assistance from another non-profit with a government contract to provide housing services. When the government housing voucher was too slow in arriving to make Marisha's first month's rent, the family support caseworker provided the first rent payment through a special fund available for these types of emergencies.

Marisha continues to work with a combination of government and non-profit service providers in order to re-establish herself in Kenosha. Through close communication between Marisha and these various helpers, she has received a variety of services for herself and her children.

The service providers work as a team, contacting other agencies when appropriate in order to make sure that Marisha's family gets the services they need.

This team partnership between non-profits and government is an important aspect of social support in Kenosha. I next look at the dynamic between government and social service agencies in providing for families in Kenosha.

Social Capital Links Between the Job Center and Non-profit Agencies

The job center services are linked into a wider array of human services offered by government and non-profits. In a community the size of Kenosha, a small number of agencies provide social services. Most participate in regular network meetings. The Prevention Services Network includes seven community-based organizations, the Department of Human Services and the Kenosha Unified School District. This network provides an array of services to the most at-risk families in the area, like Marisha and her children. The Emergency Services Network focuses on housing, shelter, disaster relief, Women Infants and Children's program and other support services. Children's Services Network focuses further on children at-risk. Many of the same organizations participate in each network.

In addition to formal social service agencies, there is a network of churches providing emergency housing in connection with the homeless shelter. Some churches also provide social services. These church-based activities seem to be less formally linked to the official safety-net networks, but there does appear to be some overlap in individuals participating in various kinds of community supports.

These coalitions create strong social capital links among organizations well established in Kenosha to provide assistance to the needy. As in Marisha's case, these networks can facilitate information across agencies through patterns of trust and shared information. In other cases, government uses non-profits to gain access to closed social capital communities. For instance, the Kenosha County Job Center placed a medical assistance employee at one of the Hispanic/Latino organizations in an attempt to reach the newcomer Mexican population that they acknowledged was reluctant to enter their facility due to fears of deportation. This initiative preceded sending county employees off-site with laptops.

As W-2 transitioned more people into the ranks of the working poor and many people failed to apply for supplementary assistance when W-2 was implemented due to confusion in eligibility requirements, use of non-profits for basic needs increased dramatically. For example, the homeless shelter reported a twenty-four percent increase in families using the food pantry. The number of families receiving assistance at holidays through a partnership of non-profit organizations has risen from 1500 to 2100 for Thanksgiving baskets. These figures suggest that devolution has led to more burdens on the private sector. As the Kenosha County Job Center turns to non-profits to provide even more services with no government funding due to its most recent budget cuts, reliance on an increasingly stressed non-profit system is likely to rise. To date, the Kenosha social support system for the very needy has begun to turn from a partnership between governments and non-profits to reliance on non-profits that provide services previously shared with government. The nature of the coalitions and their ability to provide holistic services may be compromised as this pattern of increasingly limited government support continues.

The close network of non-profits and government also worked to enforce government eligibility rules and limit assistance. For example, Kenosha residents were not allowed to apply for energy assistance at a non-profit organization if they were not legal residents of the United States, limiting use of this government service. Caseworkers at the Hispanic/Latino organizations knew not to refer their undocumented program participants for a wide array of government services. The non-profits providing housing assistance under government contract also had close ties to the Kenosha County Job Center that structured the way they provided service. While these close ties enabled good service and cut down on people trying to gain additional services through multiple providers, it also created a closed system for people outside of these closed social capital networks. This particularly became a problem for undocumented Hispanic/Latinos.

The closed social capital networks also limited connections between insider organizations, outsider organizations, churches and government. The link between agency social capital networks and government funding will be discussed in more detail later in this report. Two elements of the dynamic between government and the African American and Hispanic/Latino communities are relevant here. First, while some organizations actively participated in the government/non-profit coalitions, most organizations associated with communities of color had limited participation in these meetings. As one government administrator remarked, the coalitions were made of well-established organizations with strong ties to Kenosha's mainstream political and social service structure. As relative newcomers or organizations considered invisible to the rest of Kenosha until recently, the African American organizations were less likely to participate in these networks. Some of the Hispanic/Latino organizations had stronger ties due to connections

63

with government in earlier decades while others had little contact with the Kenosha County Job Center.

Churches in these two communities had little or no contact with the government agencies. Several pastors reported that they only went to the job center if they were trying to help their members find work. Government made little effort to formally reach out to the churches to facilitate access to government services.

In agencies like the homeless shelter, non-profit referrals to government had a special weight because receipt of non-profit services was tied to applying for government aid. Connecting non-profit program participants to government was far more tenuous in cases without this requirement. Some agencies would not refer their program participants if they knew that they would have trouble with government eligibility requirements. Others would go with their program participants to ensure that they received appropriate government assistance. In other cases, caseworkers could not guarantee that the people that they served, who came from closed social capital communities suspicious of government, would follow through on referrals. One non-profit agency worker commented:

> Yes, I've told them and they're aware that they can go there. I can't say for sure if they've gone to [the Kenosha County Job Center]. All I can do is suggest. Like I say, you can take a horse to water but you can't make him drink from the trough. You know what I'm saying? So I'm not sure if they're sincere about it, but it's not for me to say.

This comment suggests that the use of government services depends on the willingness of the participant to use those services. Willingness, in turn, depends on the reputation of the government agency in the communities needing service. The final part of this section examines the ways that African Americans and Hispanic/Latinos use the Kenosha County Job Center.

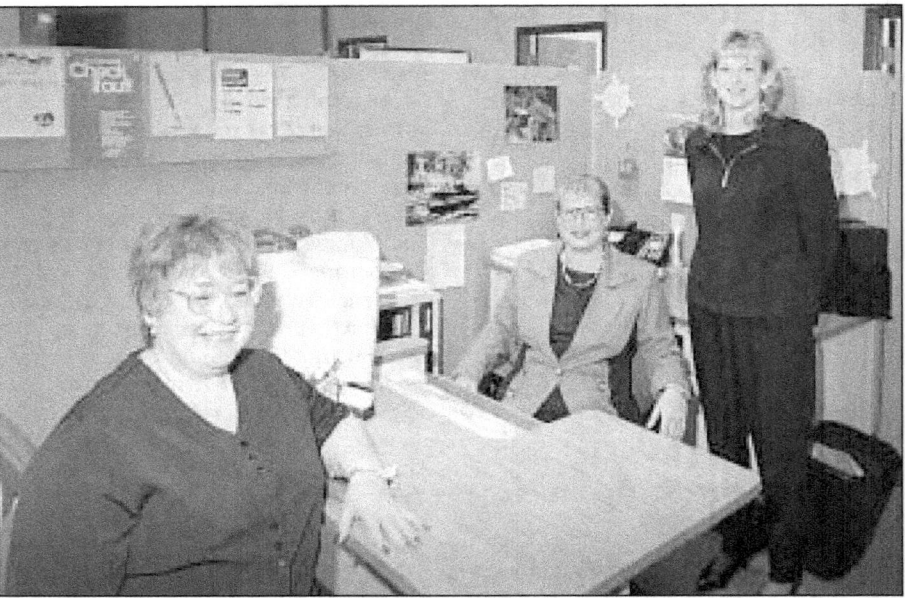

Family Use of the Kenosha County Job Center

W-2 began in the fall of 1997. Local W-2 agencies had until March 30, 1998, to convert all AFDC cases to W-2. Case conversion meant that everyone receiving AFDC had to report to the W-2 office to complete an employment development plan in order to continue to receive benefits. As in other parts of the state, Kenosha found that roughly fifty percent of their caseload came in for processing. The remainder lost benefits as of March 30.

Conversations with Kenosha County Job Center administrators during the *Kenosha Conversation Project* revealed that many of the families on AFDC that did not apply for W-2 were working and using government assistance to supplement meager wages. Of the 750 cases that Kenosha had to convert into W-2, half were already employed. Some others were AFDC cases of relatives caring for children that were converted into kinship care. Until recently, none of these families were eligible for cash assistance under W-2. Many still could qualify for food stamps and Medicaid and may be receiving this form of government assistance. These

low-skilled workers had a history of packaging work, government supports and supports through churches and non-profits to meet their needs. W-2 eliminated one source of income for these families. These cuts contributed to these families' increased use of food pantries and other programs to obtain basic food, clothing and shelter.

Kenosha has experienced a dramatic drop in people receiving W-2 services. As of September 1, 2000, only 302 cases were officially enrolled in W-2. One hundred and seventy-six were receiving a cash grant. Most of the remaining families had someone working and received case management in order to help them stay on the job.

The drop in cases are part of a long-term trend. The 1996 Department of Human Services annual report noted a sixty-six percent drop in caseload from 1990. Kenosha human services and job center people believe the change was caused by their implementation of the work-first JOBS program and the upswing in the local economy.

The population served by the W-2 program has changed in the last few years. The Kenosha County Job Center programs serving low-income populations under the predecessors to

W-2 had a constant ethnic make-up of sixty percent white, twenty-five percent African American and fifteen percent Hispanic/Latino. Forty-five percent of participants did not have a high school diploma or GED. In the first six months of 1998, forty-six percent of the people enrolled in W-2 were white, forty-one percent African American and thirteen percent were Hispanic/Latino. This means that the population has shifted to more people of color. The proportion of participants without a high school diploma was 24 percent in September, 2000. This means that more W-2 recipients have finished high school than in the past, but that the racial make-up of the population has changed.

Both government and non-profit agency staff that work with the W-2 population say that these remaining cases have many barriers to employment. For example, thirty-seven percent of the W-2 cases on cash grants are in the W-2 transition part of the program.[23] Some of these people have substance abuse problems, developmental disabilities and/or were victims of domestic abuse. Others have many children or new babies and are unable to find work that will support large families. In these cases, commitments to caring for young or sick children also limit the ability to work for wages. These families need the kind of intensive services provided to Marisha. Most staff working with W-2 participants worry that these families may never become self-supporting, or that it will take more than the five years currently allowed for welfare to help them find and keep jobs.

Research for this report on employment suggests that many people still using W-2 cash assistance may also lack the social networks to find stable work. For example, one agency worker reported that the people she worked with just "go in and fill out applications at the same places with no results." Interviews

with welfare recipients either new to Kenosha or living in closed social capital communities where few people had stable jobs reported the same thing. Without ties to people or organizations that could refer them to stable work, they were unable to find family supporting employment.

While both government and non-profits involved in the government sponsored coalitions increasingly worry about this small group of people who remain in the cash assistance system, the increasingly larger pool of working poor have begun to re-evaluate their relationship to government assistance. Some people told us that they did not want to bother with government assistance due to the hassle of reporting to government systems and the shame they felt due to demeaning questions by some government workers or negative attitudes toward government assistance by the general public. For example, Theresa, a Latina currently in the stable working-class reported her experience using public assistance when her husband was laid off as follows:

There was the job center; they gave us medical cards for six months, because we had no insurance. And they gave us food stamps about a hundred dollars and something and then the shelter paid one month's rent, because for about three weeks we had no income. As soon as I realized that we were looked at, I felt shame [for the food stamps].

Her shame comes from the way that Kenosha culture views the use of government aid. As a number of people commented, Kenosha residents are happy to help the "deserving poor" in need of assistance due to illness or unemployment but presume that people on welfare are lazy because most people in Kenosha have no trouble finding stable work. In the community, people using government supports may have trouble in stores, finding housing with government vouchers or in other ways. For

example, one of our fieldworkers, a white, stable working-class Kenosha resident, reported this experience when she approached an apartment complex rumored to accept government Section 8 housing vouchers:

I decided I would approach the office to get a feeling of what a person on welfare might have to deal with. I asked how much a two-bedroom apartment would be and if they would accept a voucher from [the housing agency]. She said she didn't know what I was talking about; the apartment is $570 a month, and I have to earn at least $1710 a month to fill out an application. After I said I would be receiving money from W-2, she really didn't want to deal with me.

We found similar experiences throughout the project. White Kenosha residents often had no experience with government assistance and wanted nothing to do with people who used this kind of aid. The people in the homeless shelter without other ties in the community often found that it took a long time to find housing for this reason. Others, with social supports through either family or agencies, were able to locate housing because their closed social capital networks provided information on landlords who accepted government vouchers. The same was true for food stamps. As in other cases in Kenosha, communities accepting of the need for government aid offered support to their members using these services.

Unlike the established white population, we found many more African Americans and Hispanic/Latinos who were familiar with government supports. While some stable working-class and educated middle-class families felt similar to mainstream whites about welfare, in many more cases, families understood the need for government aid because they, their family members or friends had used this system. This finding highlights the fact that people using government supports are not separated from other families in the community. We found stable working-class elders who received kinship care for grandchildren whose parents were unable to care for them. A number of stable working-class and a few educated middle-class families reported that they had used government aid earlier in their lives.

The *Kenosha Social Capital Study* found that educated middle class, stable working-class and low-skilled workers viewed public assistance differently. While most educated middle-class people considered using government resources only when their personal networks failed, they were more likely to consider the Kenosha County Job Service a positive resource available in times of need. Like Mark, they used the job referral sections of the job center most frequently and felt no stigma in using citywide services paid for by their tax dollars.

Stable working-class families were least likely to use government aid. In most cases, they simply reported that they did not need Kenosha County Job Center help because they now had strong networks and stable jobs. A few others echoed the common negative sentiments toward people who use public assistance. Some simply reported that they knew they made too much money and were likely to be ineligible for aid or would not want to experience the shame of public assistance. Some of these experiences came from times when eligibility requirements were stricter than they are today. For example, Jorge reported:

Since we got married we have worked, we have not had the opportunity or the necessity to use any of those services. Thank God. Once when they laid me off, I went. The company was giving food and other things. But they said I did not qualify because my wife worked and we had two cars and therefore I could sell one and buy the basics they

were offering. When I left there were people outside selling what they had obtained for free. I, who had gone with the intention of actually using it, was denied and they, who went there with the sole purpose of selling it, they qualified.

Despite raising the income limits for medical assistance and childcare, many families still do not qualify because their low wages are still above the cut-off points for this program. For example, while undocumented Hispanic/Latinos do not qualify for government assistance, their U.S. born children can get aid. Maria's family falls into the low-skilled worker category. She reported:

We work and we pay taxes but we do not get any services. That is [the] problem one has for not having a social security number. But one is paying all the same. When I applied for Medicare, they told me that if we had income they would take it away. The baby is a citizen, but they told me that I should be working and bringing income.

Low-skilled workers were most likely to need government assistance and have used the Kenosha County Job Center in the recent past or present. These families were persistent about getting aid if they felt that they qualified for assistance. However, their view of the Kenosha County Job Center was far more ambivalent than the educated middle class. Some people reported good experiences with their caseworkers. Others told us about workers who were demeaning or hostile. These front-line workers were most likely to hold opinions that people using public assistance were morally deficient. People of color sometimes interpreted these negative interactions as racist. For example, Marisol told us about one bad experience with the Kenosha County Job Center:

I was in such [a] bad situation economically, I went to apply for the medical card and that and I had such a social worker, so racist, that she asked me questions that even a person who went with me to interpret and [the questions were so] inappropriate that she and I almost tore up the pages and left. After that I had a right to qualify because I did not have a job but the woman made

us feel like.... Now my social worker is a very nice person, but in that occasion the person [I talked to] there is nobody more racist than her. One could see her anger and the way in which she was trying to pry into my private life, things I do not like to talk about.

Notice that Marisol reports that her regular caseworker is nice. This highlights the fact that the team approach to case management used by the Kenosha County Job Center can soften negative experiences with one welfare caseworker. We found many people who told us about caring, thoughtful service from Kenosha County Job Center staff. For example, Marisha told us that:

[One worker] was really nice; she even sat down with me. She had a book with all the different kinds of jobs and people that they work with too—but the ones she had me look at were the ones they were having volunteers at and then they would be hiring within the near future. She said she could easily send me to a site for the volunteer work where I would easily get my check every month. She wanted me to find one in there that would have work I would like to do and being as they would be hiring. So she went through all the clerical cause that's what I want to do. Data entry and all that. She found all those and now she's going through calling them. She's waiting for them to call her. That's all I'm waiting for with her. She told me that she has her voice mail set up for twenty-four hours a day and to just call her. She can always call and check and she'll give me a call if something's wrong.

These differences in experience with Kenosha County Job Center staff come from a combination of factors. Negative experience partly comes from interactions with caseworkers or intake workers, who hold to the working-class Kenosha culture view that outsiders, particularly welfare recipients, are the undeserving poor who need to either learn how to work or leave the community. Among Kenosha mainstream communities, many people believe that most of the welfare recipients are poor people from Illinois who move to Kenosha to use county resources. Others feel that those still on welfare simply do not want to work. Asking about lifestyle details like the caseworker that Marisol encountered is a way to find out how the person seeking government aid is deviant from what the caseworker considers "normal" family practice.

Lack of staff also contributes to difficulties in obtaining cash assistance. Limited staffing combines with Kenosha's practice of providing a number of steps to get cash assistance and clarifying work expectations in the hopes that people will find work before turning to government aid. For example, Marisha found that she needed patience to get through the W-2 application process. She told us:

> [The caseworker] was like, kinda like, rushing, trying to hurry up and get through. I've dealt with her type before. So I was just taking my time and I'm like, any more papers? I just fill them out and when I turn them in. I see someone else and that's when they told me that when I do come back I can apply for child support and cash assistance and the court would send me a notice in the mail and gave me an appointment for W-2 orientation. That's to tell you more about the W-2, which paying thing you were going to be on since there's three of them, like one you work and you get paid so much, another where you do volunteer work, you don't get paid from the site

> but you get your check once a month, work just to get your check for that month. The third is just if your baby isn't three months old, you receive a check for $673 a month. So be at that orientation and after that, she send me thing saying she needed something from my kids' school, showing that the kids were in school. Cause they got this thing called learnfare, the kids have to be in school, they have to be there on a daily basis or they take it out of the check at $5.50 an hour for any hour that's unexcused.

Like other low-skilled workers unable to work, Marisha complied with these steps to get into the W-2 system. When applying for cash assistance, she had a new baby and qualified for a cash grant without work requirements until the baby became three months old. Unfortunately, she applied for assistance halfway through a benefit period and did not get a check for another few weeks, keeping her in the homeless shelter longer. The W-2 practice of treating welfare like a job may provide the boundaries of a regular paycheck to some recipients, but it does not offer much flexibility in emergency cases like this one. We met others in the research process who lacked basic necessities because of diversion tactics at the Kenosha County Job Center. Others experienced problems because checks were slow to arrive.

As with many low-skilled workers, Marisha wants to move into the stable working class through training. In her case, her employment specialist has agreed to work with her to meet this goal. Through helping Marisha find a community service placement that might lead to a job, her caseworker attempts to offer bridging social capital through her own social service networks. Marisha's other caseworkers offer similar assistance by connecting her to after-school programs for her children, good schools and training opportunities.

This kind of partnership among people needing assistance, government and non-profits is an important component of the Kenosha system at its best.

However, as with the young man who did not go to the Kenosha County Job Center because he thought that he did not qualify for services due to localized knowledge from his closed social capital network, many others do not use government aid because they presume they do not qualify. Others stay away because they do not like the sometimes demeaning treatment from caseworkers who "had to know everything about your business." Still others try to access services but, like Kinesha, are turned away by front-line workers giving false information or following the wrong rigid guidelines to determine who can access service.

Depending on their social networks and available resources, Kenosha county residents of color viewed the Kenosha County Job Center in a variety of different ways. Community experiences with the Job Center influenced when and how they used government benefits. Since support for government services comes from a combination of community perception and government's estimations of the needs for the system in the community, community perceptions and use of the Kenosha County Job Center, in turn, influenced availability of services. Funds to maintain the job center were cut when fewer people used the government W-2 program. Community perceptions of the need for the job center depend on their knowledge of the system and their own experience with it. Since established Kenosha mainstream employers and employees are not familiar with the center or use it often, this government facility must rely on the perceptions and use patterns of a small percentage of community residents. Given the facility's mandate to provide service to everyone in Kenosha, its ability to fulfill this mission will ultimately depend on expanding knowledge about services to a broader community constituency.

Implications for Policy and Programs

68

Like many government systems, the Kenosha County Job Center has much promise but sometimes fails in executing its program fully. As discussed above, problems come from: 1) a combination of limited funding that in turn limits services; 2) Kenosha cultural views about government aid that influence staff behavior; and 3) limited information about Job Center services stemming from localized knowledge within closed social capital networks. Low-income eligibility cut-offs associated with many government programs also limit the ability of the job center to provide assistance to a wide range of families that would benefit from assistance in Kenosha. Kenosha County Job Center's challenge involves creatively expanding its networks so that community residents increasingly use needed services while contending with budget cuts, as the state presumes that the working poor are completely self-supporting because they do not use government aid systems. The following changes to government policy and programs would help the Kenosha County Job Center and facilities like it throughout the United States better serve community residents:

- *Determine funding for government services based on community income figures rather than government program use.* The Kenosha partnership between government and non-profits that provides holistic service to some low-income residents is currently at risk because the government center has had to cut services due to funding which is formula-based on the number of people using W-2. If the goals of welfare reform are to support
low-income families through work, then case management supports, childcare assistance, medical care and other services available through government become increasingly important in order to maintain these families in a secondary sector economy. Basing government funding to communities on data on families with incomes below the median wage or the number of workers employed in firms offering low wages and limited benefits would allow government to better meet this goal.

- *Raise income limits for support services like medical assistance, childcare assistance and training.* As with many other studies of working people in the United States, the Kenosha Social Capital Study finds that the lack of universal benefits common in most countries for health care, education and assistance raising children makes life difficult for all families. Given political realities which suggest that universal benefits will not be developed soon in this country, we recommend raising income eligibility levels so that more families who do not have access to these resources through work or other income sources can get the help they need to thrive. Allowing more families to qualify for assistance may, in turn, increase support for government services throughout the community.

- *Ensure that staff providing information to the public seeking services have full training and have developed empathy for people using government aid.* One of the weaknesses of the Kenosha County Job Center system involves poor services provided by front-line workers. Bad experiences reverberate throughout the community as people share them in their closed social capital networks. Paying extra attention to the training and behavior of these workers would increase use of the Kenosha County Job Center and improve perceptions of the agency in the community.

- *Enlarge networks of organizations involved in coalition activities with the Kenosha County Job Center in order to improve service and expand community knowledge of government services.* The project found many examples of good service provided through a team of non-profit and government providers. However, agencies likely to be most in touch with the closed social capital communities needing services are sometimes left out of these networks. Creating bridges to agencies within communities of color and their churches may improve supports for families in need and enhance knowledge of government services throughout Kenosha.

- *Use social capital links through agencies, employers, churches, schools, unions and other venues that are used by a wide array of Kenosha residents to share information about programs and the Kenosha County Job Center.* While anti-poverty agencies had information about government programs that as shared with program participants, many other organizations either did not have information or did not readily share it with all Kenosha residents. As with the program that sends government human services workers out into the community to sign up aid recipients, the Kenosha County Job Center needs to better advertise all of its services through presentations to people at places that they regularly congregate. In order to best facilitate use of services throughout the community, education sessions for gatekeepers within the organization such as teachers, floor supervisors, counselors, pastors and agency staff might best serve this goal. Providing information to trusted individuals in local institutions can best use closed social capital networks to spread correct information throughout the community. Given Kenosha's emphasis on providing employment supports to all Kenosha residents, information fliers and presentations should stress the egalitarian goals of government services to help everyone eligible for assistance. Stressing the universal availability of many Kenosha County Job Center services is particularly important given Kenosha culture's focus on support for those who work.

Social Service Agencies and Social Capital

70

The *Kenosha Social Capital Study* concentrated on Kenosha's non-profit organizations that provided a service to families in need or who were understood as located within the African American and Hispanic/Latino communities. The research focused on three organizations chartered to serve everyone in Kenosha with a particular need and five non-profit organizations identified with the African American and Hispanic/Latino communities. One of these organizations was a citywide program that merged with an organization designed to serve communities of color in Kenosha during our research project. Project staff and students observed participating organizations for a number of months to understand how they operated on the ground. We also interviewed key staff and board members, collected agency reports, attended board meetings and fundraisers, and gathered information on these organizations from the newspaper. Through class projects,

we also gathered more limited information on several other organizations. This section reports on these findings from an organizational standpoint.

Kenosha History and Organization Development

Kenosha's history as a unionized, heavy industrial town meant that this small city did not develop, until recently, many of the anti-poverty organizations and organizations for people of color commonly found in cities in the United States. As a community offering good paying jobs to most people, and where job contacts and social supports were provided through closed community networks centered on church, union, ethnic group and local neighborhood, Kenosha residents felt little need to organize networks of citywide non-profit homeless shelters, training programs and anti-gang activities until

the factories began to close in the 1980s.

Kenosha did have a number of organizations that offered recreational activities for youth, care for the elderly and social clubs like the Elks in addition to churches and unions before the economic shift. In keeping with the Kenosha cultural practice of preference for local control, even the youth development activities were held by local organizations that performed activities similar to national organizations. For example, there were two recreational organizations that provided all of the activities usually offered through the YMCA. However, Kenosha did not have a YMCA chapter. Kenosha residents preferred to create their own organizations to fulfill common needs rather than turn to outsiders for organization models.

The Kenosha homeless shelter developed in the 1980s in response to the changing economy. The domestic violence shelter reflected national trends toward development of similar organizations to support victims of domestic abuse in the 1970's.

While most social and support activities were focused through the churches and several social and recreational agencies, Kenosha's communities of color did develop a series of organizations to support newcomers and their more vulnerable members. Most of these organizations were local chapters of national organizations. Three of the non-profit organizations for communities of color were based in adjacent Racine, with satellite offices in Kenosha. While most of these organizations have existed longer than anti-poverty activities for the general community, they remained mostly invisible to mainstream Kenosha until recently.

Invisibility came from three related reasons. First, communities of color kept to themselves as is common in Kenosha's pattern of closed social capital networks. Second, these organizations were organized and run by communities of color for their members: Kenoshans belonging to other communities within the city had little reason to pay attention to the organizations. Third, since most of these organizations were actually satellite offices of organizations located in Racine, governance issues were not centered in Kenosha exclusively. If aware of these organizations at all, the average Kenosha resident would consider them as "belonging" to Racine.

Despite the fact that these organizations were largely invisible to the average Kenosha resident, local government officials were aware of the activities of three minority-based organizations. Connections between minority organizations and local people came through bridging individuals who worked well with Kenosha officials. Each of these bridging people was a woman who served in an assistant director capacity in the organization. Two of these leaders had recently died as the study started and the third person had retired from her paid staff position a few years earlier. She remained an active volunteer in the community, but held no paid staff or board position associated with the non-profit agency.

Relying on individualized networks, these women became symbols for their agencies and communities. One white community leader commented:

> They were symbols the community could rally around, constants in an ever-changing picture. Because they were good folks and good spokespersons for the community, and the community knew they had help in that area and with all the change they stayed there.

These women developed strong social capital relationships with Kenosha officials that allowed them to garner resources for their agencies. They practiced a bantering, informal persistence characteristic of bridging social capital in Kenosha. For example, one government official reported:

> I would always laugh with Grace. She would come in and say, 'Mark, I need this.' It'd be kind of like, 'Grace, I can't do this.' Two months later, she got what she wanted. It was just one of those things. She was just persistent until she got what she needed.

By the time we started this study, the organizational picture in Kenosha had changed dramatically. These community leaders had died or retired and each of their organizations was in transition.

Current Kenosha Organizations

We found two types of organizations that provided services to the African American and Hispanic/Latino communities in Kenosha. In order to protect confidentiality for individual agencies, the rest of this section will describe each type of organization in aggregate form. On the one hand, citywide anti-poverty organizations provided services to a population that disproportionally consisted of people of color. These organizations were considered "strong" and "well run" by the city power structure.

On the other hand, organizations based in communities of color actually served people throughout the community because they each had contracts for citywide services. Minority-based organizations had contracts for energy assistance, work permits for teens and other county services. These organizations struggled more for funding than the mainstream organizations. These organizations had their core mission activities aimed at their communities, but also provided these services to people outside of their communities. While citywide opinion of each of these organizations varied, all had a reputation for "weak" governance and most had experienced financial scandals in the past. People in the Kenosha power structure were less sure of the quality of these organizations.

As discussed below, part of this difference of opinion regarding these minority-based organizations came from the fact that they did not have uniformly good social capital relationships with the city power structure. Concerns also came from media perceptions. Finally, community perceptions of "good" leadership and citywide criteria for governance were not always the same. These factors together influenced citywide perceptions of these organizations. Perceptions, in turn, influenced the ability to get funding and staff for these organizations, creating a self-fulfilling prophecy that made it difficult for these organizations to successfully fulfill their missions.

Before discussing each type of organization in more depth, I will outline issues common to all non-profits in Kenosha.

71

Characteristics of All Kenosha Nonprofits

Expectations of Charity and Church Mission Patterns

Since Kenosha non-profit organizations developed out of church, local community and union activities late in the city history, these organizations reflect religious-based expectations of charity more than non-profits in communities with a longer history of non-profit activity. This tendency took several forms. First, Kenosha residents expect people to survive through work when possible and find social supports in times of trouble through church and other closed community networks. Both minority and majority community members viewed these social service organizations as important extensions of the community ethos to provide for the deserving poor. However, the community leaders I spoke to equally expected these organizations to find supports from private sources.

Financial Support

Since community members viewed support for the needy as charity, organizations were expected to rely heavily on in-kind contributions and

run their organizations on low budgets. For example, board members focused first on finding volunteers to provide such services as driving vans or unloading goods. Organizations were expected to locate in-kind donations for many basic necessities like vehicles, office furniture and computers. As a result, agencies without strong social capital connections to local businesses and people of means constantly struggled to keep worn out computers, furniture and vehicles functioning. Most organizations had older furniture and buildings, outdated computers and limited resources for their staff.

On a more positive note, organizations with strong social capital links found that community businesses and individuals gave generously to support organizational activities. This included both in-kind and cash donations. For example, when the newspaper reported that one organization lost some checks because of a theft in the agency, a community leader called the executive director and offered to donate a safe.

Fundraising followed a combination of church charity models and expectations of business community

support. For example, the annual fundraising luncheons and dinners for most of these organizations were primarily organized around efforts to get businesses to buy tables for their employees. This strategy succeeded for organizations with strong ties to the business community, but was less successful for organizations that lacked these ties. For example, one citywide organization had sold tables to a number of major city businesses as well as the colleges. On the other hand, at a minority community organization benefit, many of the tables had not been bought by businesses. Instead, fewer tables were purchased overall and the contributors primarily consisted of the colleges, government social service entities and stronger non-profits. This difference stemmed from the fact that the citywide organization had strong social capital ties to business while the minority-based organization primarily drew its support from citywide social service entities.

Most of these fundraisers also included raffles, talent skits and other activities common in church fundraising. Most of these organizations also practiced traditional community fundraising activities like selling goods, memberships and other similar activities. These patterns may still be common in small non-profits throughout the United States, but most non-profit organizations currently rely on a combination of grants, the United Way and government support to fund their activities. Kenosha organizations also got some of their funding from these types of sources. However, in Kenosha, church and informal community donation patterns accounted for larger percentages of organizations' budgets than in most cities in the United States. As a result, few Kenosha organizations had much surplus and many ran on budgets much lower than the executive director felt was needed to adequately fulfill the mission

Activities

This ethos of informal church and community organizations also influenced staffing and activity levels in all Kenosha organizations. Like voluntary church and grass-roots community activities, non-profit organizations with an anti-poverty or community of color focus were expected to provide holistic services through a small cadre of staff and volunteers. All of these organizations offered a package of services to meet the needs of their program participants which included basic necessities, counseling, work assistance, educational programs for children and other types of assistance felt important for these communities. While each of the organizations had a specific mission that focused their activities on one population, the holistic expectations pervaded each institution. In many ways, this expectation was a plus—these Kenosha organizations worked with families as whole units rather than focusing on problems in a fragmented way.

However, organization leaders also had to constantly resist expectations that they would provide every need for an individual and accept any kind of donation. Newer executive directors in several organizations reported shutting down food or clothing pantry operations. Another executive director showed me a basement full of broken computers and ragged clothing donated by community residents. While he appreciated community support, useless donations simply took up space in buildings already too small for their operations.

Staffing

Kenosha cultural expectations that social service agency workers were similar to church and grass-roots volunteer activists combined with the egalitarian and anti-intellectual ethos of the community to influence staffing patterns and wages. People in Kenosha presumed that non-profits should primarily function through volunteer efforts and donations. As a

result, all agencies struggled to fund needed professional staff. Every one of the organizations we observed was chronically understaffed. Key staff people fulfilled several functions. Several newer executive directors complained that they could not adequately perform their primary job functions of representing the agency in the community, fundraising and overseeing operations because they also had to perform direct service and clerical functions due to lack of staff. The same multi-tasking expectations were true of other full time staff in all of these agencies.

Non-profit sector salaries tend to be lower than in government organizations or the private sector. Kenosha non-profits paid less than similar agencies in other communities. They were also more likely to offer part-time wages and limited or no benefits. This meant that agency staff either had to rely on spouses with more lucrative jobs or get by on limited incomes. We found that key staff often stayed with the agency for long periods of time but had other sources of income. Some other agency jobs experienced constant turnover as staff lacking alternative financial support or less committed to the ethos of the organization sought family supporting work elsewhere. Staff were often expected to put in long hours much beyond normal working hours.

In keeping with Kenosha patterns of hiring through closed social capital networks, most front-line agency staff got their jobs through word of mouth referrals. For example, one woman recalled:

I had a friend who was a secretary working for [the agency] in Kenosha and we used to socialize on weekends. And one day she called me and said, "You know we have an opening, why don't you come and apply." It was a job placement something or other. I can't even remember. And I was so sick of factory work and so on and I went and I applied. And I really believe that it was because of her

recommendation, because they really liked her there, that I was able to get in and get that job.

This word of mouth referral system meant that front-line staff were likely to know their closed social capital communities well and provide appropriate services to their neighbors in need. On the other hand, these front-line staff may lack the professional training and demeanor to adequately fulfill their jobs. We found this tension among many front-line workers in Kenosha social service agencies.

Executive directors and upper level staff found their jobs through a combination of more general searches and word-of-mouth referrals through social capital networks. These individuals were more likely to have training and experience appropriate for their jobs. However, due to the understaffing, these individuals were also more likely to be spread too thin running to meetings and taking care of clerical duties, in addition to performing the primary duties in their job descriptions. Availability and quality of work sometimes suffered as a result. Others simply worked long hours and cheerfully focused on their commitment to the organization to perform their jobs well.

Volunteers

Each of these organizations relied heavily on volunteers to supplement paid staff functions. Most of these organizations had "working" boards where board members actively volunteered in either direct service or supplementary staff activities such as bookkeeping or fundraising development.

All of these organizations drew creatively on community volunteers through local social capital ties, the two colleges, churches and other informal service organizations. All of them used several formal volunteer systems through senior volunteers, W-2 community service workers, community service parolees and prisoner work-release programs (community service parolees are people who have either committed offenses like drunk driving or are on parole after sentencing for white-collar crimes like check fraud). We found volunteers from these programs doing clerical duties and performing janitorial work in every agency we observed.

Collaboration Among Agencies

Kenosha agencies worked together in many ways to fulfill community needs. We found strong social capital networks among most agencies in this community. Government also worked closely with non-profits through partnerships and contracting. Agencies felt that collaboration was necessary in order to meet community needs. We found many instances of agency workers calling another organization to help a program participant when the need was beyond their capability. For example, one long-term agency employee commented:

> We work a lot with the homeless shelter because of the services they have. We need their services. We work a lot with [another agency], very closely with town hall throughout the years. We work with [another minority based agency], with [their assistant director], very good friends. In the last few years
>
> [another citywide agency]....
> working with them very closely, referring people back and forth. I think, you should go to this other agency. You have to use all the resources. It just doesn't work like we need the help, they need the help.

This quote shows several factors typical of interaction among social service organizations in Kenosha. First, resources are shared in a partnership fashion. Organizations feel that they need to work together to meet community needs. Second, interactions occur mostly on an informal basis. While a number of

organizations had formal relationships through coalitions of agencies involved in one activity and some wrote joint proposals for funding, most of these formal relationships were cementing already existing informal connections. Third, like this employee going to another agency key staff person for assistance as "very good friends," most interactions were on an individual and personal basis. Staff at different agencies would call each other based on social capital trust developed through common activities, not as formal representatives of their particular agencies. Connections among individuals were based on personal social capital networks rather than institutional social capital.

At the same time, agencies involved in government-funded services did divide up activities based on who had what contracts and designated catchments areas for services. For example, anyone who needed energy assistance or housing was sent to the agency that offered those services. While both the homeless shelter and one Hispanic/Latino agency participated in the federal commodities program and Second Harvest food distribution systems, all Spanish-speaking people were sent to one Hispanic/Latino organization because it was designated as the agency to provide services to this population.

Goods and services also were shared between agencies. For example, when one organization got a food donation too large for their population from a local company, they sent some of the surplus commodities to another organization to distribute.

These examples of collaboration illustrate strong social capital networks among organizations and their staff. This came from well-developed networks among non-profits through a combination of coalitions established to address a specific need and long-established personal connections among agencies. Most of the organizations involved in helping with basic needs were part of an

"emergency services" network. Similar coalitions existed for at-risk youth activities and many other types of services. Personal networks and formal networks intertwined to encourage collaboration among area agencies.

Government Support for Non-profits

Government supported non-profits in Kenosha through both formal and informal mechanisms. Informal mechanisms included occasionally helping agencies find funds for programs as in the example with Grace above. More often, city government and business leaders helped key organization staff find private resources to fulfill a need. This involved citywide leaders using their social capital networks to help an organization. Organizations based in communities of color relied on strong social capital ties to these leaders through trusted bridging community representatives like Grace. African American and Hispanic/Latino based organizations that lacked these individual social capital ties seldom received this kind of social capital support.

Formal mechanisms included contracting for citywide services and formal volunteer programs like the W-2 and work release programs. While government services were let out for bid in a formal process, government also acknowledged their need to support services to many constituencies in the community. For example, if only one organization provided a service in the community, government contracts would not take the fee for service form common for government today. One administrator commented that in several cases:

> ...technically [it's] a contract relationship, but in reality it is a grant. I mean it is administered as a contract, but it is not a unit of service based contract, it is a flat amount that we give them each
>
> year.... just for general

programming uses. Because we know that that's a very basic needs service.

While government was careful to offer all contracts to bid and supported agencies based on performance, they simultaneously included minority community organizations in contracting for citywide services. Some politicians acknowledged that this support was one way to provide government funding to communities of color. For example, one community leader acknowledged that one weak organization continued to get government funds: "Because there was a recognized problem in the community, no one was willing to step in and ask for strict accountability. No politician was willing to be accused of being a racist."

This comment shows two related elements. Citywide politicians look for ways to support organizations in marginalized communities through the regular contracting process whenever possible. This showed a consciousness about needing to spread city resources among closed social capital communities in keeping with Kenosha's wide spread ethos of supporting people within its community on an equal basis. At the same time, community leaders recognized the potential for discrimination based on closed social capital and racism. In this case, they continued to fund an organization even though they had doubts about its ability to perform well due to fears of being labeled racist.

This sense of responsibility to communities of color existed simultaneously with widespread beliefs that organizations should be judged on formal criteria rather than as representatives of a particular group. Despite cautiousness about pulling funding from administratively weak organizations identified with communities of color, recent Kenosha history reveals several instances where minority community non-profits lost key contracts and United Way dollars

due to citywide concerns regarding mismanagement. In both cases, Kenosha leaders quickly stepped in to rescue the floundering organizations. Strategies to save these organizations will be described later in this section.

Every city leader interviewed for this project stressed that organizations got contracts because they provided the best services to the most people. Each of these leaders thought that an organization that served mostly African American, Hispanic/Latino people, or both was as much a provider for these populations as organizations identified with these communities of color.

For example, during the study period, we witnessed a community-wide dispute regarding contracts for Community Development Block Grant (CDBG) funds. Unlike many communities where CDBG funds are earmarked for housing, Kenosha gives out CDBG monies for a wide array of community programs. That year, large contracts were given to several citywide organizations while none were given to organizations based in communities of color. Representatives from the African American- and Hispanic/Latino-based organizations cried racism. However, community politicians uniformly denied this charge saying that they simply gave out funds to organizations that had the best records and submitted the best proposals. The fact that the CDBG committee chair was African American also did not help the organizations' assertions of racism in grant decisions. Since the organizations that received contracts served large numbers of African Americans and Hispanic/Latinos, city leaders felt they were providing for these two communities. They simply could not see organizations as "belonging" to one community or another. Relying on Kenosha understandings of individuality and formal criteria to make decisions, leaders could not understand how minority communities thought of themselves as groups represented by specific organizations.

While, on the surface, privileging funding to citywide organizations did not represent individualistic prejudice against organizations based in communities of color, the way that proposals were evaluated did reflect structural inequality in this community. Decision makers relied on their own social capital understandings of these organizations. Organizations with a record of good service and where decision makers had personal knowledge of the quality of the organization's service received more support than organizations that had weak social capital ties to funding sources. The resources available to various organizations throughout Kenosha influenced many of the criteria used to make decisions such as the presentation of proposals, units of service and so forth.

This project found significant differences between the citywide organizations that we studied and those based in the African American and Hispanic/Latino community. I next compare these organizations on key criteria.

Comparisons between Citywide Organizations and Organizations Based in Communities of Color

The *Kenosha Social Capital Study* found that social and cultural capital issues profoundly affected the nature of the operations in these two types of organizations. Issues related to funding, staffing, provision of services and relationships to the Kenosha power structure all differed between the citywide organizations and those based in communities of color. Each factor is described next.

Funding and Community Connections

Kenosha expects its organizations to obtain the majority of funding from their constituent communities. Citywide organizations had better access to individuals, businesses and city leaders with resources to support

75

their organizations. African American and Hispanic/Latino based organizations needed to either bridge into mainstream social capital resources or find funding and in-kind supports from within their communities. Since their communities generally included fewer people of means and fewer professionals to provide in-kind services, most of these organizations had less financial and in-kind support than their citywide counterparts.

76

As with Grace developing strong relationships with Kenosha power brokers, some community organizations actively created these links. Another key staff person describes gathering in-kind resources in the same way:

> When you start working in one area, you start first step, like a baby step, that step was good or it was not good and you follow that. So since I been here so many years, since I worked here I knew so many people [that] I knew who to ask because one time or another I had to ask for something. We found very good people, a lot of very good attorneys on our committees and doctors who were very sensitive to our needs. You can share with them your needs. A doctor is not an attorney but he knows someone, you have to know your resources.

African American and Hispanic/Latino organizations practicing closed social capital lacked these kinds of relationships. Partly this was due to informal practices characteristic of Kenosha culture. Meeting times were communicated through word of mouth exclusively within the closed community, mainstream community leaders were not invited to regular organization events, and leaders did not establish social ties with mainstream power brokers.

Instead, African American and Hispanic/Latino organization leaders would only interact with the mainstream when they needed money or there was a community crisis.

Community power brokers were less likely to support people they saw only in confrontational or crisis situations. Often, organization leaders approached the mainstream using racialized language asserting discrimination or using identity politics strategies of claiming authority to speak for their community. This form of racial performance is common in the United States. Whites, particularly in a working-class community claiming an egalitarian ethos, often look askance at any accusation of racism or expectation of racial authority based on their own history of inter-group relations.[24] For example, I first met Grace at an event where I presented my research on welfare reform. I had prefaced my talk by saying that the research had been done while I was a non-profit administrator developing welfare reform programs for a multi-cultural community. Despite this, Grace loudly accused me of being an academic who did not understand the community. Others in the room quickly came to my rescue, assuming I needed to be protected from "rude" behavior. When I called her up the next day to talk about this, she told me not to worry, she understood who I was and had made that statement because "I felt

you could take it." People like Grace could play both sides of the racial divide because they established bridging social capital ties into mainstream networks and also partially adhered to Kenosha majority cultural practices. Other African American and Hispanic/Latino leaders failed to develop these connections and social skills. Mainstream whites often resented these closed community leaders.

Staffing, Volunteers and Ability to Provide Services

Limited resources meant less staff and lower wages for paid staff. While all Kenosha organizations were under-staffed, we saw much more multi-tasking, due to under-funding, at the organizations based in communities of color. Every executive director performed direct service. All staff had several jobs and constantly had to choose between offering direct service and attending coalition meetings essential to garner resources to carry out direct service functions. The quality of proposals, planning and direct service all suffered as a result. Citywide organizations were able to successfully beat out these smaller minority-based organizations, in part, because they could afford to use staff in more effective ways.

Organizations based in communities of color also used formal volunteers differently than citywide organizations. While all organizations used people from W-2, Court Community Service, and Senior Citizen Volunteer programs in support staff functions, African American and Hispanic/Latino community-based organizations were more likely to use these people in visible clerical or direct service activities. In some cases, using formal volunteers in this way had a strong positive effect on service provided through the organization and offered a second chance to people in need that they might otherwise not have received.

For example, a number of counselors and support staff were drawn from the senior volunteer pool of older residents who had worked in low-wage jobs for most of their lives. The senior volunteer program supplemented social security payments for low-income seniors. These individuals knew their communities well and were able to offer appropriate individualized service as well as create a sense of warmth and care that helped the organization provide quality service on a low budget.

In other cases, African American and Hispanic/Latino leaders used community service placement volunteers in direct service or key clerical positions. This tendency came from a combination of a real need for extra staff and an ethos of looking beyond the rigid rules of the community when judging people. Some organizations used W-2 community service workers in direct service positions, hiring those who performed well on the job when funds became available. Others used community service parolees in the same way. For example, our fieldworker in one organization reported her agency placed a community service parolee intern into a direct service position. As in several other instances, this individual was eventually offered a job in the agency.

On his first day at the agency, she reported that:

> We also had a new helper today, his name is Matthew. He came here through a program set up through probation and parole. He is an ex-convict, on parole and he will be working here part-time in order to receive two years of college tuition. This is an incentive program through probation and parole, but I also know that not many of the parolees take advantage of it. They have to be on parole, that means coming out of jail or prison and they have the choice of either doing
> full-time for three months or part-time for six months. Matthew is doing part-time for six months because he works another full-time job. This is volunteer work, so they do not get paid; they get tuition for college or technical school. Matthew is in his early twenties, white and from the lower class. He worked very well with the kids and seemed to really enjoy himself playing with the kids.

While using formal volunteers in direct service positions provides a creative way to supplement staff and offers a second chance to deserving individuals in need, sometimes the need for people to fill staff functions overrode the ability to offer quality service. People hired because they had a connection to the agency rather than credentials or experience needed for the job may offer limited service simply because they lack expertise. Low-paid agencies are less likely to offer these employees the time or financial incentives to gather additional education in direct service fields.

More importantly, the quality of service may suffer if a revolving group of volunteers fulfills key functions. For example, one organization used probation community service and W-2 community service workers to answer the phone. These people often did not know the staff and services well enough to serve as the first contact for the agency. Sometimes, they did not

have the communication skills to answer phones. Decisions to use volunteers in this way ultimately hurt the agency as both citywide professionals and potential clients found it difficult to get messages through to appropriate people.

Taken together, staffing strategies both maintained these organizations' place as resources for their local communities and hindered their ability to perform their missions adequately. Other aspects of staffing decisions characteristic of these organizations based in communities of color also influenced the nature of administration in the organization. I next look at this difference between the two types of organizations.

Criteria for "Good" Administration

Understaffing combined with closed social capital expectations of "good" service further influenced who was hired by an organization in the African American and Hispanic/Latino communities and how they provided service. Citywide organizations made executive director and key staff hiring decisions primarily based on objective ability to perform a job. While community contacts helped people find work in these agencies, education and related work experience were equally important. As a result, managers and key staff knew how to oversee administrative functions essential for non-profit credibility. They also knew how to write proposals, plan and work with city leaders.

While citywide organization key staff still carried out multiple functions due to understaffing, their boards rarely expected them to perform direct service. Boards followed hierarchical organizational practices, presuming that managers mostly managed while staff provided direct service.

Opposite tendencies were foremost in the African American- and Hispanic/Latino-based organizations. Here, agencies often sought staff with

78

administrative experience, but had to resist community expectations that everyone in the agency should provide direct service like the church mission workers they were familiar with. For example, one person said that her favorite candidate for an executive director job came first because:

I like him a lot because he worked with the [organization] for years. He was very nice. He did his job and when there were emergencies, he always listens and cares. He didn't hesitate, when he found information about a family, he didn't say it's not my job. He cared, if could help, he did. He had a good rapport with the families and the kids. I think he would have done a very good job.

The result of years of hiring choices based on an ethos of direct service rather than administrative capacity, combined with expectations that managers would spend much time providing service, meant that administrative records received less attention than they should in some of the minority-based agencies. Government officials reported sloppy record keeping in many of these agencies. Citywide power brokers lost patience and trust after years of inattention to accountability issues. This led to crises in these organizations just before the study began. Others relied on key staff to do all of the record keeping in the agency on top of direct service and their managerial duties. Records were kept properly, but at the expense of other activities.

While most minority-based organization boards today looked for people with management qualifications, they still expected executive directors to be the lead direct service provider in addition to being the manager. In one case, an executive director quit after a mixed review from the board because she was not eager to offer direct service. The next executive director hired by the agency had direct service expectations as part of his contract. These mixed

expectations limit the ability of organizations to fulfill their missions and build the social capital relationships and trust with funders and the community that are needed to help the organization thrive.

Insider/Outsider Issues

Kenosha's emphasis on closed social capital also influenced the ability of staff to serve various sub-communities. We saw several differences in staffing patterns between citywide organizations and those based in communities of color. Citywide agencies tended to hire people from within their closed social capital networks. This meant that most staff was white, stable working and middle class. Sometimes these staff viewed participants from low-skilled worker families or communities of color as different from themselves in ways that portrayed these individuals as "undeserving" poor in need of re-socialization.

For example, one fieldworker was completing a degree in early childhood education and, as a parent herself, had experience in judging parenting capabilities and their affects on children. Staff constantly told her in her agency that the clients lacked basic parenting skills. But she noted good interaction between parent and children and appropriate level child development.

Even when these staff expectations were not voiced, program participants felt this hidden disdain. For example, one program participant reported that white staff treated her "like I was four [years old]." More importantly, sometimes these expectations influenced the way that staff behaved toward their clients. For instance, in one agency a person working with children expected quiet, calm, speak-when-you-are-spoken-to behavior from children. A curious African American child was viewed as disruptive and severely punished, causing a traumatic experience for that child. The staff person justified her actions based on presumptions that

children in the program did not know how to behave properly and needed to be re-socialized.

Other white staff did everything they could to help the families in their agency succeed. For example, Mary, a mainstream social service agency white case worker, served both as a mediator when problems occurred in her own agency as well as going out of her way to help a person of color in need. In several cases, she interceded to make sure that agency participants were treated fairly by other staff. She spent much time talking with Kenosha County Job Center staff and other organizations to make sure that the people she worked with got special care or services that they needed. In one case, Mary called another mainstream agency to connect a client, who had particular trouble adjusting to Kenosha, to a youth program for her children. She also suggested schools where the children would be well-treated. In other cases, white caseworkers would serve as advocates for people of color both in their agency and through citywide initiatives. Sometimes these people recognized their own limitations of crossing boundaries. Sometimes white staff called staff from organizations based in the appropriate community of color to help when a citywide organization staff person could not solve a particular problem. In still other cases, program participants were treated as equals in need and offered many different kinds of support.

Organizations based in communities of color, on the other hand, tended to hire from within those communities. Staff had the advantage of knowing the communities they worked in first hand. For example, a staff person found out about a problem in a program participant's family by running into the participant on the street. This informal support bolstered staff ability to appropriately help their program participants.

On the other hand, staff in organizations based in communities of color faced an extra measure of suspicion from various closed social capital networks within those communities. Staff with college educations were sometimes treated as outsiders even though they grew up in these communities. Staff who came from outside of Kenosha's African American and Hispanic/Latino communities, even though they came from the same racial or national background, were treated with suspicion until they developed strong links in that community. Outsiders were often hampered by closed social capital practices that did not share information outside of the network. Several people who left positions in these agencies commented that they felt that they could not carry out their jobs because of mistrust from established Kenosha residents in these communities.

Conclusion

The affect of insider/outsider issues on program participant perceptions of direct service will be discussed in the next section. Taken together, these differences between citywide organizations and organizations based in communities of color led to very different perceptions of these organizations in Kenosha. Citywide power brokers with social capital available to support agencies often justifiably viewed African American and Hispanic/Latino community organizations as weak and not offering documentation for support. Part of this came from objective criteria such as record keeping or number of people served. These factors were influenced by the cultural and social capital differences described above.

At the same time, this perception of weak organizations came from lack of visibility for these organizations and their constituent communities in citywide social capital networks. As the city power broker quoted in the section *Understanding Social Capital* observed, decision makers often are leery to believe these agencies' reports

because they have no direct knowledge of their activities.

Often, non-profit organization analysts attribute poor organization performance to weak boards. This is not the case in Kenosha. In fact, we found overlapping board memberships including some of the same competent power brokers in the city on most Kenosha social service organizations we studied. All of these boards were racially integrated. In several cases, we found strong boards working actively for their communities that lacked the social capital resources to easily realize their missions. In other cases, boards consisted of people with access to citywide social resources who were on several boards. Torn between multiple obligations, these individuals were more likely to put their energies into fundraising and governance for the organizations they perceived as providing more consistent service. They remained on community of color organization boards because they felt an obligation to community self-support despite misgivings about the direction of the organization. As a result, they did little to help the weak organizations improve. This continued limited performance of these weak organizations became a self-fulfilling prophecy as under-funded organizations struggled to meet their mission.

Citywide power brokers supported organizations in communities of color through contracts to provide services to everyone in Kenosha. These contracts had two opposite effects on these organizations. On the one hand, contracts brought needed funds into these organizations. Since people in the communities of color needed these services, organizations were also helped to fulfill their missions in this way. On the other hand, since much of the funding for these organizations came from Kenosha-wide contracts, agencies already pulled in several directions found more and more of their resources focused on activities outside of their core mission.

Community-wide support sometimes limited their ability to serve their closed social capital networks. In an effort to offer bridging social capital, citywide power brokers created tensions in these minority community-focused institutions that were not easily resolved.

Citywide solutions to crisis in these organizations also reflected efforts to broaden social capital through connections to mainstream networks. In one instance, the United Way and other city power brokers preserved the autonomy of the organization, but insisted that they diversify their board to include people beyond the closed social capital networks that had previously governed the agency. At one point, these citywide agents suggested an executive director candidate. They have also supported agency actions to hire key management positions from outside of this particular community. As a result, the agency is developing rapidly in a manner appreciated throughout the city. However, this has changed the culture within the agency.

In another case, a struggling agency merged with a strong, citywide organization. This case may be the best of both worlds because the hosting agency maintained staff from the community-based organization. This entity had both strong social capital ties throughout Kenosha and equally strong ties within the community of color.

Other organizations associated with communities of color continue to struggle to maintain their mission activity and build bridges to the larger Kenosha community. The next section discusses the way that program participants interact with organizations. These organizational structure and dynamics issues play a role in providing service. Additional factors discussed in the next section also influence program provision and participant satisfaction.

Implications for Policy and Programs

- *Nonprofit funding levels in Kenosha are too low to ensure adequate staffing, salaries and other tools to meet agency missions.* Nonprofits become one employment source for workers, particularly in the African American and Hispanic/Latino communities. All agencies suffered from limited staffing of programs due to insufficient funds. In order to adequately serve its community, funding and salary levels for small Kenosha non-profits need to rise to levels common in similar organizations elsewhere. Given generous community support already, additional resources may need to come from outside Kenosha.

- *Citywide contracts need to be better integrated into mission-based service provision in order to better fulfill agency mission and build bridging social capital.* Citywide services sometimes stretch the mission of the organization as well as its limited staff resources. Boards and staff at these organizations need to develop stronger mechanisms to link these programs to the core programs for the agency.

- *Organizations based in communities of color need to develop mechanisms to bring mainstream stakeholders into the agency to become more familiar with activities.* African American and Hispanic/Latino organizations sometimes lose out on citywide funds because key decision makers do not have direct knowledge of their activities. Mechanisms like placing these individuals on boards, inviting them to view activities and regular conversations can better develop these links.

- *Agency heads need to develop strong personal social capital connections throughout Kenosha.* Bridging individuals were able to obtain resources for their agencies because they participated in citywide activities and made a practice of cultivating trusting relationships with politicians, businessmen and others throughout Kenosha. Newer key agency staff need to develop similar relationships in order for their agencies to thrive.

- *Frontline contacts like receptionists need to be paid staff with strong knowledge of agency programs and good communication skills.* Often agencies lose out on both funding and use of service because the person managing communications is a constantly revolving volunteer. While considered expendable by many agencies, front-line communication staff are often key agency representatives.

80

Social Service Agency Use and Social Capital

found that under-staffing did impact on service provision in agencies. For example, one woman compared a youth agency that her son attended to a similar organization in other communities where she had lived, noting:

I don't think they had enough activities for a thirteen or fourteen year old. Other than the open gym, they don't have enough organized activities for the teenagers. I've been in there a couple of times after getting off work and there's just nothing for them to do there. There's video games, there's pool tables, the TV, the videos. But as far as having some arts and crafts, something the kids could be interested in doing. I don't know if they're understaffed or they don't have good planning or they don't have a good recreation director.

Analysis of non-profit agencies providing services to the needy or to communities of color revealed a mixed picture. On the one hand, agencies received strong support from their community and worked together well. On the other hand, Kenosha organizations suffered from chronic underfunding typical of small non-profit organizations that was exacerbated by Kenosha's understanding of non-profits as charity for the deserving poor. The resources available to each institution depended on the resources of the social networks it was tied to. While citywide power brokers were concerned about caring for African Americans and Hispanic/Latinos, they judged these organizations by their ability to obtain resources from the wider community and create strong social capital ties throughout Kenosha. This section first explores the impact of these organizational dynamics on the

services provided by community organizations.

Kenosha organizations consisted of two types: mainstream organizations serving predominantly communities of color with primarily white staff, and organizations based in communities of color that served a mix of Kenosha residents due to the fact that they had contracts to provide fundamental services to the entire Kenosha community. After outlining the effects of organizational structures on services, this section compares service in the two types of institutions.

Kenosha Organizational Structure and Service Provision

Understaffing and Service Patterns

While many people reported getting good service from the Kenosha non-profits that we worked with, we

This particular agency turned out to offer mixed quality services depending on funding and the quality of the individual staff person. We witnessed a number of high quality programs which provided opportunities not otherwise available to children in this community. However, due to low wages and under-staffing, some parents' expectations were not being met.

Other people observed that they had to wait a long time to get services or could not reach the staff person they needed to find. For example, one person tried to obtain a specialized service, only to have the appointment time reset over and over because staff would be pulled away for other emergencies. She reported:

I called about five times and it was later, later, tomorrow and so on. I could never find somebody to help me for the time at which I had the

appointment. I think it also depends on who it is. They tend to help people who are there all the time. They are there, they drop in, and so on. Those of us who have needs only occasionally and go only occasionally, have problems finding people to help us when we need it.

82

This observation shows that Kenosha social service organizations also follow Kenosha culture patterns of working with people as they appear, not according to appointments. This example also illustrates a tendency for some organizations to provide better service to people who are known to them. This pattern is similar to preference in employment to known individuals. As a result, people needing help would identify a helpful staff person and rely on them to provide access to a variety of services.

However, we equally found organizations that would go out of their way to help someone that they had never met before. Staff would use their contacts to gain service throughout the city. In this way, Kenosha social service agency staff became the social capital conduit between people who lacked jobs, goods and services, and those who could fulfill that particular need.

Collaboration Across Social Service Agencies

Analysis of agencies revealed strong collaboration among agencies primarily based on individual social capital ties. These connections proved helpful for program participants. For example, the homeless shelter gave their residents the tools that they needed to find housing, financial assistance through the job center, schools and work. However, they initially expected their clients to use these tools to find these basic necessities on their own in order to encourage self-sufficiency. In some cases, Kenosha's mistrust of outsiders and resistance to providing to people perceived as the undeserving poor, like an African American welfare recipient from Illinois, meant that shelter

residents had trouble finding housing. For example, Marisha spent several weeks filling out referred housing applications with no response. Shelter staff had connected her to another agency connected to the community of color to provide youth services to her children. The second caseworker at the community-based organization called a landlord she knew who promptly offered Marisha an apartment. Local landlords were not willing to take a chance on an unknown person, but immediately offered assistance when a known caseworker used her social capital resources in support of this outsider.

We saw many examples of collaboration among agency staff to meet a need for a particular client. Schoolteachers and counselors referred children to youth programs they felt would be helpful to them. Like the agency staff person quoted in the last section who called another agency to find goods for her client, caseworkers knew which agencies had contracts for which services and who might have a better connection for furniture or other basic needs.

Usually, this involved a combination of direct referrals to other agencies and, if program participants had trouble navigating the communication practices at the other agency, caseworkers stepping in to ensure that their program participant received the requested service. This two-step process became necessary when the front line staff at the second organization did not relay messages to the requested caseworker due to limited time and training. Sometimes a new applicant to an agency had trouble accessing service because they did not fit into the social and cultural capital community of front-line agency staff. The front-line gatekeeper ignored newcomers or treated them badly because they were different.

The result of Kenosha's collaboration patterns is that successful agency caseworkers developed strong ties in a number of organizations and learned

to help their program participants navigate through their networks to gain the services they needed. This informal aspect of Kenosha organizations also influenced the ways that program participants used organizations. I examine this aspect of organizations next.

Ways that People in Need Access Services

People accessed services at a particular agency in Kenosha for two reasons: 1) that agency was the only one providing the service, or 2) they had heard through closed social capital networks that an agency worker provided good service. As with employment and other aspects of Kenosha life, information was spread largely through word of mouth referrals. Social capital provided most of the information that people needed in order to find services. Within communities needing particular services, there was little need to advertise because people told others in their social capital network where to go and what they would need to obtain service.

We saw this kind of social capital at work in many ways. For example, a homeless woman in Illinois knew about the Kenosha homeless shelter because a friend had found out about it from a relative who lived in Kenosha. Hispanic/Latino women found out about prenatal care in the same way.

People coming to an agency to obtain a specific service often simply came to achieve their goal and left. For example, student fieldworkers kept a daily log of who came to the agencies where they interned as part of their observation research. In the organizations based in communities of color, an average day saw two-thirds or more of the traffic into the agency consisting of people coming to receive services such as energy assistance or work permits. Traffic flow into the agency depended on the annual or monthly cycle of service provision. For example, people may come to the agency for energy assistance during the intake period for that service, and for commodities on the days when the food pantry usually gave out these goods. People using the agencies for these services would wait their turn, present the required documen receive the service and leave.

We rarely witnessed people coming into an agency for these spe services asking about other programs offered by that ager This observation implies that, while government contracts to provide citywide servic brought money and people into these small community-based agencies, these activities did little to expand the number of people who used other programs or enhan bridging social capital among closed communities.
Without trust between participant and agency, transactions simply involved a trip to unknown territory to process paperwork. Kenosha residents tolerated the need to go to these organizations because they had no other choice. However, they sought services for other, more personal needs like youth development programs, or for assistance finding housing or work from agencies that they trusted because they had a good reputation in their closed social capital community.

The bulk of program participants using core program services or caseworkers at both mainstream and community of color-based organizations came to that organization through a direct referral. This referral either could be from a friend or family member or another agency caseworker. After-school enrichment programs tended to be filled with children drawn from a few networks of extended family, neighbors and friends. Low-skilled workers needing basic necessities would go to an agency known to help others in their community and ask for the same

staff person who had helped their friends and relatives in the past.

This pattern shows that closed community patterns extended to nonprofit organization use. People in need would first turn to their churches and then to organizations with a reputation for supporting people in their social capital networks. Organizations needed to establish trusting relationships in the same way as individuals. For people of color, this often meant going to a trusted staff person at one of the organizations based in communities of color.

Results of Service: Comparisons Across Types of Agencies

Closed communities and closed social capital do not simply come from minority communities isolating themselves. These patterns arise from subtle processes in the wider community that tell people of color that they are not respected by people in another class or racial group. For example, another fieldworker, a woman who was a participant at this particular

mainstream organization, reported a conversation with a white patron of her organization. The organization leader cordially answered her questions, but spent the entire interview watching a sports event on the television placed on a shelf behind the chair where the fieldworker was sitting. We interpreted this double message as indicating that people of color did not have the same trusted status as whites associated with this organization. These kinds of subtle messages led to patterns like people coming into an agency to receive services and leaving as soon as they had achieved their goal.

In another example, one fieldworker in a mainstream organization reported that the direct service worker offered an

array of services to clients, but presented advice in a rigid and patronizing manner. While offering help, the worker maintained a boundary through her manner that suggested that the clients were objects to serve, not neighbors in need. No social capital connections or trust were offered or built through this transaction. The program participants patiently accepted the service, but did not try to bridge the gap between provider and individual.

After years of subtle messages, people of color using these mainstream organizations found that it became best to pretend to be passive and unintelligent, saving individuality for activities within the trusted, closed community. This same suspiciousness of outsiders was extended to other organizations serving different parts of the same community of color or another minority community. For example, we found that different groups of children used the array of youth programs we witnessed in this research project with similar successful results. Parents chose a particular agency because someone they knew said it was a good program. They were unwilling to venture outside their network of known people and organizations to try something different.

This tendency influenced the ability of organizations to attract program participants as well as the kinds of services that program participants received. If people only went to organizations tied to their closed social capital community, organizations based in those communities had little success garnering participants through wider advertising. The only way to expand the participant base involved developing networks with staff people at different sending organizations. Developing bridges, in turn, depended on the limited time and available social capital networks of agency staff.

Since different agency staff also came from closed social capital networks, ability to build bridges varied enormously among agencies. Often, this heavy reliance by both program participants and staff on closed social capital networks leads to cementing existing inequalities and divisions within the community. For example, we found that a small group of elderly residents participated in one senior program. They were likely to send their children and grandchildren to the youth program at that same agency. Most children came from the same schools. As a result, they developed social and cultural capital that would later influence their education and career choices. This recreated the class system as young people without ties to people in other networks followed the same patterns as their friends and family before them.

The tendency for organizations to provide help, but not always a step up, varied based on several factors. The first factor involved the relationship between staff and program participants. In most cases, we found that people of color in need seldom developed strong egalitarian relationships with mainstream white agency staff because those staff held

subtle beliefs that program participants were culturally different from themselves. This led to advice that helped people resolve the presenting problem, but did not build bridges into a new way of life because that kind of support was not offered. Like teachers who believe that a child does not qualify for an advanced placement program because he "does not communicate well" even though the student has "straight As," these subtle boundaries remind program participants to trust each other rather than staff. Program participants take what they need from these programs and focus their energies elsewhere.

On the other hand, agency staff that see program participants as potential equals and promote their development can make a real difference in the lives of the people they serve. For example, Janice, the young woman from a welfare-dependent family described in *Understanding Social Capital*, drew support from helpful counselors at both mainstream organizations and organizations based in communities of color. She reported:

I was quite young, that was middle school age when I got involved in [an African American based organization]. I got involved in that was through being at [a neighborhood-based after-school program at another African American community-based Organization] I know that my mother volunteered there somewhat. You know how they have adult classes and that was part of what she had to do [for welfare]. I was there, getting involved in the after school things, the little drill teams, the after school outings that they had.

I would say it helped me with some positive development as a child. It helped me be focused and be out of trouble, not wander around aimlessly doing some things. I know some of my friends got into [trouble]. It helped me have structured time outside the home and outside the school. It helped me in those aspects.

Some positive structured time. And again, building in my self-confidence, my self-esteem, especially the dance teams that we did performed publicly, that was a good experience for that.

[At the second organization], we had our young membership, this young coalition group going on and we met twice a month or once a month. We talked about different issues going on in our community and in school. It just gave us a chance to get together and there were times we got together with a little group from Racine and it gave us a chance to network and meet other young people. Talk about our different experiences and share. We talked about future goals; the what would you like to be when you grow up? We learned some history about each organization, which was like at the time, cool.

This positive experience with the African American based organization, combined with efforts by school counselors in the African American multi-cultural programs, encouraged Janice to change direction and go to college. If she had only attended the neighborhood-based after-school program and had not had additional encouragement to join the second organization, she may have developed discipline, self-esteem and stayed out of trouble as a young person, but she may not have built bridges into other social worlds. Other people who only attended the after-school programs at agencies like this one remained in low-skilled worker communities and are still in the marginalized working class today. This extra measure by supportive staff to build bridges rather than maintain good behavior within the closed social capital network through supportive staff makes a major difference for program participants.

The second factor involved the culture and closed social capital networks bringing program participants to the agency. Notice that Janice only got involved in the neighborhood based non-profit organization because her mother went there for classes. In Kenosha, people are often limited by these closed social capital ties. If her mother had not learned about the youth programs through positive involvement in the agency, Janice may not have had the opportunities she found through these social service agencies.

The third factor involves the social and cultural capital networks developed within programs among agency participants. For example, while observing at one anti-poverty program, our fieldworker found that the program participants had developed a close network that continued after participants finished the program. These participants worked together to find childcare and housing, and to fulfill other basic and social needs. While these networks provided important support for these individuals, they also limited the ability of network members to seek additional outside supports. Since all of these people were low-skilled workers returning to low-skilled jobs, they did not develop either networks or skills to move beyond their current social and economic status.

Organizations based in communities of color and mainstream organizations often have different social and cultural capital related gifts to offer people in their programs. While mainstream agency staff often did little to create bridges across class and race boundaries, sometimes these organizations offered important social and cultural capital support that changed the lives of program participants. While staff at organizations based in communities of color were more likely to offer holistic services to program participants with an egalitarian ethos, these organizations did not always have the social capital ties themselves to build bridges into other communities.

If the goals of social service are to support families through services in keeping with their current closed social and cultural capital networks,

both types of non-profit organizations in Kenosha achieve this goal quite well, though sometimes in different ways. Both organizations and participants relied on their established closed social capital networks to achieve these goals.

If non-profits also intend to foster bridging social capital, the extra ingredient of social trust between program participant and staff needs to exist in order to make links into different worlds. In many cases, people of color from the same communities as program participants, but who worked in mainstream organizations, provided the important link between closed social capital communities and other opportunities. Since Kenosha was only beginning to hire people of color in professional social service positions, and most African American and Hispanic/Latino professionals came from outside Kenosha, common communities usually developed outside of the social service agency context. In many cases, churches provided that additional source for community. The next section examines the role of churches in developing both closed and bridging social capital.

Implications for Policy and Programs

- *Making concrete connections between citywide services and core agency services is an important way to build agency use and create bridging social capital.* Given that people using non-profits for citywide services do not pay attention to other services offered by the organization, staff should pay special attention to introducing these people to other agency programs. Since this is best done through social capital networks of participants, introducing people who use the agency in a casual way to people in core programs may achieve this goal.

- *Enhancing the circle of care throughout the community and building bridging social capital through mentoring.* Many people receive strong social supports through agency staff they trust who connect them to goods and services in related organizations. Strengthening this process by drawing on successful people within the community to work more closely with program participants may achieve this goal. Agency board members and church volunteers are important resources in this process.

85

Churches and Social Capital

86

Policy makers and some researchers think of churches as an alternative form of support for families. Some policy makers think that churches can do a better job of providing for poor families than either government or non-profit organizations. These people think that churches have social capital that government and non-profit organizations lack. Others see churches as teaching appropriate values. These people see churches as purveyors of cultural capital. This section looks closely at the role of Kenosha's African American and Hispanic/Latino churches in the lives of African Americans and Hispanic/Latinos in this community. The ways that communities support their churches is also discussed.

Kenosha Churches Serving the African American and Hispanic/Latino Communities

The *Kenosha Social Capital Study* identified several African American churches (two Baptist, one AME congregation, and several independent churches), several Protestant Hispanic/Latino churches, and a Catholic Hispanic/Latino congregation hosted by a white parish but which maintains a separate social support and committee structure within the host congregation. Two of these churches had mission projects to their local communities attached to them.

Faith communities for African Americans and Hispanic/Latinos developed differently. In the African American community, people drew on their established church traditions to first develop Baptist and AME congregations. In addition to these

formal denominational churches, Kenosha's African American community also includes several larger Pentecostal churches and a few small storefront churches. One of the Pentecostal churches runs a thrift shop, the only formally recognized spin-off organization directly related to the churches. Most of the Pentecostal churches tend to serve the most marginalized parts of the Kenosha African American population.

People flow between these various churches. In several instances, we found families where one spouse belonged to one of the Baptist churches while another belonged to the AME or another Baptist congregation. The same was true within generations. Family members would switch between churches based on current preferences. We found less movement between the Pentecostal congregations and the traditional denominational churches. Barriers related primarily to class rather than religious orientation. This was particularly true for one Pentecostal church, where many of the members consisted of the children of welfare-dependent families or low-wage workers. Several social service agency workers described how these children would get themselves dressed and go down to this particular church. Religion became a self-motivator for these children, providing them with a variety of social, material and spiritual supports. Despite the class boundaries between the Pentecostal churches and the mainstream denominations, the pastors worked together and social service workers who belonged to either the Baptist or AME congregations were very familiar with the Pentecostal churches and their members.

Most people in the Hispanic/Latino community are Catholic, though a number of established residents describe themselves as "Catholic by tradition." The Catholic Hispanic/Latino congregation started as a mission to the migrant workers. Until Hispanic/Latinos started settling in Kenosha in large numbers, priests came to the farms to celebrate Mass.

As the population moved into the city of Kenosha and neighboring Racine, the Hispanic/Latino Mass moved into established community Catholic churches. In Kenosha, the Hispanic/Latino Mass was first hosted by a parish near where most newcomers lived. However, about five years prior to this research project, the original host church requested that the congregation be moved elsewhere.

Another church with a liberal priest friendly to a Hispanic/Latino mission, but outside of the population center, became the congregation's new home. However, the established white population still sees the Hispanic/Latinos as simply using their space. There is little interaction between the two congregations, and the Hispanic/Latino congregation maintains a separate parish council and Sunday school in the guise of the advisory committee to a social welfare organization for new Hispanic/Latinos also hosted by the parish. The current priest commented that "you could cut the umbilical cord between the [social service agency advisory] committee and the established congregation and have a fully functional parish council."

As established Hispanic/Latinos became acculturated, a number have joined Catholic parishes in their neighborhoods. Several Protestant Hispanic/Latino congregations also exist, drawing primarily from already Protestant migrants. The Hispanic/Latino Mass largely serves newcomers from Mexico, but the church officers and choir consist primarily of more established families.

The Catholic Church developed social mission activities to their Hispanic/

Latino parishioners in a separate center that offers transitional services and translation to Hispanic/Latinos in need. To a large degree, the church mission center provides a lay employee to perform social support activities started by the first priest who served the migrant parish. For example, families reported that this priest would help them find jobs and housing. The Center employee performs the same work today. The center is funded by contributions from all of Kenosha's Catholic parishes and is overseen by the parish church committee mentioned above.

The relationship between church and social service activities in the African American community appears more tenuous on the surface. With the exception of the one church mission activity, none of the churches offers a formally constituted social welfare organization. However, churches actively offer a number of informal activities and the staff of many of the social service organizations come from various churches. As discussed in the next section, churches provide training and, more importantly, faith-based understandings of social welfare activities for its members regardless of where they carry out their work. This pattern blurs the distinction between social welfare service through congregations and that provided by organizations.

The majority of Kenosha African American- and Hispanic/Latino-based churches practice closed social capital patterns in recruiting members and carrying out their activities. Following Kenosha culture patterns, information is not published in ways readily available to outsiders. Members are recruited primarily through word-of-mouth referrals and information about services and benefits are given out within the community through individual contacts.

For people connected to these communities, closed social capital practices work well in offering

information about church resources. None of the newcomer Hispanic/Latino migrants had any trouble finding churches because the friends and family who encouraged them to come to Kenosha already knew about these resources. Newcomer African Americans who met established members of this community had an easy time finding a church home. For example, one newcomer reported that her neighbor invited her to church.

On the other hand, since none of these churches actively advertised in the community newspapers, newcomers without direct ties to the established African American and Hispanic/Latino communities had a difficult time finding local churches. For example, one African American family first started attending a white church because they could not locate an African American church from the denomination that they belonged to. While they found the worship practices in the white church different from what they were used to, this family stayed with that church for several years because they could find no alternative. Eventually, their children met other African American children in school who invited the family to the African American church from the same denomination. The family was comfortable in this church and quickly switched membership.

These closed social capital patterns were beginning to change for the large denominational churches in the African American community during this research project. The change occurred because the ministers in these churches became more active in the wider community. These individuals and their churches were more often featured in the newspaper in a positive light. Other African American churches were only mentioned in the newspaper when a financial scandal occurred.

More importantly, the ministers and some church members participated actively in inter-faith coalitions, community social service activities and Kenosha politics. These coalitions will be discussed in more detail in the next section. Through visibility in the wider community, information about the churches began to spread outside of closed social capital networks.

88 Despite these changes, none of the churches did a good job of advertising their activities. Signs with dates and times for services were missing or difficult to find. For example, one fieldworker reported that the times for bible study were wrong during the three months that he attended one church. This meant that outsiders who wanted to attend the church would arrive at the wrong time and miss activities.

All of these churches recruited members through closed social capital devices. The smaller churches for both communities simply relied on word-of-mouth personal invitations to draw members. For Catholic Hispanic/ Latinos, white churches might tell them about the Spanish-speaking Mass if they did not already have a connection. The two larger and more visible African American churches primarily relied on word-of-mouth referrals through other members. One church encouraged members to "bring friends." Another developed a series of "contact ministries" that they used to gather members. These ministries included door-to-door recruiting in African American neighborhoods as well as encouraging members to invite acquaintances to church.

Once people found their way to one of the churches, they mostly found a welcoming environment. Like our fieldworker who was warmly welcomed to the church, he attended as a class project, newcomers were encouraged to join these established communities and become part of their closed social capital networks.

Church Finances

With the exception of the Catholic Church Hispanic/Latino Mass, all of Kenosha's African American and Hispanic/Latino churches relied primarily on their members for financial support. As a congregation hosted by a white parish and as the designated Spanish mission for Catholics in Kenosha, the Catholic parish could draw on wider resources within the Catholic community in addition to member support. In all cases, the amount of money available for the churches to do their work depended on the financial means and generosity of their members. Given the lower incomes of many Hispanic/Latinos and African Americans in Kenosha, this meant that churches had less to work with than some comparable institutions in the white community. In addition, several pastors in both communities commented that Kenosha's African Americans and Hispanic/Latinos had not developed a practice of giving generously to their churches. Pastors often spoke from the pulpit encouraging members to give in order to be able to expand church activities.

The Catholic Church was able to rely on established funding sources within that denomination in order to fund mission activities. Nevertheless, church funding only allowed for part-time staff. Two of the African American churches had applied for funding for church mission activities that had incorporated separately as non-profit organizations. In both instances, these projects were turned down by citywide funding organizations as conflicts between church and state. Conversations with white community leaders revealed two problems with these minority community proposals. The first was a strong sense that local communities should support themselves, which translated into a belief that government and citywide funding sources should not support religious community activities. Second, community leaders judged some proposals on their format. Proposals that did not follow the expected forms were discounted as "not well put together." Third, since community leaders had no direct knowledge of minority community organizations, they had less confidence in the merit of these proposals.

Church funding requests were turned down, in part, because social capital connections between these churches and the funders were missing. Lack of social capital, combined with the fact that churches requesting aid from the wider community violated the cultural capital norms in Kenosha that ethnic and racial communities take care of their own. These patterns may change as some African American pastors develop bridging social capital with white community institutions. As discussed in the next section, these bridging activities are slowly changing both social and cultural capital in Kenosha.

Instrumental Supports through Churches

Each of the churches offered a variety of social and economic supports to their members and the wider community. For the most part, these ministries took two forms. Formal mission committees of both women and men visited the sick, provided spiritual and emotional support to families facing hard times, and gave away goods and sometimes cash to people in need. In the African American churches, the pastor usually served as the source of most monetary contributions.

The amount of cash support needed by community members had climbed dramatically since implementation of

W-2. For example, one pastor remarked that his church had given out $12,000 from the benevolence fund in the last year. The largest problem seemed to be covering rent costs for people about to be evicted because unstable low-wage jobs did not provide enough money to reliably cover costs. In one case, several pastors together had helped save one family from eviction. People helped through church instrumental support included both parishioners and others in the community.

One hallmark of church instrumental support involved the circle of giving and receiving in the African American congregations. Most families active in helping others through church and their work had received similar support themselves. For example, the Clarks, a middle-class family active in their church, served the community in a variety of ways. The wife worked as a teacher's aid in one school and her children tutored younger pupils at home. Through the church, this family volunteered in one of the social service organizations. They were also active in several church ministries involved in social uplift and political change.

Despite their image as established pillars of the community, when asked about the role of the church in their lives, they responded that "God provided." One key example included a time when their van broke down and they had no means to buy another one. Somehow, someone associated with the church quietly gave them another vehicle. These kinds of stories were repeated throughout the fieldwork. The circle of care ranged from social visits when someone was ill to long-term financial or mentoring support.

Church instrumental support took a more formal shape in the Catholic parish. Here, ministry was provided either through the center for the Spanish-speaking population or the St. Vincent de Paul office. Givers and receivers often differed by generation and sometimes race. For example, most of the people receiving aid were newcomer Mexicans or African Americans.

Churches as Training Ground and Developers of Cultural Capital

Faith-based ministries for youth development, education and political activities eclipsed the instrumental ministries in importance in the minds of people participating in these activities. Both of the larger African American churches strove to involve their members in several ministries. Some of these were subtle activities organized as part of worship. Parishioners were encouraged to participate in both worship and service.

Organized ministries were available for people of all ages in the African American churches. Activities like youth groups, men's ministries and women's ministries combined bible study with discussion and connections to life in the real world. For example, one bible study group started with a bible verse and then used this to talk about savings and money management. More relevant to the connection between faith and works, ministries, through discussion and example, taught ways to rely on God to provide for others. As Angela, a member of one of the two large churches, remarked:

> Definitely, what I've been taught plays a role. It helps me raise my son to be a better person. I look at a lot of things differently. Even being an adult, temptation is out there, big time. There's a lot of things I have to keep a religious perspective.

Angela worked as a nursing assistant, finding that her faith helped her through the rough spots in her job. Faith played a large role in the work life of most people involved in social service. Karen, a teacher's aid, commented:

> My faith is that God made every child different, just because this one isn't so quiet and this one over here is. God made every child different and He loves that one just as much

as the quiet one over in the corner. You know, their home life might be different. There might be some reason that child—sit down and talk to him.

We found that the churches' role as training ground and spiritual well for people involved in social welfare activities in the community was far more important than direct social service because of the range of social welfare activities provided by congregation members. Most of the African Americans working as teachers, counselors, social service agency employees, and in other helping roles in Kenosha were active in church and came from religious backgrounds. Churches taught leadership, values appreciated by mainstream culture and the patience to work with difficult populations. Churches encouraged both education and work that offered more than financial remuneration.

The evolution of both African American and Hispanic/Latino participation in social welfare and political activities in Kenosha stemmed from the mainstream community noticing people active in their churches. For example, one African American family became the link between the white mainstream social welfare system and the African American community. The mother in this family had started in ministry work in her church, gradually becoming known throughout Kenosha for her works. Her visibility to the white community led her to be hired by one of these organizations and she eventually became an assistant director of a key non-profit organization centered in the African American community. Several of her children have followed in her footsteps. These children are active both in church and non-profit social service activities.

The values and leadership education taught through church were always connected to a strong faith base. The various narratives on the relationship between faith and works stressed that

God and faith played a prominent role in the way people carried out their work. Faith provided sustenance to go on in difficult times. Faith showed how each program participant was also part of the family of God. Faith provided an unseen support and creative solutions through good times and a sense of being part of a larger plan on bad days. Faith moved social service workers beyond the often-petty machinations of human events.

90

We saw the same relationship between faith and works in the Hispanic/Latino Catholic community, though less frequently. Given the formalized nature of social support, church-based activity often involved individuals who either were asked to participate in social welfare activities or volunteered to help others. Examples include nuns or priests asking someone to take on a faith-based social welfare job or Anglos who helped out Hispanic/Latino families through a church-sponsored activity. In both cases, initial participation in church-based service led to a life of work for others through non-sectarian social service venues. For example, several employees and board members of the Hispanic/Latino social service organization had started out in these kinds of mission activities. While Catholics did not speak as often of God or faith in carrying out their works, they readily acknowledged the link between faith and works in their activities.

How Do Churches Build Social Capital?

Kenosha African American and Hispanic/Latino community churches built social capital through a slow and consistent process of developing community and establishing trust among their members. One example illustrates social capital development in action. This field observation of a meeting at one church shows how one young person, a newcomer to the church, is offered a combination of emotional, spiritual and instrumental support:

We wrapped up the meeting with prayer. Mary said the prayer and she asked that the Lord continue to give Tasha the strength to work hard, stay active in the church and not worry about being a slower learner than most of us. Tasha was a younger woman who was at the meeting; she didn't say much during the meeting. I learned after the meeting that she is just out of high school and is Mary's niece. She has a learning disability and has struggled with ridicule from others for most of her life. Before anyone left there were lots of hugs to go around. At the end of the meeting we took up a donation for Carolyn because her father passed away last week. Mary also asked who was going to make a meal for her; people of the church always prepare food for those who lose a family member in order to help eliminate the stress that they are facing.

This example shows several forms of social capital development. Tasha is welcomed into the church community through prayers and caring words. Hugs and encouragement to stay in school help develop trust in this supporting community. With this trust, Tasha hopefully will feel comfortable asking church members for help if she is struggling in school. Church members learn that Tasha has

a real problem that requires their assistance, understanding her as a member of their community in need rather than a young person who fails at school for an unknown reason. They are more likely to help her because both relationships and trust have been established.

Mary puts social capital in action to provide instrumental and emotional support to Carolyn after the death of a family member. This example shows that a word of mouth announcement in a church meeting mobilizes resources for a community member in need. As an example of a caring community, resources are activated without the church member specifically asking for help.

Churches built both closed and bridging social capital. Examples of mechanisms to develop each kind of social capital follow.

Bridging Churches

Two churches that participated in this project developed bridging links as organizations and fostered bridging social capital among their members. A number of members of these churches talked about how their church provided a strong sense of self for African Americans. These churches were most likely to have members who went to college, were employed in professional jobs and were involved in social service activity throughout Kenosha. These churches also were most likely to draw members from newcomers to the area.

In both cases, the leadership for the bridging churches came from outside Kenosha. These pastors felt that they should provide strong supports for their members and serve as spokespeople for their racial communities in Kenosha. One pastor explained:

> My whole context for the church is that the church would be an empowering agent, that the church would be used to build what I would say is self-independence. You need to be in a situation not only that you feel good, but also that your fullness would be illuminated.

Implementing this vision included involving church members in active ministries to develop themselves and community, an active practice of joint worship and advocacy activities with both white and African American churches, and participation in community social service and politics. As a result, for the first time, African American churches and their members are becoming a visible presence in Kenosha.

Church ethos and direction comes from a combination of activities initiated by the pastor and supported by key members of the congregation. When this pastor accepted the call from the Kenosha church, he found a small congregation full of "a very passive, take anything people. The only thing they could think about was they worked at American Motors." While he has built the congregation and empowered its members, this has been a slow process. He recalls an older member counseling him, "I'm afraid you're leaving the [train] station without some passengers."

These churches also participated actively in several church coalition activities in Kenosha. As discussed in the last section, the pastors and some members were involved in non-profit

boards and city politics. These activities slowly but surely changed the nature of inter-group interaction in Kenosha from 1997 to 2000. For example, during the *Kenosha Conversation Project*, I approached one church coalition asking to do a focus group with their members. A white pastor sternly told me that the coalition would appreciate an educational talk on welfare reform, and I could ask for people to participate in the focus groups after the event. The pastor informed me that, "We want people to educate us, not ask us to do something." This meant that the churches were closed social capital systems that did not engage in any version of social change as a coalition.

By the end of the *Kenosha Social Capital Study*, this coalition and several others like it had changed this established point of view. In fact, the same pastor who so sternly advocated against social change had become a leader in Congregations United to Save Humanity, the Alinski[25] based organizing project that started in Kenosha during this study. On several occasions, he chided people in meetings who used terms that were not inclusive of all races or acted in ways that were hurtful to people of color.

This individual change would not have occurred if the African American pastors in these bridging churches had not developed bridging social capital in order to enable these shifts in attitude. They took leadership positions, attended meetings throughout the city, and otherwise developed positive, equal and trusting relationships with leaders in other churches, political circles and social service networks. Through leaders becoming bridging agents, in combination with the active support of their congregations, these bridging churches were able to begin changing the nature of inter-group interaction in Kenosha.

Closed Social Capital

Members of all churches practiced closed social capital, as was common among most people of color in Kenosha. Closed social capital involves equally strong networks that people rely on for social, economic and emotional supports. However, community boundaries are carefully guarded and social capital networks maintained within the network. These organizations and their members become invisible to outsiders. All of the churches serving people of color practiced closed social capital. The bridging churches exhibited both bridging and closed social capital, while leaders and members of closed communities only went to outsiders when they needed something.

While closed social capital may cause problems when community members need to cross race/class boundaries, it serves to provide a trusting environment where people often treated badly by the majority world can find sustenance, trust and support. Arising from the Kenosha socio-economic structure, fed by persistent racism and where resources were allocated through neighborhood, workplace and ethnicity, closed social capital is the logical response to community conditions. Closed social capital is facilitated through dense networks that share information through word-of-mouth.

Recall the warm welcome that our fieldworker received the second time he visited one closed social capital church for his class project. Members of the church proceeded to welcome him to church from the pulpit and began a consistent campaign to recruit him as a member. He later discovered that the church members also knew where he worked and a number of details about his life. He never figured out exactly how the knowledge was transmitted, but I suspect that friendship networks, which crosscut the church and his other networks, provided these details to the church members.

91

These strong communities provided instrumental support to people in need. All of the churches and church-related social service organizations seemed to magically know when a member was in trouble and would step in to provide aid. For example, in one church, green forms for Christmas baskets began quietly appearing in the social mission project office a few weeks before Christmas. The mission staff person and our fieldworker assembled and delivered baskets. We witnessed similar mission activities at other churches.

Both churches and community organizations based in African American and Hispanic/Latino communities closely guarded these activities, practicing the strategies of evasion and passive resistance that are the typical "weapons of the weak."[26] Closed community practices came into play among whites and most people of color in efforts to provide social services or generally involve people from closed communities in wider Kenosha activities. People from closed communities would simply not show up or be unresponsive. This was particularly true of the Hispanic/Latino community, which one community leader described as "a proud people" who do not go to outsiders for help.

Building Cultural Capital

Churches built cultural capital in a variety of ways too. Most mechanisms were subtle encouragement for certain kinds of behavior. For example, one church listed the names of all the college students who belonged to the congregation in the weekly bulletin. Fieldworkers found that they were praised for dressing in ways considered appropriate for the congregation. For example, one fieldworker received much praise when she came to church dressed up with a matching hat. Another found herself uncomfortable when the pastor commented from the pulpit that

congregants should learn to tolerate women wearing pants. She looked around and found herself one of the few women dressed in this way.

Church members carry this cultural information out into the world with them. Announcing college attendance encourages others in the congregation to seek higher education too. Sanctioning women wearing pants suggests that casual clothing is not appropriate in some contexts. Hopefully, church members will learn to dress well in work environments too. Supporting fancy dress may have the opposite affect. Women who go to job interviews dressed in lacy outfits rather than plain suits or dresses may not be accepted in the workplace.

Occasionally, pastors would use the pulpit to preach cultural attributes that they considered appropriate. We heard sermons about divorce, education and many other aspects of behavior. Promoting cultural capital from the pulpit went hand-in-hand with more subtle mechanisms to encourage certain kinds of behavior. Cultural capital combined with social capital to identify insiders and outsiders. Everyone in the church community was considered a potential insider and encouraged to develop the

spiritual, cultural and social patterns that were respected in the community.

While most of these examples show support for education and advancement, the smaller, working-class and low-skilled social capital churches did not always support behaviors valued by mainstream society. For example, one of our fieldworkers, Raymond, was an African American from a low-income community seeking a college education. While he supposedly fit in every way into the church community where he did his research because he came from similar class, race and faith traditions as church members, he still found himself unwelcome in subtle ways. He reported to me that he felt that they resented him for going to college. Appropriate cultural patterns in this community meant not getting above everyone else through advanced education.

Churches as Providers of Social Welfare Services

This study suggests that churches provide a wide array of instrumental supports through formal and informal mission activity. Churches also offer spiritual and moral guidance that helps their members develop social and cultural capital appreciated by employers, schools and other aspects of mainstream society. Examples like Tasha being welcomed into a church community show that churches provide a special kind of support through the circle of care in a welcoming community.

However, these positive examples do not necessarily mean that churches automatically provide appropriate supports to needy people. Three separate factors can create situations where churches fail to provide the combination of loving support and "appropriate" values that will lead to economic self-sufficiency.

The first factor involves the nature of the values taught by a church. For example, recall the coments by Marcus, the agency youth worker profiled earlier, that the children in his youth program did not show appropriate respect for elders. Some people presume that these children would have learned these values if they attended church. In fact, all of these children did attend church. Some of them went to the same lower class church where Raymond performed his fieldwork. Some of these children dressed themselves and went to church every Sunday without their parents encouraging them to go. In this church, they learned to respect and support people from similar class and race backgrounds as themselves. However, college-educated people in positions of authority were considered different from themselves. People like Marcus, even though he came from the same racial background, were not treated with respect because they were presumed to be managers or intellectuals out to exploit

working-class people like themselves. These children practiced adversarial relationships with people in authority or who had higher education than themselves in keeping with long held beliefs and behaviors stemming from both class interactions in the workplace and race-based discrimination in many aspects of life. In this case, church taught values, but not the values expected by mainstream society.

The second factor is the nature of the relationship between the church and people in need receiving service from that church. Children in low-income neighborhoods in Kenosha were picked up for church by a bus from one of the larger, white churches. Some of the children in Marcus' program went to this church. Other families we met in our interviews and fieldwork reported that their children went to this church. While the church supported middle-class values, the children were not welcomed into the church community as full members like the families where both adults and children attended. The church may have offered cultural capital, but it did nothing to provide social capital to these children. It is unclear whether or not the children absorbed the cultural capital values taught at church. One mother recalled that her now adult children attended this church because she made them go. She reported:

> It's way out [in the suburbs]; it's a white church. They would send a bus every Sunday. I wouldn't go but I would send them every Sunday because the bus came by and picked them up. It came to the whole neighborhood, white, black and all. They would pick them up, a whole busload every Sunday. They didn't really want to go but I made them go. They got treats on the bus so that kind of made up for them not wanting to go.

Both children and adults coerced into church activities may not absorb the intended messages because they are

not part of the community of that church. The circle of care depends on all parties willingly working together to create a community. The same factors play a role in any other kind of church-based activity.

The third factor also involves the nature of relationships within a church. Some people may attend churches that offer a combination of community, social capital and cultural capital valued by mainstream society. Nevertheless, church members whose lives do not meet the standards common in that church may feel left out due to gossip or more subtle sanctioning in the community. Churches are human communities, subject to the same failings as other places where people gather together. For example, Crystal was a welfare-dependent woman who came from a religious family and was raised in a church. Her faith remained strong despite troubles with health, work and boyfriends. She talked about joining a church, but was leery of trusting the faith-based community. She commented,

> Some people in the church kinda feel they're there to help you but others are like there to get in your business and spread it here and there. I'm like, you know, me and my kids, we been subject to a lot of stuff and people these days are like so cruel. So I choose not to tell them at all.

Crystal's observations show that trust within a social capital network needs to go both ways. People with problems need to know that they will be accepted in the church community without being judged, in the same way that Tasha was welcomed into her aunt's church. People who have been hurt by church gossip in the past may go to a church for instrumental support, but they will be slower to join and become part of communities of care. This example suggests that churches can only reach out to the needy if they treat them as equals and

93

are careful to create communities that do not support the kind of gossip that Crystal reported.

Taken together, this research shows that churches are natural sources for instrumental support, social and cultural capital. However, churches can only provide the kinds of resources available through the collectivity of that community.

Low-income churches will not have lots of extra money to care for the less fortunate. Their ability to develop schools and other support programs depends on both financial and technical resources within those communities. Since those communities reflect the class and race-based values of their members, churches may not necessarily offer mainstream cultural capital or bridging social capital. At the same time, middle-class churches may not be welcoming homes for people who experienced multiple misfortunes or who have trouble maintaining community standards. Churches have much potential to provide for people in their communities, but they are not the only answer to social problems.

Implications for Policy and Programs

I will discuss implications of findings regarding churches and social service provision in more detail in the next section. These suggestions focus on the role of churches in communities.

- *Churches offer training in many social support activities.* Volunteer work in churches provides on-the-job training in a variety of social welfare occupations. Organizations seeking new volunteer and paid leaders or employees would do well to strengthen relationships with active churches to locate appropriate people.

- *Churches offer social and cultural capital to their members who meld well with the congregation.* This research found that churches created social and cultural capital supports for their members when they were welcomed into the church community. This means that churches can have a positive influence on their members. At the same time, churches do not necessarily foster bridging social capital or cultural capital valued by "mainstream" society. Nor is everyone who attends a church activity invited to fully participate in the community of care offered by that church. This finding suggests that churches in and of themselves are not an automatic solution to social problems.

- *Bridging social and cultural capital through churches can only be developed when people meet as equals with mutual respect for each other.* This research project found many examples of churches helping low-skilled workers move into the stable working and middle class. Churches that worked together with other churches in trusting relationships can change a community.

- *Church support is limited to the resources of those churches.* Kenosha's African American and Hispanic/Latino churches had much to offer their communities. However, their resources are not limitless. Finances depend on the means and generosity of the congregation. Formal programs depend on the time and talents of leadership and members, combined with the limits of financial resources. While churches could provide additional formal programs if additional financial support is provided, churches are interested in providing supports on their own terms. For example, one pastor offers food or financial assistance only if an individual agrees to church counseling. This finding means that churches cannot take over all social welfare provision or substitute for government or non-profit providers.

94

Connections between Churches, Social Service Agencies and Communities

I read in the paper about a meeting at [one church] with [a parishioner] talking about hunger in the community. I went over there being interested in that subject and she had a vision and we kept telling her, she didn't understand reality and what can we be doing? And she just said, "We're going to do this." What she wanted to do was provide a hot meal, seven days a week. She was just an active person in her church. Her church was always known as a very active church in the community.

Links Among Formal Organizations, Churches and Community

Forming Non-profit Organizations

This recollection from a community leader shows the link between churches, social service organizations and community in Kenosha. This meeting was early in the development of a soup kitchen that gradually developed into a formal organization providing a variety of services to the hungry and homeless. The evolution of this organization shows the way that Kenosha residents draw on church and other formal and informal community

groups to support those in need.

This initiative started in the early 1980's as the automobile plant was beginning to shut down. Everyone in the community was concerned. This initiative started in the churches, but rapidly drew in the union and every other service group in the community. Working together, they developed a system where one organization a night would provide volunteers to make and serve a meal. Nearly twenty years later, the organization still provides its soup kitchen in the same way. This pattern of community members working together to address a need widely recognized in the community is common in Kenosha.

The soup kitchen story is also unique in Kenosha. In most cases, organizations are focused on one or several closed social capital networks in Kenosha. For example, the Catholic Church, the Hispanic/Latino non-profit organization, the Hispanic/Latino church mission project and people in the Hispanic/Latino community all support each other. The support comes from a combination of the churches, informal organizations and individuals in these smaller communities. The same partnership among formal organizations, churches and community exists as with the soup kitchen, but in a much more localized way.

The homeless shelter/soup kitchen is one of the few organizations in Kenosha that has formal relationships with churches. A number of community churches provide shelter for single people in the church on a rotating basis. This kind of church housing for the homeless is common throughout the United States. Most of the churches involved in this program have provided this service for a number of years. We encountered several other community churches during the research project who expressed interest in contributing to this activity, but whose buildings did not meet the housing safety codes required to provide shelter.

Connections among Coalitions

As discussed earlier, the various non-profit organization coalitions had little formal connections to the churches. Until very recently, the same was true for the churches. Church coalitions focused on joint worship or educational activities, not creating links to social service organizations. However, during the study period this began to change. The major church coalition started inviting people involved in various forms of social service to present to this organization. Presenters included the school district, the homeless shelter and organizations involved in adoption, among others. Most of these presentations included direct appeal to the churches to offer assistance to the organizations through in-kind donations, volunteer labor or other means. Individual pastors shared this information with their congregations as needed.

More churches became actively involved in social service. An urban outreach mission, founded by one of the mainstream churches along with several others, became more visible throughout the community and was able to get some funding from citywide sources. Other churches were encouraged to help with this organization.

Churches also became more involved with politics during the study period. Churches were involved in elections and, most important, the liberal white churches and bridging African American churches developed Congregations United to Serve Humanity (CUSH) as an organizing effort focused first on economic opportunity and related issues. The CUSH effort brought together people from many different churches, including many staff from non-profit organizations. As a more political activity than the soup kitchen, this organization brought a different style and more formal organization to church involvement in social welfare in Kenosha.

Informal Ties Among Churches and Non-profits
As with other non-profit organizations, we found many more connections between churches, non-profits and community through informal ties. This study found multiple connections between churches and non-profits serving the African American and Hispanic/Latino communities in Kenosha. Churches provided the base

communities for many of the board, staff and participants in non-profit organizations. Particularly in the smaller organizations, overlapping religious and neighborhood ties became the resource for employees, board and participants. More important, churches often served as initiators of non-profit activity and training grounds for service. Several of these organizations started out as church missions. Many key staff moved from active church mission work to paid non-profit casework. This was especially true for people lacking professional educational credentials.

Church mission models also pervade service and fundraising strategies for Kenosha organizations. Kenosha egalitarian culture expects most non-profits to rely heavily on church and neighborhood-based volunteer resources. On the negative side, each of the African American and Hispanic/Latino organizations is expected to fulfill every need for their constituency, just like the church missions would find food, clothing, financial assistance, work and other resources for parishioners and other community members in trouble. Executive directors complained that they were expected to do everything in the organization from fundraising to direct service to fixing dead car batteries. Many Kenoshans thought of non-profits as voluntary grass roots organizations providing charity work for the deserving poor and social supports within closed communities. In some cases, non-profits were seen as a substitute for the earlier church work; in others they became a supplement to church activity or a necessity due to the changing economy.

On a more positive note, church models provided creative alternatives to fundraising through grants and other more standard mechanisms. For example, one minority community organization filled the inevitable gaps in operating budgets due to limited

government funding with the tried and true parish fundraising technique of bingo games. African American and Hispanic/Latino organizations also turned to churches for volunteers to supplement paid staff.

Two examples clearly show how these links develop within churches. Marjorie recalled that she got involved in a number of organizations because of encouragement from her church to become an active participant in both her faith community and the wider community:

> I found a lot of organizations through the church. When the pastor would come to us and said there was a need. I would always come forth and say I want to serve on this committee, I want to be in this organization because I thought I had
> something to give.... [I found]
> organizations through the neighborhood too. Knowing your neighbor and having issues that need to be addressed, and from there we formed different kinds of organizations.

As with many other people, Marjorie first began to take an active interest in her church community, developing leadership skills within the closed social capital networks of the church community. Her pastor encouraged her to participate in other activities, most of them associated with her ethnic group. Again, closed social capital supports meant working with others both informally and in formalized organizations. Marjorie translated this experience into participating in other organizations associated with her neighborhood. When we met her, she had branched out to working in citywide organizations.

People like Marjorie most clearly show the links between churches and organizations through individuals. Kenosha churches have developed strong, but mostly informal, partnerships with organizations that share common goals and come out of common social and cultural capital communities. This partnership among church, non-profit organizations and community is a real strength in Kenosha.

However, given that resources are limited, pastors are selective in what they recommend as organizational activities to their members. When asked about branching out to support a citywide organization, one pastor who supports organizations within his community noted:

They have volunteers; we have volunteers from our own church [who help out there]. One of the things when we started looking at what is happening, like even our church, cause we have room in our budget coming up for this year. And I made sure that we get in the budget. And then a lot of churches don't get involved because their financial base is so low and they don't feel like they can. And another thing, this whole thing of connecting. We have tried to, my efforts are about connecting, we want to connect with [that agency]. When we start looking at a church like this and everything that we are connected in, its very difficult to be able to get all the resources and things that you need. Because there are a lot of people who come to us [for the same services]. And so there is a lot of things that we don't get involved in because it takes so much.

As with any other activity in Kenosha, resources are limited to the time, energy and financial resources of those that care about a particular part of the Kenosha community or a particular issue. The partnership among churches, organizations and community also requires the active participation of government to provide additional funding and offer the formal supports through education, social welfare and other services that are beyond the capability of non-profits and churches.

The Role of Government

We saw many ways that government supported local communities. In keeping with Kenosha's focus on individual effort, Kenosha politicians would often do small fundraising activities themselves to support local organizations. Politicians would also set the tone for behavior for a community. For example, when one organization associated with the African American and Hispanic/Latino communities was covered with graffiti, several white politicians went down to the building and repainted the wall themselves to show that this kind of behavior would not be tolerated in Kenosha.

While government would not provide funding to churches, organizations received support through contracts and other means. Government support reflected Kenosha ideals that goals were achieved through work. For example, one person reported:

There was this abandoned school building and so we tried to negotiate with the school district. There's this building, it's abandoned, can we have it? "No, no, if we give you this building for free, everyone will want a building, we'll get sued by people

because we gave something away. But we'll sell it to you, we won't give it to you." So we had to negotiate with the school system to get this building. It was something called the 880 Club, something, it was everybody had to pledge $8.80, so we paid off the mortgage on the building.

This is just one example of Kenosha residents working together to achieve a goal. These strong links among churches, organizations and community show that Kenosha creates a circle of care to support organizations that share the ethos within that community. How then does this circle of care work for individuals who participate in organization programs? The section of organization participation suggests that some organization participants get more out of local organizations than others. I next look at ways that organizations, churches and community work together to create positive outcomes for program participants.

Connections between Churches, Non-profit Organizations and Communities for Individuals

This study suggests that organizations, churches and community work together to create a circle of care that enables people to develop stable careers and otherwise meet their goals. I begin with an example from a youth program to show this process in action:

The executive director of Youth Rising had decided to let the young members participate in the board meeting during their spring break.

This board meeting revealed much about the dynamics of social service, social capital and community in Kenosha. The multi purpose room where the board meeting was held was set up like a dining room. The board member seats were set up with silverware, wine glasses and white, imitation china. But every other seat was set with a paper plate and plastic utensils. The children seated the board member "guests," and other children from the program sat next to us in the seats with the paper plates. Lunch was provided by program participants. The gang prevention coordinator, whose students had cooked lunch, reported that, "she was shocked when she started phoning around that all the kids came in at nine a.m. on a vacation day to help." Dessert was provided by the teens from the organization.

Most of the children seated with us were African American, with a few Hispanic/Latinos. Our table included three African American girls: Alicia, her cousin (another African American girl) and a Hispanic/Latino. Most of the children only spoke when spoken to.

Alicia was different from the other children at the table. Alicia wanted to know all about the meeting and the adults near her. She then looked around, pointing to adults and other children in the room and saying, "they go to my church." She proudly pointed out her pastor, who is on the Youth Rising board. Another board member she identified as part of her church family is one of the few prominent African American professionals, who also serves on most nonprofit boards in the area. As Alicia pointed out people throughout the room, I discovered that many Youth Rising African American staff people went to that church.

I asked Alicia what she did at church. She talked about being in the youth group and doing plays, bible readings, etc. She said that Youth Rising activities were kind of similar. I next saw Alicia at a church fundraising dinner to celebrate the pastor's anniversary, surrounded by her parents, siblings, aunts and uncles. She performed a musical solo at the church event.

The board meeting went on in the middle of lunch. The executive director had one of the children helping to hand out materials. The helper handed things out to the board members, ignoring the program participants. Alicia kept looking at my copies. A staff person quickly provided copies of reports for Alicia when I requested them for her, saying that they did have copies for the children. That staff person was also from Alicia's closed social capital community.

The board meeting also featured presentations. Two African American officers in "Career Exploration Organization," a high school club, gave a halting presentation about what the group did. One reported that they "help each other out, do kids birthdays, visit seniors, do lawns and shovel snow for seniors and do bingo." The other teen started by saying that he was "nervous speaking in front of big people." At another more informal Youth Rising event, this young man was much more self possessed and articulate.

This fieldwork vignette illustrates many facets of community and social capital generation through organizations. Youth Rising's 1998 annual report describes the club as "impacting Kenosha's future...one child at a time." This board meeting presents many positive ways that club programming helps its largely low-income, minority participants become engaged future citizens with the ability to bridge between class and race. Children show ownership in the organization through eager participation in the board event and teens are taught to provide community service.

On the other hand, this event shows an organization that sometimes reinforces class/race-based boundaries through subtle messages. Showing that the deserving poor are not quite the same as their benefactors, the children eat from paper plates and the officers in the teen group have trouble speaking in front of this group.

As with Alicia and the people from her church involved with Youth Rising, this event shows that church and nonprofit organizations are often intertwined. As with the staff, board and program participants active in both Youth Rising and the church, organizations and churches provide opportunities to practice community. The communities of church and organization overlap with each other and with other communities in Kenosha. These fluid communities provide the initial connections, enforceable trust and places to learn cultural capital necessary for social capital both within the African American community and between majority and minority.

Activities through non-profit organizations like Youth Rising and churches reinforce each other. Both church and youth organization provide children like Alicia with support to develop into confident and successful adults. Church and non-profit both offer a variety of activities that foster educational development and teach values and behaviors appreciated in mainstream workplaces.

Church and youth group activities stress slightly different values and behaviors. The church focuses on spiritual development while the youth group offers a variety of other activities.

While these overlapping activities encourage positive development, a third factor makes the difference between simply learning a set of skills and developing bridging social and cultural capital. That third factor is comfort and trust in the community that an individual is involved in. Recall the older teens that gave a halting presentation to the adults. The two African American young men gave their largely white board audience a presentation that suggested that they were grateful recipients of youth services, not proud young men moving toward a positive future. However, when I met one of these presenters at another event, he demonstrated a much greater level of confidence and communication proficiency. The difference was that in the second event, someone introduced me to him from his home community and church. He felt more confident to present his full capabilities within the safety of his closed social capital community.

The presentation to the board represented sharing one's skills with outsiders. Kenosha culture teaches children of color that it is safer to conform and appear as a good, willing worker. To stand out from the crowd like a leader would not be appreciated. To become leaders in the outside world, these young people need to feel confident that their gifts will be truly appreciated by their adult audience.

Unlike these teens, Alicia felt confident enough at the Youth Rising board meeting to behave like the bright and curious child that she is naturally.

That confidence came from the combination of several factors. First, her church community and youth program encouraged her development. Alicia belongs to one of the bridging churches, where members are actively encouraged to move beyond closed social capital networks. The youth group promotes the same kind of bridging through some of their activities. Second, she recognized people in both Youth Rising and her church as coming from the same community. Since people that she knew as neighbors and congregation members were clearly evident as Youth Rising staff and board members, she felt the trust of her social and cultural capital communities available to support her even though she was sitting at a table with four white adults whom she had never met. The availability of her home community provided the support for Alicia to expand her horizons.

It is precisely the three-way links between church, non-profit and common, caring community that creates the circle of care that people need to develop the skills to bridge across social capital networks in a community like Kenosha. The strength of these three-way links becomes even clearer through examples of adults who have moved into the stable working and middle class from low-skilled worker and welfare-dependent families. Janice, introduced earlier in this publication, was raised on welfare by a single parent after her mother stopped working to care for a sick grandmother. She grew up in a poor neighborhood and was labeled as learning disabled by the schools. This background meant that she had deficits in mainstream measures of economic, human, cultural and social capital. However, she had strong supports through her church, activities from a minority community-based non-profit organization, and youth group activities in another African American community-based organization. The encouragement of

both closed and bridging social capital connections through church and organizations led her to go to college and become a teacher. She now teaches children labeled "at risk" like she was and actively volunteers for both church and the non-profit organization that provided further support to continue her education. Janice's story suggests the value of both closed and bridging social capital. Without the support of the financially weak African American non-profit and her closed community church, she would not have developed bridging social capital. However, without the equally strong ties to people who bridged between communities, she would most likely have remained in the closed communities like her peers.

In recent years, policy makers have debated whether non-profits, churches, for-profit organizations or government can best provide for people in this society. Policy makers also debate whether or not community participation is on the decline. This research study suggests that social capital and community participation is alive and well in communities like Kenosha. However, community and individual development is not a simple thing that happens through one strategy. Instead, communities come out of the dynamics among organized institutions like churches and non-profits, situated with communities of people who share common values and goals. In most communities, like Kenosha, society is made up of many smaller communities with closed social and cultural capital.

Strategies to develop more inclusive communities must get beyond simply counting memberships; asserting that church, non-profit or for-profit providers are "better"; or debating the value of minority versus majority controlled organizations. Strong communities need a combination of all of these things, and people who can bridge between the necessary closed communities.

Implications for Policy and Practice

- *Supporting families involves creating strong partnerships among government, non-profits and churches that recognize the strengths and unique contributions of each type of institution.*

- *Developing partnerships starts with recognizing the assets in communities identified as in need of service.* Many of the books on church involvement in social welfare presume that church members come from economically, spiritually and socially stable communities while the people they aim to help lack spiritual and social supports as well as basic needs. In fact, communities always include a combination of people with different assets and needs. Working with these assets is the first step in building connections among the haves and the have-nots in this society. This means seeking community leaders and drawing on the strengths of the people receiving service.

- *Developing strong individuals involves expanding communities of trust through overlapping networks among non-profits, churches and government.* Programs and policies need to encourage the creation of communities of care like these positive examples in Kenosha through developing shared staff and volunteer connections among divergent communities and organizations. These connections need to include shared power and respectful interactions. Including partners from targeted communities at all levels of organizations is the first step in fostering these kinds of positive experiences. Providing adequate assets to build bridges across communities is also essential.

Conclusion: Social Capital and Supporting Families through Organizations and Churches

The *Kenosha Social Capital Study* shows that social capital is an important ingredient in understanding how families find work, instrumental supports like childcare and education, and social supports. Social capital is equally important for organizations, churches and communities. Formal institutions and groups of people also need trusting connections to survive and grow.

There are two kinds of social capital: closed and bridging social capital. Closed social capital is essential for any individual or group. These are the primary relationships that provide strong supports at all times. Bridging social capital involves intentional efforts to extend trusting relationships across closed social capital groups. Bridging social capital is essential to expand horizons and develop new career paths or directions for an agency. However, bridging social capital is not better than closed social capital. Nor is bridging social capital a substitute for closed social capital networks. Bridging and closed social

capital networks work hand in hand to build strong individuals and communities. Examples of the circle of care involving both bridging and closed social capital networks among churches, non-profits and occasionally government highlight the importance of both types of social capital. The trust relationships developed in closed social capital networks allow supports for individuals and organizations. Combined with bridging social capital through organizations, churches and other mechanisms, community change and individual growth occurs. The CUSH initiative is one example of this type of growth for organizations. Individuals like Janice and Alicia show how closed and bridging social capital together can develop strong individuals committed to education, positive career paths and supporting their communities.

Social capital is linked to cultural capital. Each section of this booklet shows how connections are shaped by the history of Kenosha, its socio-economic structures and its

cultural values. Individuals and organizations that practice Kenosha culture develop strong social capital networks while those without approved cultural capital remain on the outskirts. Organizations and individuals who practice other forms of cultural capital —like the leaders who use race-based identity to claim rights—fail because their statements run counter to the egalitarian and individualistic ethos shared by those in power in Kenosha. They also fail because these leaders lack bridging social capital ties. However, by slowly becoming part of mainstream social capital networks, present day African Americans and Hispanic/Latinos are changing what is acceptable cultural practice in Kenosha. References to race and cultural habits different from the Kenosha mainstream have become more acceptable now. Expanding cultural capital and bridging social capital go hand in hand, as trust is needed to change a community.

This study suggests a number of general implications for policy and programs. While these concluding ideas are focused on Kenosha, they hold for many local communities looking for ways to better support their families and organizations.

Implications for Policy and Programs

- *Developing strong families and communities involves creating equal partnerships among non-profits, government and churches that recognize the different strengths of each type of organization.* The sections on the role of organizations, churches and government in supporting families show that a circle of care that involves churches providing basic instrumental, spiritual and social

102

supports; formal organizations offering professional services; and government providing income supports and connections to other services work best to support families. Sections on organizations show that neither churches, organizations nor government can do the work of the other adequately. Furthermore, the strength of Kenosha's public/private partnership involved adequate funding for all partners. The circle of care fails when one partner relies on the other to provide services due to lack of funding or other resources.

- *Both organizations and communities enable social capital through individual networks.* Each of these sections shows that people obtain work, services, social supports or resources for organizations through connections among individuals. Strengthening ties among communities and organizations in Kenosha involves expanding these individual connections. The challenge for Kenosha and other communities like it involves the fact that these connections are grounded in suspicion of the other. Through mutual activities, organizations and communities need to first break down the negative aspects of closed social capital if they intend to build bridging social capital.

- *Bridging social capital is built through key individuals moving across closed social capital lines.* Each section of this report shows individuals or key organizational staff developing links into closed social capital networks. Sometimes this involves a bridging individual creating links for a closed social capital church or organization. In other cases, mainstream leaders insist on diversifying an organization's board and key staff when they are in trouble. As the citywide contracts for organizations show, bridging social capital only develops when people develop trust across networks through personal contacts, not simply by using an organization. The same is true for coalition activities or organizational growth.

- *Community strategies must be grounded in local culture and community practices.* The efforts that succeed in Kenosha draw on community ethos for supporting everyone as equals through work, connections among closed social capital networks, and localized knowledge. Ideas coming from the outside or that do not appeal to all of these elements achieve less success. For example, a church initiative aimed at simply giving things to the needy received limited support while another activity that spoke of helping people find work or other mechanisms to get on their feet met with more success. Appeals to programs for all Kenosha residents rather than race-based organizing was more successful. While community culture will necessarily differ in various localities, it is important for planners to identify key cultural traits and understand how the community puts them into action in their organizations and programs.

- *Change comes from drawing on established social and cultural capital to expand into new territory.* The successful programs for individuals drew on the circle of care already established in community churches and organizations to help people find new directions. As with Janice, positive participation in one activity led to movement into another related activity through individuals trusted in each organization. Without these already established ties, new growth would not occur. The same is true for organizations. The church coalitions that are slowly changing the political and social landscape in Kenosha developed through years of joint worship and participation in activities that drew on older Kenosha cultural forms. The trusting relationships developed in these closed networks provide the foundation for more radical change.

Books, Articles and Reports Cited in this Report

Bourdieu, Pierre and Loic J.D. Wacquant. (1992). *An Invitation to Reflexive Sociology*. Chicago: University of Chicago Press.

Buenker, John. (1976). "Immigration and Ethnic Groups." In *Kenosha County in the Twentieth Century: A Topical History*. John Neuenschwander, editor. Kenosha: Kenosha County Bicentennial Commission: 1-50.

Coleman, James. (1988). "Social Capital in the Creation of Human Capital." *American Journal of Sociology*, 94 Supplement: S95-S120.

di Leonardo, Miceala. (1984). *The Varieties of Ethnic Experience: Kinship, Class and Gender among California Italian Americans*. New York: Cornell University Press.

Dudley, Katherine Marie. (1994). *The End of the Line: Lost Jobs, New Lives in Postindustrial America*. Chicago; University of Chicago Press.

Foley, Michael and Bob Edwards. (1997). Escape from Politics? Social Theory and the Social Capital Debate. *American Behavioral Scientist*, 40 (5): 550-561.

———— (1999) "Is it Time to Disinvest in Social Capital?" *Journal of Public Policy* 19, 2:199-231.

Gans, Herbert. (1982). "Symbolic Ethnicity: The Future of Ethnic Groups and Cultures in America." In *Majority and Minority: The Dynamics of Race and Ethnicity in American Life*, Norman Yetman and C. Hay Steele, editors. Newton Mass, Allyn and Bacon: 495-508.

Goode, Judith and Jo Anne Schneider. (1994). *Reshaping Ethnic and Racial Relations in Philadelphia: Immigrants in a Divided City*. Philadelphia, Pennsylvania: Temple University Press.

Gordon, David, Richard Edwards and Michael Reich. (1982). *Segmented Work, Divided Workers: the Historical Transformation of Labor in the United States*. Cambridge: Cambridge University Press.

Keehn, Richard. (1976) "Industry and Business." In *Kenosha County in the Twentieth Century: A Topical History*. John Neuenschwander, editor. Kenosha: Kenosha County Bicentennial Commission: 175-222.

Newman, Katherine. (1999) *No Shame in My Game: The Working Poor in the Inner-City*. New York: Alfred A. Knopf and the Russell Sage Foundation.

Kenosha Area Business Alliance (KABA). (1999) *Kenosha County Overall Economic Development Program Plan, Annual Report*. Kenosha, WI: KABA.

Portes, Alejandro. (1998). "Social Capital: Its Origins and Applications in Modern Sociology." *Annual Review of Sociology*: 1-24.

Portes, Alejandro and Patricia Landolt. (1996) "The Downside of Social Capital." *The American Prospect*, 26: 18-21.

Putnam, Robert. (1995) "Bowling Alone: America's Declining Social Capital." *Journal of Democracy*, 6 (1): 65-78.

———— (2000) "Bowling Alone: The Collapse and Revival of American Community." New York: Simon and Schuster.

Schneider, Jo Anne. (1997). Dialectics of Race and Nationality: Contradictions and Philadelphia Working Class Youth. *Anthropology and Education Quarterly*, volume 28 (4): 493-523.

———— (1997). *The Social Network Study Technical Report*. Philadelphia: Institute for the Study of Civic Values. Available on-line at <http://www.chss.iup.edu/jschneid>.

———— (1998). *Social Capital and Welfare Reform: Lessons from Philadelphia and Wisconsin*. Unpublished paper presented at the 97th annual American Anthropological Association Meetings, Philadelphia.

———— (1999). *Organizations, Communities and Social Capital: Exploring the Dynamics Between Community Based Organizations, Churches and the Communities they Serve in a Milwaukee Neighborhood*. Unpublished paper presented at the 28th annual Association for Research in Nonprofit Organizations and Voluntary Action Meetings, Arlington, VA November.

———— (1999). "Trusting that of God in Everyone: Three Examples of Quaker Based Social Service in Disadvantaged Communities." *Nonprofit and Voluntary Sector Quarterly*, 28 (3): 269-295.

104 ———— (1999). *Kenosha Conversation Project Education Booklet.* Kenosha: University of Wisconsin-Parkside.

———— (2000) "Pathways to Opportunity: The Role of Race, Social Networks, Institutions and Neighborhood in Career and Educational Paths for People on Welfare."*Human Organization* 59 (1): 72-85.

Scott, James. (1985). *Weapons of the Weak: Everyday Forms of Peasant Resistance.* New York and London: Yale University Press.

Stack, Carol. (1974). *All Our Kin: Strategies for Survival in a Black Community.* New York: Basic Books.

———— (1996). *Call to Home: African Americans Reclaim the Rural* South. New York: Basic Books.

Yancey, William, Eugene Erciksen and Richard Juliani. (1976). "Emergent Ethnicity, Review and Reformulation." *American Sociological Review* 41: 391-402.

Yancey, William, Eugene Ericksen and George Leon. (1985). "The Structure of Pluralism: 'We're All Italian Around Here Aren't We Mrs. O'Brien?'" In *Ethnicity and Race in the U.S.A.: Toward the 21st Century*, Richard Alba, editor. New York: Routledge and Kegan Paul.

Zophy, Jonathan. (1976). "Invisible People: Blacks and Mexican-Americans." In *Kenosha County in the Twentieth Century: A Topical History.* John Neuenschwander, editor. Kenosha: Kenosha County Bicentennial Commission: 51-82.

Notes

1. Kenosha Area Business Alliance (KABA). *Kenosha County Overall Economic Development Program Plan, Annual Report.* Kenosha, WI: KABA, p. 24 (1999).

2. For discussion of undergraduate student involvement in ethnographic research, see Milosky and Schneider, 1999, *Field Method Guide for Undergraduates.* Available from the authors.

3. Putnam's discussion of social capital can be found in two major works:

   "Bowling Alone: America's Declining Social Capital." *Journal of Democracy,* 6 (1): 65-78 (1995).

   Bowling Alone: The Collapse and Revival of American Community (New York: Simon and Schuster, 2000).

4. The concept of social capital became popular in social science literature in the 1980s. In France, Pierre Bourdieu used social capital in his studies of social mobility and education. He saw closed social capital networks that were maintained by cultural capital behaviors and attitudes as maintaining the status quo in society. For Bourdieu, social capital works hand in hand with economic capital. In the United States, Coleman saw close, face-to-face networks helping people and organizations to meet their goals in similar ways. In the United States, Alejandro Portes combined Coleman and Bourdieu's definitions in his own explorations of the concept. My definitions draw primarily on Bourdieu and Portes.

   People interested in reading more about this concept will find additional resources in:

   Bourdieu, Pierre and Loic J.D. Wacquant. *An Invitation to Reflexive Sociology.* Chicago: University of Chicago Press, 1992.

   Coleman, James. "Social Capital in the Creation of Human Capital." *American Journal of Sociology,* 94 Supplement: S95-S120 (1988).

   Foley, Michael and Edwards, Bob. "Escape from Politics? Social Theory and the Social Capital Debate." *American Behavioral Scientist,* 40 (5): 550-561 (1997).

   "Is it Time to Disinvest in Social Capital?" *Journal of Public Policy* 19, 2: 199-231 (1999).

   Portes, Alejandro. "Social Capital: Its Origins and Applications in Modern Sociology." *Annual Review of Sociology:* 1-24 (1998).

   Portes, Alejandro and Patricia Landolt. "The Downside of Social Capital." *The American Prospect,* 26: 18-21 (1996).

   Readers interested in further discussion of my definition of social capital will find more in depth discussion in:

   Schneider, Jo Anne. *Social Capital and Welfare Reform: Lessons from Philadelphia and Wisconsin* (1998). Unpublished paper presented at the 97th annual American Anthropological Association Meetings, Philadelphia.

   "Trusting that of God in Everyone: Three Examples of Quaker Based Social Service in Disadvantaged Communities." *Nonprofit and Voluntary Sector Quarterly,* 28(3): 269-295 (1999).

5. Readers interested in learning more about Kenosha history will find information in:

   Buenker, John. "Immigration and Ethnic Groups." In *Kenosha County in the Twentieth Century: A Topical History,* ed. John Neuenschwander. Kenosha: Kenosha County Bicentennial Commission, 1976: 1-50.

   Dudley, Katherine Marie, *The End of the Line: Lost Jobs, New Lives in Postindustrial America.* Chicago; University of Chicago Press, 1994.

   Keehn, Richard. "Industry and Business." In *Kenosha County in the Twentieth Century: A Topical History,* ed. John Neuenschwander. Kenosha: Kenosha County Bicentennial Commission, 1976: 175-222.

   Zophy, Jonathan. "Invisible People: Blacks and Mexican-Americans." In *Kenosha County in the Twentieth Century: A Topical History,* ed. John Neuenschwander. Kenosha: Kenosha County Bicentennial Commission, 1976: 51-82.

6. KABA, 1999, p. 58.

7. Zophy, 1976.

8. Numbers do not add to forty-two percent because not every business answered this question.

9. Numbers do not add up to one hundred percent due to rounding.

10. David Gordon, Richard Edwards and Michael Reich, *Segmented Work, Divided Workers: the Historical Transformation of Labor in the United State.* Cambridge: Cambridge University Press, 1982

11. The median is the middle of a range of responses to a particular question and is more likely to show typical patterns than a statistical average in cases where one company's answer can make the average much high than the rest of the answers. I give the range of responses in cases where the median differed substantially from the mean.

12. Numbers do not add up to one hundred percent due to rounding.

13. The KES was unable to get data on the racial breakdown of the labor force due to resistance found to answering this question by employers when we first tested the study. Questions about race and ethnicity were not included in the final questionnaire.

14. Numbers do not add up to one hundred percent due to rounding.

15. The federal poverty level is calculated based on family size using a formula including the costs of goods and services considered necessary for family support.

16. Numbers do not add up to one hundred percent due to rounding.

17. I found similar work and resource use patterns in several larger scale studies in Philadelphia. Readers interested in reading more about the role of work experience, training and social networks will find this material in *Pathways to Opportunity: The Role of Race, Social Networks, Institutions and Neighborhood in Career and Education Paths for People on Welfare.* Human Organization, volume 58(4).

18. Kenosha County statistics as of 9/1/2000.

19. Kenosha County statistics as of 9/1/2000.

20. Wisconsin W-2 contracts allotted a set amount of money for use to aid W-2 recipients through cash grants. Agencies that did not use all of this allotment received a portion of this money back to invest in programs to aid the community. Kenosha used these community reinvestment funds to offset cuts in the new W-2 contract.

21. According to the Kenosha News (12/3/1999, C3), the new contracts reduced funding from $7.3 million to $4.6 million. Interviews with Kenosha County employees during the project reported that community reinvestment funds returned to the county through W-2 cash savings on the first W-2 contract cut the shortfall to $1 million. The number of people laid off due to budget cuts comes from interviews.

22. Kenosha County statistics as of 9/1/2000.

23. Kenosha County statistics as of 9/1/2000.

24. See Goode, Judith and Jo Anne Schneider. *Reshaping Ethnic and Racial Relations in Philadelphia: Immigrants in a Divided City.* Philadelphia: Temple University Press, 1994: 209-240, for in-depth discussion of working-class white approaches to race and racism.

25. Saul Alinski's community organizing activities focus on developing community interest on specific issues and then training community residents to confront government and other power brokers to change policy to help their communities. A number of Alinski style organizing activities center on churches, and continue in the United States today.

26. Scott. *Weapons of the Weak: Everyday Forms of Peasant Resistance.* New York and London: Yale University Press, 1985.

www.ingramcontent.com/pod-product-compliance
Lightning Source LLC
Chambersburg PA
CBHW081552280526
45788CB00011B/3448